DEADLY BLESSING

DEADLY
BLESSING

STEVE SALERNO

◆

WILLIAM MORROW AND COMPANY, INC.
NEW YORK

Library of Congress Cataloging-in-Publication Data

Salerno, Steve.
Deadly blessing.
1. Daniel, Marion Price, 1941–1981. 2. Murder—
Texas. 3. Politician—Texas—Biography. I. Title.
HV6533.T4S25   1987   364.1'523'09764155   87-19105
ISBN 0-688-06565-1

Printed in the United States of America

2   3   4   5   6   7   8   9   10

BOOK DESIGN BY MARIE-HÉLÈNE FREDERICKS

Prologue

Zero minutes of sunshine were officially recorded by the *Houston Chronicle* on January 19, 1981. It was a chill gray day of forty-degree temperatures and intermittent cloudbursts, of drizzle and fog and pungent, oppressive air that reached out and cast a pall over East Texas. It was a day on which, in the small town of Liberty, some forty-odd miles east of Houston, laborers looked up and cursed the sky for the heaviness of their workshirts, and even the eager young women who stood at the cash registers in the Main Street shops might have paused, during a lull between customers, to gaze out through the misty windows in wistful contemplation.

It was, also, a day that served as an apt metaphor for the darkening mood at the large, ranch-style house about two miles out of town, along what was popularly known as "the Governor's Road"—this, in honor of the town's homegrown political superstar and most celebrated resident. The house belonged to the Governor's son, who was something of a local legend in his own right, as well as an enigma. A legend, because he had leaped right out of the chute and gotten off to a brilliant start in politics; an enigma, because he had unaccountably stalled somewhere along the line. In recent years, his precipitous decline and virtual disappearance from the political scene had been the basis of many conversations among Liberty's small but influential Democratic fraternity.

But politics was not the subject of the discussions at this house on this night. The animated conversation between the Governor's son and his wife focused on matters of a less lofty nature: matters having to do with the divorce action that the wife had filed, in supremely ironic style, amid the gala atmosphere of New Year's Eve.

They had lived their separate lives, he the son of patrician circumstances, she the girl from the neighborhood Dairy Queen, in near-exile from the rest of Liberty. Their marital ups and downs—downs, mostly—had been apart from the scrutiny of the town's dedicated corps of gossips. Thus nobody knew much about the circumstances that had spawned the divorce action, or the issues that were at the heart of the heated debate between Liberty's oddest couple on that gloomy night.

But when it was over, they knew this much: that the man who, some felt, should never have been in politics, had been killed by the woman who, many felt, he never should have married.

Soon everything would come to be known. Much more, certainly, than the Governor and others in the immediate family might have wished. The revelations in the tragic aftermath of January 19, 1981, would vary in flavor from the scandalous to the infuriating to the poignant. And yet the major theme to emerge would be that of one man's failed attempts to reconcile the demands of being born to political royalty with the demands that rose up from within himself—of privileged circumstances that became, for Price Daniel, Jr., a deadly blessing.

Chapter One

I f the likelihood of political success can be gauged by bloodlines—and those steeped in Texas's grand traditions of horse breeding and cattle raising tend to believe it can be—then Marion Price Daniel, Jr., born in June 1941 to Mr. and Mrs. Marion Price Daniel, Sr., of Austin and Liberty, Texas, should have been a sure winner.

The boy's mother, Jean Houston Baldwin, was a direct descendant of Sam Houston, avenging spirit of the Alamo and the first president of the Texas Republic. She was also a daughter of the oil-blessed Partlows, a family that had exerted its own share of influence on Texas politics. Though she herself had never been involved directly in campaigning—women being generally proscribed from such roles in Texas—she was no stranger to getting things done. In later years, people would describe Jean Daniel as the matriarchal rock of the family; the quiet one who just sat and listened, but who wielded ultimate authority.

Still, it was the father who set the standards against which Price Daniel, Jr., would be measured for the rest of his life. Price Daniel, Sr., began his political career auspiciously in 1938, with three consecutive terms in the Texas legislature. He was appointed by his colleagues as speaker of the House in 1943; won election as Texas attorney general in 1946, 1948, and 1950; went to Washington as a senator in 1952; and returned to Texas to take the governor's chair in 1956 (a chair he held for a record-equaling three terms). In 1963 he took his place as an associate justice of the Texas Supreme Court. As impressive as the offices themselves was the manner in which he won them. Daniel's victory in the 1950 Democratic primary was by the largest margin in the history of Texas politics—the Republicans did not even bother to mount a candidate against him in the general election. His selection as speaker of the House was *unanimous*. When he ran for his Senate seat, the Republican party, lacking anyone willing to serve as a sacrificial lamb, threw him its support as well. Four years later, he trounced his gubernatorial opponent by a million votes—this in an election in which a total of just 1.6 million votes were cast.

During his term as senator, Price Daniel, Sr., engineered the passage of what would be recorded as perhaps the most important piece of legislation ever passed on behalf of a single state. The Tidelands Bill was an outgrowth of Daniel's unshakable belief in states' rights. (Indeed, during his first term as attorney general, he had caught the eye of segregationists for upholding the right of the University of Texas to bar a black student from attending its law school.) In this case, Daniel believed his state was entitled to the potentially enormous revenues to be had from oil drilling off its shores in the Gulf of Mexico. Upon becoming attorney general, he began the process of filing the complex legal briefs to achieve this.

The early odds were against him. In 1947, the U.S. Supreme Court had set a precedent by denying California's similar claim to Pacific tidelands. And although all states' claims were being reviewed on a case-by-case basis, a movement was afoot in Washington to draft legislation that once and for all ceded such offshore resources to the

8

federal government. The Supreme Court then handed down a ruling favoring the government's right to resources located in the waters off Louisiana and Texas, and Daniel's crusade began in earnest. Here, after all, was more than a matter of principle; it was a golden opportunity. The question of tidelands ownership was the kind of issue upon which a man could build a career.

Daniel dispatched an ombudsman to Washington to present his argument, only to be rebuffed by President Harry Truman. Realizing the measure would require more intensive politicking than he could manage at long range from Austin, he decided, in 1952, to run for the Senate.

In the midst of his campaign, Democratic presidential nominee Adlai Stevenson announced that he concurred in the government's right to the oil. Daniel took a bold step, one that could have been political suicide had it backfired. Despite his role as a leading figure in the state's Democratic party, he announced his intention of withholding support from Stevenson; he proclaimed that Texas Democrats could feel free to vote for Eisenhower and Nixon, the Republican presidential ticket, without losing status as Democrats in good standing. In so doing, he was bucking not only his party but a regional prejudice against Republicans dating back to Lincoln and the Civil War. Just once, in 1928, had Texas gone Republican in a national election.

The risky move worked. Eisenhower won, carrying Texas by a significant margin. Daniel was hailed as a prophet, a "take no guff" individualist in the Texas tradition. Some years later, the extraordinary influence he had wielded to upset the political sensibilities of an entire state would come back to haunt him. But arriving as a fledgling senator in Washington, an emboldened Daniel described himself as a "Texas Democrat, not a national Democrat." If this inflammatory remark raised eyebrows in the capital, it served only to expand his following back home. Texans shook their heads in admiration and approval over their brash new man in Washington.

To no one's surprise, Daniel's first Senate address in the spring of 1953 was devoted to the tidelands issue. As a freshman legislator, he had few friends in Congress, and relatively little influence with which to log roll. Yet within a month he and several allies from other coastal states had, through intensive politicking, ensured passage of the landmark bill. President Eisenhower, the grateful beneficiary of Daniel's disaffection with the Democratic presidential ticket, promptly signed it into law. Texas's territorial boundary was set at ten and one half miles offshore, more than three times the customary three-mile limit. Billions of dollars of revenues from future offshore oil and gas finds were thus guaranteed to Daniel's home state.

Daniel took many stands thereafter: in favor of conservation; against Senator Joseph McCarthy's witch hunt; in favor of a strong, well-funded national defense; against statehood for Alaska and Hawaii; in favor of vigorous enforcement of drug statutes. Yet, he never again equaled his inaugural act. Nor, with his slightly roguish image, was he ever taken to the national bosom—in contrast to the other Democratic senator from Texas, a fellow by the name of Lyndon Baines Johnson.

No matter. When he left the Senate to run for governor of Texas in 1956, it was, in the words of one Houston newspaper, as if he had rolled up his sleeves, gone to Washington to do a job, done it, and come home to glory. A landslide victory gave Daniel the governorship, an office he held by equally impressive margins until a party power struggle derailed his chances for an unprecedented fourth term in 1962.

Ironically, a victory that year might have given Price Daniel, Sr., the national attention that had largely eluded him. For had Daniel been reelected in 1962, he—and not John Connolly—would have been seated in front of John F. Kennedy when Lee Harvey Oswald took aim in Dallas the following fall.

Little Marion Price Daniel, Jr., was born during the heady days of his father's second term in the Texas Statehouse.

In a society where anyone who was anyone was either oil or politics, "Little Price" was both. Any child would have been spoiled in such circumstances, and Little Price was no ordinary child. Handsome, obedient, and quickwitted, he was doted on and showered with gifts.. From the time he could crawl, he was taught that life held some special promise for him, as though his first steps would lead right up into the Oval Office.

Pressure to succeed came early. Growing up in Austin and Washington, Little Price was seldom permitted to indulge a child's normal inclinations for getting down in the dirt and getting gritty. Years later, his wife Vickie would notice the zeal with which Price abandoned himself to such activities as playing with a toy train set. It caused her to wonder how much of his boyhood had been stolen from him by the "privileged" circumstances into which he had been born.

But Little Price appeared to embrace the trappings of adult responsibility. While most of his friends were watching cartoons and deciding what to buy with next week's allowance, he had a successful paper route going. He was convinced, as a woman who knew him well in the last years of his life would put it, that "his daddy's money was his daddy's money. Price always wanted to make it on his own, to establish his own identity."

Early on, a special bond developed between Price and his sister, Jean, who was a year younger. In vitality and intelligence, Jean was her brother's equal. The two shared a ready, barbed wit, and were closer than Price was with either of his two younger brothers, Houston and John.

As Price and Jean got older, they double-dated often, and, in fact, Price and Jean saw nothing wrong with going out and having a perfectly fine time with each other.

"What was uncanny was the degree to which they were on the same wavelength," one of Jean's dates recalled. "We had gone out to the movies, and then afterward at the restaurant, they just went off on one of their little tangents, with private jokes and all. They'd just look at each other and start to laugh, like they knew right away what the other was thinking. It got so that the girl Price was with and I were looking at each other too and wondering, like, what's the deal here?"

Price enrolled in Baylor University in Waco, Texas, where attendance was all but compulsory for members of the Daniel family. Jean, John, Houston, and an array of cousins would follow Price to Baylor, just as Price had followed his father.

He quickly earned a reputation as a conscientious student, one who got straight A's and studied to the exclusion of almost all else. One girl Price was dating remembered how she had spent Saturday nights in his off-campus apartment, while Price studied his lawbooks. When it got close to curfew, he'd take her out for a quick bite, then drop her off at her dorm. And that was the routine, week after week. She watched TV, he studied. She liked Price well enough and considered him a good catch because of his family, and his classy, wholesome looks—but before long she frankly just couldn't stand the boredom any longer. She began spending her Saturday evenings with others.

Price's fanatic devotion to schoolwork was characteristic

12

of his approach to most undertakings. In everything he did, Price junior was a perfectionist. "He prepared for each day as if it were a space shot," recalled one friend. It was no exaggeration. While Price was at Baylor, a cousin spent a benumbing twenty minutes watching him set his wristwatch so that the hour hand, minute hand, and sweep second hand were all in perfect synchronization. When Price finally looked up, satisfied that all was in order, the cousin confronted him.

"Would you mind telling me," he asked, "how in the world you could spend twenty minutes doing that?"

"I like to be punctual," Price replied, as if a few seconds one way or the other made a difference.

But it *did* make a difference to Price. If he said he would be back at 3:00 P.M., he arrived not at 2:59, or 3:02, but *precisely* as the clock struck three. It was as though he had parked somewhere nearby to wait for the precise moment he had promised.

Price was no less fastidious about his grooming. At Baylor he engaged the services of a maid to iron his shirts, because he was unhappy with the way laundries handled the assignment. He wanted the collars left ironed straight up, so each day, after he had selected his wardrobe, he could hand-iron the collar down to match the lay of the jacket and the knot of the tie.

For such reasons, Price never quite fit in with the collegiate crowd. One got the feeling he was always on his way to a job interview. At the end of the day, when everyone else was looking wilted or disheveled, Price was still daybreak fresh.

Nor was it just his dress. About everything, he was obsessively, ostentatiously neat. His books, for example. He lined them up next to one another, shoulder to shoulder, with no book pushing the slightest bit father forward than any other, or arranged them in a perfect pyramid with the largest on the bottom, and each successive book centered exactly in the middle of the book below it. A cock-eyed lampshade or a picture hanging askew drove him to distraction. Discovering a typo or a grammatical error in the college newspaper, he would whip out his pen and actually correct it right there in the margin.

The image fellow students had of Price junior was augmented by his delicate features and his gait, which exhibited a certain stiffness. A *correctness.* Even his stubble seemed to grow in perfect order—uniformly, with no dark or light spots. Among the Baylor crowd, "he tended to look like a shiny new pair of shoes in a closet full of worn slippers," noted David Parker, a classmate who would marry Price's cousin Susan.

Nor was Price the kind of person you warmed up to with a friendly chat. Rather, his ear was keenly attuned to information from which he might profit, preferably in the financial sense, and particularly through real estate, a life-long preoccupation. A fraternity type who accosted him with a choice piece of gossip about an available co-ed would be turned away smartly. "I don't have time for that kind of stuff," Price would say as he straightened his lapels and strutted off.

There were moments, though, when the decorous facade would crack. Price would gather up two or three trusted cronies and head off somewhere to raise hell in one of the small towns near the college community.

Occasionally his driving, too, would reveal a certain affinity for living on the edge. Another cousin, Ann Daniel Rogers, attended Baylor with Price, and was dependent on him for local transportation. He would pick her up, and they would tear off in his Riviera to challenge the serpentine backwoods roads at speeds often in excess of ninety miles per hour. Ann would shut her eyes tight and scrunch down in her seat to approximate the brace position that stewardesses demonstrate on airplanes. Thus, she would wait for the shattering impact that, praise the Lord, never happened—at least not with her in the car.

After a while, Ann learned to take Price's driving a bit more in stride. She could relax enough to keep one eye open. It was then that she noticed that Price could emerge from the terrifying Riviera joy ride with not a hair out of place. *Not a single hair.*

As Price neared the end of his prelaw course, his political aspirations began to crystallize. He decided it was expedient to have a wife. In typical Price fashion, he drew up a list of specifications, as though he were inviting bids on a government contract for a new fighter plane. List in hand, he broached the subject during one of his wild rides with Ann Rogers.

The list, as Ann would remember it, called for a woman who was pretty, bright, vivacious, well-groomed, and socially adept. She should also be from a good family and have some interest in politics and world affairs. Price asked his young cousin to help locate this ideal woman.

Ann was overwhelmed. Being finicky about your shoes, or about the editorial standards of the school newspaper—well, that was one thing. But this was ridiculous. Besides, Ann didn't run in those kinds of circles. "I'm just a freshman here!" she protested, shaking her head. "I'm not even in a sorority or anything, Price. . . . I just don't know many girls like that!"

Unfazed, he told her to do her best. Over the next few weeks and months, Ann half-heartedly looked around a bit, but nothing much came of it.

Chapter Two

L iberty, Texas, is located along U.S. 90, midway between Houston and Beaumont. Leaving Houston, U.S. 90 is a dismal two-lane industrial road that yawns into a four-lane backwoods highway and finally becomes something resembling a genuine freeway in the short stretch between tiny Dayton and the Trinity River, which defines the westernmost edge of Liberty's city limits.

The Liberty in which Price junior grew up and reached manhood was in many ways a surprising town, occupying a place in Texas history belying its size (population: 7,900) and sleepy demeanor. Fought nearby in 1836 was the Battle of San Jacinto, wherein eight hundred Texans routed fourteen hundred Mexicans and captured General Santa Anna, villain of the Alamo. The victory led directly to the formation of the Texas Republic under the leadership of Price's ancestor Sam Houston, hero of San Jacinto. Shortly thereafter, a Liberty resident penned Texas's first constitution—an accomplishment not lost on Price.

The town also prided itself on its self-sufficiency. True, its occasional touches of refinement—its Cadillacs, jewelry, and other niceties—tended to be imported during regular forays to Houston. And a few of its more prominent citizens were Houston expatriates. But Liberty remained, overall, remarkably independent for a town that lay in such close proximity to a blossoming megalopolis. Especially compared to most of the other satellite towns Houston had thrown off like seeds around itself since the epochal Spindletop oil find of 1901.

Further, Houston of the sixties was a relatively "new" city, a city that through the constant infusion of new blood was forever expanding and redefining itself—and, many would tell you, not always for the better. Liberty, on the other hand, was rooted in a stable core of founding families. It was the kind of place where people who had lived there for two and three generations were still regarded as newcomers. Such was Liberty's kinsmanship that all town residents seemingly drew from the same pool of two or three dozen surnames.

There were other, more fundamental differences as well. Whereas Houston could boast many of the people who owned the oil, Liberty's populace mainly tended to the machinery that extracted it from the soil. Houston was management, Liberty was labor. Thus, in the daytime, the town was dominated by men in stained blue coveralls, driving pickups: large men of equally large stomachs and biceps and sun-scorched necks with deep horizontal creases that climbed halfway up the backs of their heads before disappearing into haircuts of boot-camp severity.

Another segment of Liberty's population—smaller than in times past—consisted of people indentured to the land they farmed, and accustomed to backbreaking labor.

In Houston, a city where bigger was automatically better and ostentation was taken for authenticity, people admired success and were duly impressed by its trappings. Not so in Liberty. The laborers and the farmers found it hard not to begrudge people who did no more to deserve their riches than to happen to be standing on a certain spot when oil began bubbling up from under them.

Had Price junior launched his effort for recognition and contentment anywhere else in Texas, things might have worked out differently. In Austin, Houston, Dallas, and San Antonio, even in the multitude of sagebrush towns throughout Texas, the Daniel name was revered. In Liberty, the respect for the family's political heritage was tempered with suspicion and distrust. The folks who had seen Price's family grow up and come to its station in life thought they knew another side to the illustrious Daniel saga.

Texas remembers its heritage in many ways. There is, for instance, the prefix FM, for farm-to-market, as in FM 1011. Once, FM 1011 was one of many backwoods trails in and around Liberty by which farmers set off to sell their goods. But with the ascendancy of Price Daniel, Sr., FM 1011 came to be known as the Governor's Road.

The appellation was not merely honorific. The Daniel family owned much of the land adjacent to FM 1011. Not infrequently, when someone said "the Governor's Road," there would be more than a trace of scorn in his voice. For legend had it that Price senior's father, the original Marion Price Daniel, had accumulated much of his valuable land by duping poor, uneducated landowners.

The elder Daniel would persuade the gullible Baptists, the story went, to sign gas and oil leases. In and of itself, this was no crime. The leasing phenomenon had taken hold after the huge Spindletop gusher, and Daniel was only one of hundreds of entrepreneurs who went out there daily to make a pitch. The speculator's goal was to persuade the farmer to lease him land near recent oil finds, cash on the barrelhead. The logic was, Why not take the bird in hand in case there might not be two in the bush? If there was indeed oil down there, well, both men would

19

make a profit. If not, at least the farmer would have something to show for it.

Sometimes, the speculator might try to persuade the farmer to sell an interest in possible future royalties from an oil company. The drilling, after all, was an iffy proposition. The cash being offered—two or five or ten thousand dollars of it, right there in a leather suitcase—was not. It was a most persuasive inducement for farmers who, in their entire lives up to then, had never seen so much money in a lump sum.

But Price senior's father, the story went, did not play by the rules. When the time came to put things in writing, instead of a leasing agreement, he unfurled a *deed*. And just like that, with one signature, the farmers were reduced from landowners to tenants.

There were other dark stories, too. Despite being married, old Price was said to have an eye for the young ladies—with the emphasis on young. One tale told of his being caught in the cornfields one fine afternoon with a lass just barely into her teens. Supposedly, the matter was settled amicably enough—money took care of that. But the whispers continued.

Rumor also had it that there was an additional sibling somewhere (a brother or sister to Price senior, Bill, and Ellen, the three children of official record), who was born as the result of a liaison between Price senior's dad and a Baytown woman. The old man's will, which had mysteriously disappeared from the files in the county courthouse, was said to have provided a secret bequest for the mystery child.

The gossip also included Price senior's mother, for she was indeed an idiosyncratic woman. She would sometimes be seen wandering about, as if in a drunken stupor, screaming gibberish. Less and less was publicly seen of her until, in the last years of her life, she was confined to her house.

That particular unpleasantness might have been forgotten had it not been for signs of instability that showed
up in subsequent generations. Ellen Virginia Daniel, Price
senior's sister, was considered flaky and had never married.

And then there was John Daniel, Price junior's brother.
As a child, he had been uncommonly sharp-witted and
popular, a straight-A student. But somewhere along the
line, John started drinking heavily. He began to have automobile accidents (at least one of which, at the Lib-
erty/Dayton Bridge, was quite a serious affair), and was at
the heart of a couple of ugly public scenes. By the time
he was ready for his hitch at Baylor, John was considered
somewhat unreliable. Shortly thereafter, John was sent off
to an East Coast facility that offered more personal supervision.

In 1966, after getting his law degree from Baylor, Price
Daniel, Jr., finally found, courted, and married a woman
with the qualifications he had enumerated for his
cousin Ann.

As a descendant of Thomas Mitchell Campbell, esteemed governor of Texas from 1907 to 1911, Diane
Wommack was a political blueblood in her own right. She
was also pretty, articulate, refined, and skilled at the social
graces. "The perfect politician's wife," said one acquaintance.

The newlyweds returned to Liberty and, courtesy of Price
senior, took up residence in a mammoth, ranch-style house
on Governor's Road, just a short distance west of the Governor's own imposing home.

Price's first move was to open up a local law practice.
No one exactly fell over in astonishment, for Price senior,
upon *his* return to Liberty from Baylor in 1932, had gained
notoriety through defending a number of sensational
murder cases. Little Price was of a more mundane bent;

he preferred the intricacies of civil law to the drama of criminal law, perhaps, as some would observe, because he was more at home with writs and codes and numbers than he was with people.

With added impetus supplied by the ambitious Diane, young Price's entrance into the political arena was even swifter than his father's had been nearly three decades earlier. A mere two years after passing the bar, Price was seeking election to his father's old seat in the legislature. He ran on a platform of accountability and reform: Too much lawmaking goes on behind closed doors! You send your representatives to Austin to do your bidding but then lose track of what happens there. "We are the keepers of your trust and hopes," proclaimed Price, "and every man deserves to know what becomes, in the end, of his vote!"

It was a fresh, appealing line in Liberty County, with its ancient tradition of club politics and smoke-filled rooms. An enthusiastic electorate sent twenty-seven-year-old Price off to Austin.

He was not prepared for what he found there. Generally lacking his father's social skills, he was hardly comfortable with being "one of the boys." Price was neither one to ask favors, nor one to blithely grant them. He did not play the game. Carlton Carl, Price's assistant in Austin, noticed right away that Price preferred his own company, or that of a few close friends, to the general hubbub of the capital.

When Price did mingle, problems surfaced. Given his idealism, or rather perfectionism, he was not a man to whom compromise came easily. Bill Buchanan, a radio personality who worked with Price on the preparation of a bill aimed at expanding media coverage of legislative activity, found the young Daniel to be exceptionally candid—blunt, really—no doubt to his detriment. Price junior called things as he saw them. Compounding the problem was the platform on which he had come to Austin in the first place: removing the cloak of secrecy from governmental processes. It was an undertaking that was bound to raise hackles among the old guard.

Price also found it hard to politick. "He's the kind of guy who calls you only if he needs you," Bill Buchanan told people. By this, he stressed, he did not mean to imply that Price was a user, but that the man simply did not call you unless it was necessary, for whatever reason. Seldom did he dial somebody just to "keep in touch" or trade small talk.

Many of Price's colleagues found it odd that a man coming from such a prominent political background should be so naïve. Others, however, blamed that very background for Price's maladjustment. Liberty County Judge Harlan Friend, for example, would laugh when he heard people liken the Daniels to the Kennedys. "It just doesn't hold up beneath the surface," Friend would insist. "Papa Joe Kennedy spent time with the boys, made sure they understood everything they were about to get involved in. Which is something the old man, Price senior, did not do with Little Price, ever."

As a result Price junior was hardly a dominant force in Texas politics during his early years in Austin. "He never sponsored any major legislation," Representative Gib Lewis of Fort Worth, a close friend, would recall. "He just served and stayed quiet and showed no urge to change the world." If he stood out at all, it was by omission. The Texas legislature had a reputation as a fun-loving, devil-may-care band. Price didn't fit the mold.

Besides, his wife had just presented him with a son, Thomas, whose company he would not have traded for all the political fanfare in the world. By the end of his first term, Price had for all intents and purposes faded into the woodwork.

Fate, however, had other ideas.

A political upheaval triggered by one of Houston's regular financial scandals cast the bulk of state legislators in an unfavorable light. Even those not directly involved suffered from guilt by association. As the media seized upon the story as Texas's answer to Teapot Dome, the man in the street was increasingly incensed. The prevailing sentiment was *Let's throw the rascals out!*

Suddenly, Price's aloofness was an advantage. He was above reproach. When the call came for new leadership, Price Daniel, Jr., was the right man at the right time: a symbol of principle and independence—someone to clean up the den of iniquity. At the same time, Price senior quietly stoked the burgeoning sentiment in his son's favor through an energetic behind-the-scenes lobbying effort.

By this improbable sequence of events Price Daniel, Jr., one of Austin's lesser lights, acceded to the position of speaker of the House in January 1973.

Had Price continued as a mere representative, he might have been all right. But suddenly he and his flaws seemed to swell in proportion.

One hundred years earlier, Texas's first constitution had been penned by a man from Liberty. The timing was too ideal to ignore. Price was in position to make a grandstand play. With the objective of substantially expanding the amount of openness in government and ending the long-standing oligarchical grip of business interests over Texas politics, Price called a Constitutional Convention.

Almost immediately, he encountered resistance. His legislative colleagues resented this grand gesture from someone who had been appointed speaker largely as a public-relations move. And when the resistance came, Price did not respond well. Words like "vindictive" and "devious" began being used to characterize the speaker's office.

His allies attempted to defend him. "We were playing hardball," Carlton Carl would explain, "and that's the only way politics is played." Indeed, in Texas, political fights are waged ferociously. Accusations that would be slander almost anywhere else become slogans in Texas.

Price acted as though he were bent upon undermining his apologists' best efforts. He was prone to occasional fits of pique, which did little to endear him to his influential opponents. At the height of the convention furor, he publicly berated labor leaders, once his staunchest supporters, as being callous and selfish. Nor did he endear himself to certain convention delegates by calling them "cockroaches" and refusing to apologize.

Complained one fellow legislator, "He doesn't seem to realize that he's dealing in the realm of emotions and feelings and beliefs. You can't put those things down on a balance sheet."

Not a few of Price's opponents said his problem was a lot simpler than that. It had nothing to do with Price's personal commitment to perfection or any high ethical standards he was unwilling to compromise; it was *height*. Snidely, they painted the five-foot nine-inch Price as having a classic Napoleonic complex: a little man trying to prove himself among all those big, broad-shouldered Texans.

In the end, Price saw his new constitution fail by three votes. Detractors claimed Price was the Peter Principle at work: He had risen to his level of incompetence. In an odious comparison to his father, they began calling him "Half Price," insisting that had it not been for the financial scandal, he would never have merited such power and authority in the first place. Even his disciples felt that a more flexible man could have surmounted such a small margin. Price's father would have.

A watered-down version of the constitution was adopted the following year. But by that time, Price had abdicated his speaker's chair. He offered the same rationale once given by Price senior: It was too powerful an office to be held by any one legislator for more than a single term.

In Price junior's case, the explanation had an ironic ring to it.

Price, it turned out, was not the kind of man to leave his office worries at the office. The strain of politics took its toll on his marriage to Diane. Some said, in turn, that Diane was chagrined at her husband's failure to bring off his grandiose scheme. Whatever the case, in November 1975, they were divorced.

Within one year, seemingly, Price had lost it all: his dreams of glory, his wife, and his beloved young son.

In the spring of 1976, Price began to pursue a young woman who worked not far from his Liberty office. She was a comely blonde who could be found at the Dairy Queen on Main Street. Obviously, she wasn't from his social milieu. Perhaps, at this point in his life, Price needed an admirer—someone whose expectations, unlike Diane's, were modest.

Price made his first move on a fine afternoon in early May. Driving to the Dairy Queen, he positioned himself near the counter. Ostensibly, he was surveying the wall menu, but in truth, he was waiting for the right waitress to come to the front and take his order. When she did— the sprightly girl with the soft platinum tresses—he requested a cup of black coffee, and smiled.

Chapter Three

V ickie Loretha Carroll was the tenth, and next to last, child of an improbable union between a quiet, nomadic refinery worker and his aggressive, principled wife. The family lived in Baytown, Texas, an upgraded shantytown just east of Liberty. The parents were divorced early in Vickie's childhood, and Vickie's mother subsequently worked at a succession of menial jobs in stores or restaurants.

Mrs. Carroll was religious and industrious, and expected her children to be also. Even divided among eleven children, the household chores and responsibilities were burdensome. (The fact that Vickie one day recalled this period as the "happiest, most carefree" part of her life is a commentary on the bleakness of her adult years.)

At the age of twelve, Vickie went to live with her older brother Franklin. However, the arrangement ended because of Franklin's failing health. She returned to her mother, who by this time had taken another husband. Restless and disoriented, Vickie dropped out of school the following year. Before long, she found herself in a church-sponsored children's home in Waxahachie, a Dallas suburb.

This might have caused many adolescents to despair. For Vickie, however, the exchange of environments proved to be a blessing. She went from being one of the youngest in the group to being one of the oldest. Accordingly, her confidence soared. She cooked, dressed the girls, supervised the housework, led them by example. The youngest children responded especially well to her, and she sensed that they looked to her for guidance and protection. One day, she knew, she would be a fine mother.

Vickie admired her brother Franklin and was influenced by his strict Pentacostal beliefs. Franklin lectured sternly about sin and sinners. Foremost among the latter were women who cheapened themselves by allowing themselves to be used by men, or even *looking* as if they might allow themselves to be used by men. Only when Franklin died was Vickie able to shake off his admonitions about "those kinds of girls."

She dyed her hair blond.

Years later, she would laugh about the great symbolism of this commonplace act. But then it was her initiation into the real world, where people loved and laughed and made their own rules. And sinned.

With her new blond hair Vickie discovered she could be a coquette. She could wink her way out of traffic tickets, or persuade some redneck to let her cut in front of him in the checkout line at the Minimax supermarket.

Yet she refused to take responsibility if the consequences of such behavior got out of hand. Profound indignation was her response to any man so foolish as to read her flirting as an invitation. The winks, the coy smiles, the hair tossing—they were a southern tradition and all came standard on women in East Texas. Men who expected something more than flirtation . . . well, it was just too bad.

That is, until Vickie met Larry Moore, a tall, husky heavy-equipment operator from Dayton. Vickie and Larry had quite a lot in common: Neither of them smoked nor drank; both loved the outdoors and the same leisure activities. Together, they rode bicycles, played tennis, and hunted squirrels, rabbits, and ducks.

Larry was particularly impressed with Vickie's hunting skills. Years later (and at the most inopportune possible moment, from Vickie's perspective), he would talk of the uncommon ease with which she had taken to firearms.

In 1967, a few months shy of her twentieth birthday, Vickie became Mrs. Larry Moore. In September of the following year, she had a baby daughter, Kimberly.

Vickie was, at this stage in her life, still growing up. For the first time, she made regular use of cosmetics, visited beauty shops, wore slacks and jewelry. Some of her childhood taboos took years to die. One day young Kim came home from school and raved about her friends' earrings. She wanted her mother to get her ears pierced with her; Vickie did, but for a while thereafter, she felt wretched, unclean.

Her awakening to such vanities was also stifled mainly by a lack of funds. With Larry, money was always tight. "When bread was twenty-five cents," she would one day recall, "we didn't have the money for bread." The situation worsened after a second child, Jonathan, was born in 1971. Vickie took a job at a movie theater to help out. In hopes of avoiding further financial burdens, Larry had a vasectomy.

Vickie started to become something of a puzzle to Larry—a mass of conflicting characteristics. She was innocent and she was worldly; she was sweet, yet insensitive; she was talkative, yet private. Larry found her mood swings utterly unfathomable; her reactions defied prediction. He began to wonder whether he really knew the woman he'd married—or, whether it was even possible to know her.

He was not alone in his confusion. Vickie showed different side of herself to different friends. "Vickie?" one would say. "Why, she's as quiet as a church mouse! Withdrawn, almost." In total disbelief, another friend might reply, "Are you *serious*? Why, Vickie's a nonstop talker!"

For Larry, the marriage became a relationship of extreme highs and lows. Things never got boring, at least. And he mightily admired her spunk.

If only she didn't get so *physical* about it . . .

The fights had begun the very first year and occurred at least twice a month. (After a while, it seemed, Vickie was always exploding about something.) They would have words, and Vickie would slap or scratch him. She never used her fists, but the scratching was, in a sense, worse: fierce, animallike, frightening. Some wounds took a month to heal. One time, Larry actually held her down and trimmed her fingernails.

On still another occasion, Vickie went after him with a butcher knife. Although Larry was big enough to fend her off and escape injury, the incident was unsettling, to say the least.

By early 1976, both of them had had enough. Taking the kids with her, Vickie moved out. She took a job at Dairy Queen, and began thinking about divorce. One of the things she thought about was whom to choose for her lawyer.

This was not the first time Vickie had met the impeccably dressed man who now stood before her in the Dairy Queen. Their paths had crossed once before, several years earlier. Although the specific occasion had long since been forgotten, an unfavorable impression lingered in Vickie's mind. She had met this fellow and his wife—a lovely woman named Diane—who was as pregnant as Vickie herself had been at the time. The man sidled over and initiated a vaguely flirtatious conversation that seemed in rather poor taste considering the big stomachs of both women. She remembered having felt a little dumbfounded.

Why would a big wheel like Price Daniel, Jr., seek her out, and exactly what had he had on his mind?

The memory of that incident alone was enough to get Price off on the wrong foot. Moreover, Price was not physically the type of man to whom Vickie was usually attracted. He had a certain cerebral look, more resembling an accountant than a laborer like Larry Moore. Price was just a little too clean-cut—not that he was totally unappealing, just quieter and sophisticated. And perhaps just a trifle effeminate.

"What's your name?" Price asked, already knowing the answer.

In a playful mood, Vickie lied to him: "Misty."

"Are you married?"

She shrugged. "Sort of."

Price's eyes twinkled. "Are you sure about that?"

"I'm getting a divorce." She was immediately sorry she had said that.

"Oh? Who's your lawyer?"

"I haven't got one," she shot back, impatient with his probing.

"Well, I happen to be a lawyer," Price chirped. "Why don't you give me a call?" He handed her a business card, then swiveled on his heels and left.

No, I hardly think so, Vickie said to herself as she watched him drive off. Lord knows I've got enough problems already.

Nevertheless, Price did go on to handle Vickie's divorce proceeding against Larry Moore, and by the summer of 1976, the rocky nine-year marriage was over.

Price Daniel, Jr., approached his courtship of Vickie with characteristic zeal and single-mindedness. He filled her mailbox with letters, her vases with flowers, and her ears with whispered endearments. He sat with her for hours in restaurant booths, and often he would bare his soul, much to Vickie's embarrassment.

Vickie ran hot and cold in the face of such behavior. Her degree of physical attraction was insufficient to offset her suspicion of Price's motives. "Don't you think you're on the wrong side of the tracks?" she asked him once, on his birthday no less. Price was taken aback. "How do you mean?" he replied. She told him plainly it was her impression that men like Price sought out women like her for one reason, and one reason only. Price was sincerely flabbergasted. "Explain what you mean by 'men like me' and 'women like you,'" he demanded. "What makes you think we're so different?"

He went on to tell her she could do anything she wanted to if she really put her mind to it. She was charmed by his answer, which had seemed not the least bit patronizing. Still, she wondered. After all, he was a politician; it was his job to be convincing.

But there was something about Price that was hard for Vickie to resist, something that kept her coming back for more. She could not deny he was a wonderful suitor.

Price, in turn was thoroughly taken with Vickie's vivacity, and her utter lack of pretension. Unused as he was to small talk, he nonetheless found her gregariousness refreshing. Her lighthearted behavior was just so—*relaxed.* Which it almost had to be, given that their dates not infrequently included Vickie's two children.

Price had even come to believe that Vickie's particular charm might be of practical value. In dealing with people, she had a way of finding the common denominator. Everyone felt at ease in her presence. With grooming, she might be able to transcend her background and become a political asset.

Among the gossips, there were other, darker theories about Price's attraction to Vickie. Perhaps it was a way to rebel against his privileged background and preordained path in politics. "Looks to me like some kind of death wish," mused a well-connected friend who did not see in Vickie the possibilities that Price described. The friend saw their union as a catastrophe.

Throughout his separation from Diane and pursuit of Vickie, Price always made a special effort to stay close to his son, Tom, then five years old. Late in the summer of 1976, father and son went on a Caribbean cruise. A basket of fruit from Vickie awaited them in Miami, the embarkation point for the cruise. Vickie was rewarded for the gesture with cards and letters from every Caribbean port. Upon his return to Texas, Price presented her with a heart-shaped pendant and matching earrings.

Still, Vickie was skeptical. The mail, she told a co-worker, didn't prove anything except that Price knew where she lived. The gifts, meanwhile, looked a little bogus. Remind me to check his car for the Cracker Jack boxes, she tought.

Besides, Vickie expected someone like Price to try to win her over with fancy-looking gifts. She wondered if Price was the kind of man who bought his son toys as a substitute for reading him stories at bedtime.

"I don't know, Vick," one co-worker mused. "If I were you, I'd stop worrying about it and take things at face value."

One of his gift-giving efforts did finally find its mark. It was a tiny plastic bubble of the type usually sold in supermarket vending machines. Inside was a scrap of paper with a handwritten message: "You're beautiful." Vickie was deeply touched by the simplicity and sweetness of the offering.

Yet doubts continued to surface. She questioned whether she was confusing love with admiration—or worse, convenience. So much of what he took for granted was unfamiliar to her—there was the time she mistook his chic dinnerware for camp-out plates. She detected sometimes a certain unintentional—and therefore, she assumed, genuine—snideness in his tone. "He makes me feel like something's wrong with me," she fretted to a sister. "It's not that he means to, necessarily. It's just his way."

Driven almost to distraction by such concerns, on October 1 she filled out an application to remarry Larry Moore. But Larry, whose cooperation was obviously needed, balked at the idea of a reconciliation. He had had enough trench warfare. Besides, there was a new woman in his life.

In early October, a desperate Vickie phoned Price at his house to discuss the entire situation with him. Price's manner that night soothed her doubts as never before. He consoled her, told her not to worry—everything would work out okay in the end. She was overwhelmed at his sincerity and concern.

On Halloween, she and Price took off for New Orleans, where Price's sister, Jean, lived with her minister-husband, David Murph. The occasion marked Vickie's very first plane ride. On November 1, the marriage vows were read in Murph's church. Vickie wore a white suit, and in what would come to be a gesture of haunting irony, Jean Murph gave her away.

The couple returned to Liberty, to the large spread on Governor's Road. Vickie felt uneasy about the house, and not simply because Price had lived there with Diane. It had a foreboding air. She would later recall that the very first time she stepped inside, all the windows fogged up around her. She felt as if the walls were closing in.

As she settled into her new life with Price, Vickie could never seem to keep the place warm enough. Price, who was eternally worried about the utility bills, did not like her to turn up the thermostat too high. But even when he wasn't around and she did turn up the heat, Vickie never quite felt warm enough in that house.

Chapter Four

The marriage of Price and Vickie raised eyebrows in East Texas. People made no bones about the fact that Price and his new bride had pitifully little in common.

"I couldn't believe it," one matron explained, looking back. "I mean, here was a girl who was a high-school dropout, and whose job at Dairy Queen was the pinnacle of her working career. The general feeling was, What was Price—a political man, mind you—what was he thinking of when he did this?"

Mary Cain, a young woman who had known Price for years (and who joined his office staff some time later) was equally perplexed. "Oh, *no*, is he all right?" she whispered to friends. "What has he done?"

Generally, Price was oblivious to the snide remarks. Yet he did now and then tender unsolicited explanations in her defense.

"I know a lot of people think this was a peculiar step for me to take," he volunteered to one acquaintance, "but believe me, when it comes to life and living, there are things Vickie could teach the both of us."

"Oh, really? What sort of things?" the acquaintance snorted.

Price dismissed his friend's lack of tact with a small laugh, then turned earnest once again. "She's got a good head on her shoulders. I'm telling you, the things she puts her mind to, she *knows*."

And it was true. While she could not hope to keep up with Price and his friends in a discussion of politics or current events, she did have a certain intuitive grasp of people. She read avidly about things that interested her, such as the lives of Hollywood celebrities.

For her part, Vickie found she had to adjust to Price's more eccentric habits.

As a suitor, he had impressed her with his perfectionism, his attention to detail. Often, she just watched how carefully he dressed himself—adjusting his tie, patting down his hair—and thought, My God, how wonderful it must be to be so *perfect*!

Now Price expected her to look perfect, too. You did not, Vickie learned, emerge from the bathroom until you were completely ready to greet the world for the day. Price detested seeing her in hair curlers, or applying makeup. Likewise, one did not walk into the bathroom while Price was in there, no matter what he was doing.

Price watched over his possessions with fanaticism. Vickie would recall a time when an optometrist examining Price's contact lenses stared up at her in utter disbelief.

"What is it?" she asked, concerned.

"These," the man said in measured tones, "are the first contact lenses I've ever seen without any scratches on them."

Not surprisingly, Price loathed having others—even Vickie—handle his personal effects. Once Vickie happened to mention in passing that her eyes were bothering her and that she had borrowed his Murine. Not long after, she noticed the nearly full vial in the trash.

Almost nine months to the day after the wedding, Franklin Baldwin Daniel was born. This provoked no small amount of kidding about the robust events of the wedding night. "Sorry to disappoint you," Vickie would reply playfully, "but Price was too drunk to do anything on our wedding night." Vickie had come to anticipate the birth with great joy, and not just for the usual reasons. Early on, she had found herself complaining to a sister, Patsy Denman, about the extent to which Price doted on Tom. During his frequent talks to the boy via long-distance telephone, Price was almost beside himself with joy. He maintained a room in the house just for Tom, with toys *strictly* for Tom, to be used only by Tom on his visits. Price was most insistent about this, which Vickie thought odd.

By the time of the birth, however, a new problem had arisen.

During their courtship, Vickie had conjured up a rosy vision of what life might be like as the wife of a celebrated politician. But she had never tried to discover the reality. Then, in May of 1977, Price surprised everyone by announcing for state attorney general on a local radio station.

Vickie, who had not previously voted, simply had no conception of the demands a political life made on a politician's time—and his wife's patience. Her rude awakening came when the Governor had to drive her home from the hospital after she'd had Franklin. Price was away on business.

As the days without Price stretched on, Vickie realized she was not eager to share her new husband with the public and his political buddies. The timing was especially bad. Vickie had hoped to return to New Orleans in celebration of their first wedding anniversary. But as Price's campaign moved into high gear, she realized that she would spend that day at home—most likely alone with her two older kids and the baby.

Nor was Vickie prepared to see her home transformed into a campaign headquarters. She was impatient with the phone calls, the strategy sessions, the endless conversations in that peculiar mumbo-jumbo known only to politicians.

Their "social life" got to be a joke. On her own as often as not, Vickie tried to take an interest in the kids' school affairs. She volunteered at the church. To busy herself the rest of the time, she became a telephone addict, kibbitzing with neighbor Charlotte Daniel about their respective sex lives, and holding pleasant long-distance talks with Jean Murph (though Vickie instinctively knew that if she was looking for a shoulder on which to cry about Price's neglect of her, Jean's was the wrong number to dial).

Still she was lonely. They did not even socialize with Price's relatives who clustered about them on Governor's Road.

Larry Moore visited often to see his kids. His impression was that Vickie was "more or less unhappy most of the time," always on her way out of the house.

In fact, Vickie did walk out on Price several times as she grew increasingly confrontational at this worst of all possible times. She asked him why it was necessary to put in so much time away from home. Price sympathized; he tried to explain the demands of political campaigning, and asked her to bear with him. But he seemed distracted. And no doubt, though he was never publicly critical of her, he must have found annoying her lack of sympathy for the world in which he moved.

By the time he officially kicked off his candidacy at an Elks Lodge banquet in September, the situation was explosive.

Vickie decided that a bold move was called for. Late in October, just ten days before their first wedding anniversary, she walked into the courthouse office of County Judge Harlan Friend. Unbeknownst to Vickie, Harlan Friend was among those who had no illusions about the marriage. "He was in politics, he needed a wife, he went and got one" was how Friend sized things up upon first hearing the news of Price's candidacy.

"I'm thinking of filing for divorce," Vickie told Friend. "But I've been told that no one from around here would represent me."

"That so? And why would that be?"

"Just the way it is," said a doleful Vickie. "They tell me there's no one who'd go up against the Daniels."

That was all Harlan had to hear. There was no love lost between Harlan and Price's family. Partly it was political, partly it was personal, but mostly, Harlan was fond of saying, it had to do with a basic difference of opinion: "The trouble between Price and me is, we do not both agree that he's the most wonderful lawyer and human being who ever lived." Harlan took the case.

On October 22, 1977, a petition was filed in which Vickie claimed the marriage had become "insupportable." The wire services got wind of it, and that was how Price, in the state capital, learned of his wife's divorce complaint.

Carlton Carl, Price's chief political aide-de-camp, would not forget the twelve hours he spent on the phone with Vickie that day. "Vickie was politically naïve and political campaigns are demanding. They place pressures on the best of marriages, and Vickie had never been close to politics before."

The ensuing debate between the two principals was terse and strident.

I never see you, said Vickie.

I'm in the middle of a political comeback, said Price.

You're also in the middle of a marriage, she said.

I'm doing this for the both of us, he said.

It sure doesn't seem that way, she said. I'm the one who has to hold down the fort while you're out doing what you're doing.

It takes time, he said. You have to work at these things, to be willing to put in the hours.

A marriage is no different, she said. It takes work, and understanding, and *communication*. You never *listen* to me when I try to talk to you.

That'll change, he said. I've just got a lot on my mind now. Just trust me that things'll work out.

Vickie was skeptical. But then, with one failed marriage behind her and three kids at home, she had never really intended to leave anyway. She had just hoped to shock him a little, wake him up.

She let Price draw up a motion to withdraw her divorce suit. And just like that, it was over, roughly two days after it had begun.

By spring, Price's campaign began encountering other troubles. Polls revealed that his opponent, who had begun the race as an underdog, was rapidly gaining ground.

Zeke Zbranek, himself a former legislator and lawyer friend from Liberty, urged Price to be a little more visible.

"You've got to get out there more," Zbranek cautioned. "Shake some hands and let the people see you. This isn't the time to just rest on your laurels."

"Don't worry about it," Price said matter-of-factly. "I'll be all right." He didn't think his constituents were apt to forget him all that quickly.

Advisers, though, tended to side with Zbranek. They urged Price to blanket the state with television commercials in the critical weeks before the primary. Price listened politely, but explained that to do that, he'd have to solicit some large contributions. He didn't want to open himself up to those looking to buy influence. And anyway, he was already some $80,000 in the hole from previous campaign expenditures. As one seasoned observer later put it, "Price was the sort of fellow who wasn't hardly comfortable when he was ahead. Put him that much in debt, and he'd be downright unfit to live with."

Vickie had already learned firsthand that Price was as compulsive about keeping track of expenses as he was about many other things. Such friends as Mary Cain explained it as just an extension of his need to have a handle on things, to know that the money was being put to good use. Detractors said simply that he was a cheap so-and-so. Whatever the case, Vickie as often as not did her shopping with detailed orders from Price. A typical note might instruct her to "go to the Minimax and get the following specials: 5 paper towels, Yellow Decorator . . . $2.00; 1 bag apples and get another free; 3 cans First Pick corn . . . $1.00; 3 TV Biscuits, 10-ct. cans . . . $.49."

So it was no surprise that Price did not opt for a last-minute publicity blitz. He felt his name would carry him through. A Daniel was a Daniel. Given the inevitable blur of confusing platforms and conflicting claims, voters would be inclined to stick with what they knew.

Price lost the primary election by some 70,000 votes to his Baylor contemporary Mark White (White went on to be elected attorney general, and later, governor). Most people who spoke to Price in the days following his defeat thought he took it well—shrugged it off. Others weren't so quick to buy his impassive facade. His humor was uncharacteristically self-effacing.

"You know, I think he's really hurting inside," David Parker told his wife, Susan. "I think he's basically feeling very lonely and rejected."

In the aftermath of the defeat, Price decided to rededicate himself to building a life in Liberty, one of the few areas in the state to give him an overwhelming endorsement at the polls. With renewed vigor he turned toward his old law practice. Through the summer and fall of 1978 he won a number of cases in succession, including one in which his client, who had suffered a six-cent loss on a can of soda, recouped more than $6,600 in damages. The case generated quite a bit of attention in conservative Liberty. For some time afterward, the lawsuit was the subject of both jokes and respectful analysis among local observers.

Price also began dabbling more seriously in real estate, and as he did, his demeanor seemed to relax somewhat. Possibly he realized that through real estate, he could begin to stake a claim for himself and escape the preordained path of politics. At last he could emerge from under his father's giant shadow.

Nonetheless, Price's shift in emphasis did little to improve relations at home. The awkwardness grew between him and Vickie. He resented her for her poorly timed show of disloyalty. Price began taking his meals alone, in front of the TV. Vickie complained to a sister, "I tell you, it's like we're not even here sometimes." If Price was in a particularly ornery mood, she claimed, and didn't like what she'd fixed, the dinner tray would wind up on the floor, where it would stay until Vickie herself cleaned it up.

Worse, the initial problems concerning Price's relationship with the children had gotten worse. To Vickie's mind, Price's favoritism toward Tom had grown to absurd proportions, as had his sensitivity to any noise or commotion caused by Jonathan and Kim, her own kids.

It got so that Vickie declined to have other children in the house when Price was home. Now and then, she let Ann Rogers's daughter, Catherine, stay for the night, but such occasions were carefully planned to occur when Price was out of town.

Chapter Five

A fter a while, nothing in the marriage seemed to be working right. During the family's August roundup, at which time the extended Daniel family convened at the Governor's house for a major hootenany, Price enlisted Vickie as his assistant in a magic show for the kids. The *pièce de résistance* of the act was to be a trick, suggested by Vickie herself, in which he pierced a balloon with a needle, and yet—the balloon failed to burst. The success of the routine relied upon a trick balloon that was impervious to a needle dipped in a special oil—use the wrong balloon, or forget the oil, and the whole thing literally blew apart.

His eyebrows furrowed and his voice tinged with mystery, Price introduced the trick by explaining he would defy reality. Then, without further ado, he pierced the balloon.

Instantly, the balloon popped: Vickie, who had read the directions on the package, had neglected to mention the part about the oil. Only now did she remember, as Price stood there stupefied, watching pieces of balloon fall to earth amid the laughter of his young audience.

Giggling, Vickie confessed her oversight, but Price was not amused. It must have occurred to him as he stood there, appraising her, his lips drawn tight and his head cocked just slightly to the side, Did she do that on purpose . . . ?

In the midst of this deteriorating situation—as if to re-affirm her penchant for bad timing—Vickie once again became pregnant.

Price's sister, Jean, would contend that Price reacted in an upbeat manner; it was *Vickie,* never having really emerged from the funk that precipitated her divorce action, who was troubled. Vickie, on the contrary, would insist that Price was absolutely livid.

Whatever the case, the house was once again thrown into turmoil. The couple argued frequently and shortly afterward, Vickie found bitter solace in a Houston abortion.

For his part, Price turned to an old friend, whose sooth-ing effect he sought more and more frequently: the whis-key bottle. Vickie was alarmed by the way drinking would affect Price's personality.

It would have been helpful had she been able to go for counsel to Price's family. But their idolatry of Price did not permit them to acknowledge any facts that cast him in an unfavorable light.

At a family function Vickie made the mistake of open-ing up to Price's spinster aunt, Ellen Virginia Daniel (known as "Titha.") The subject was Price's treatment of Vickie's son, Jonathan. Even as she spoke, Vickie had mixed emo-tions, for Titha was known to have these lapses.

On this occasion, Titha just sat there expressionless, and Vickie felt that her little grievance had basically gone in one ear and out the other. In a way, she was relieved. At least, she felt, no harm had been done.

She was wrong. The very next day, she got an angry phone call from Jean Murph.

"Never," Jean instructed, *"never do that again."*

* * *

By May 1979 a change of scenery was clearly in order. The Liberty routine was driving both of them crazy, and so Price and Vickie, as had so many embattled lovers before them, sought to rekindle the flames of matrimonial bliss with an exotic vacation. Price booked a cruise to the Caribbean and South America. But diversions, no matter how captivating, were no substitute for honesty and affection.

Shortly after their return from the cruise, a bitter spat sent Vickie streaming from the house with her three children. This time, instead of going to stay with her mother or a sister, Vickie took refuge at a nearby motel, the Del Ray Motor Inn. She told the desk clerk she would be staying for a spell because she was having her own house sprayed for bugs. A day or two later, however, Price came to retrieve her.

One night shortly thereafter she woke up in the wee hours. Feeling famished, she went to the kitchen to get something to eat. Price had also awakened and followed her.

He came up behind her and slammed the cupboard shut. "You're pregnant again, aren't you?"

Vickie nodded.

On a late summer night in 1979, a dispute developed over the color television located in the children's playroom. Price had it tuned to the baseball game, but Vickie was determined to watch something else. Price told Vickie and the children to use the black-and-white television in Kimberly's room. Vickie was intransigent. The two began dueling with the channel selector in the playroom. Then the battle spread throughout the house, as Vickie and Price ambled from room to room, switching dials back and forth as they went. It might have been funny, but given the underlying tensions, the dispute escalated into a physical confrontation. By the time it was over, Price had Vickie

45

down in the master bedroom and Kimberly was pounding on his back in defense of her mother.

Vickie took off once more to the Del Ray Motor Inn.

Finally Price called a summit conference. The session produced a curious document, which served less to revitalize their marriage than to underscore the two main factors that were keeping them apart—Vickie's resentment and Price's compulsiveness.

In his preamble, Price suggested: "List 10 things that you would want me to do differently, improve on or change if we were ever to go back together. Also list 10 things that you would do differently, improve or change. Be specific. No general statements permitted."

Vickie's effort painted a vivid picture of her discontent. She named no fewer than seventeen areas in which Price's behavior could stand improvement. Many of her complaints concerned her sense of isolation/frustration: "Listen to me when I'm talking to you." "Come home to relax, not work."

Other items on Vickie's list hinted at a growing laxness in his behavior at home: "Clean up after yourself." "Cut down on your drinking for your own sake." "Eat at the table and not have me serve you in the playroom." After this last line, in a clear reference to the lack of parity she felt in the marriage, she added, "I'm not a waitress anymore, I'm your wife."

Ignoring Price's instructions to be specific, she also made complaints of a more philosophical nature: "I don't like fakes. I think you should express your own true feelings . . . to your family and friends." Of the impending birth, she wrote: "Price, I want this child, please understand. It's part of you . . . probably the only part you can give." Toward the end, in what seemed almost to be a despairing call for divine intervention, she wrote: "We should go to church regularly together."

Vickie's list of promises included fewer items than her list of grievances. Virtually the entire section was written in tart phrases meant less as sincere admissions of fault than zingers aimed at the idiosyncratic Price. "Learn to cook to your specifications" was typical, as was the facetious admission that she shouldn't be jealous "even though you go sit at another woman's table or talk all evening about how much you like a person of the fem. gender." Also: "I should never watch T.V. unless you like the show and are watching it too."

Price's effort was notable for its symmetry and order, with an even dozen items under each column. He requested among other things a "pleasant greeting when I come home from work (even if it has to be faked). . . ." "Always have a pleasant greeting in the morning (even if it has to be faked)." To both demands, he added a parenthetical note of paternal advice: "If you try to do these things and don't particularly like doing them, you will do them anyway out of habit—a good habit, not just with me but with everyone."

He made light of Vickie's chronic suspicions about infidelities on his part. "I am not running around, flirting, etc.," he wrote. "I am working my tail off." There was, he declared, no reason to be jealous, and she should stop forthwith.

Mixed in among such weighty issues were smaller grievances: "I would like a good, hot meal Saturday noon," he wrote; and then added, as though reading from a menu (and thereby lending no small amount of credence to Vickie's dismay at being treated like a waitress), that he would also like a hamburger each Saturday night. Not content merely to let it go at that, he specified that his hamburger was to have "two slices of cheese" on it.

He chastised Vickie for doing so much of her shopping in convenience stores, and for impulsively indulging the children's sweet tooth in general. Using florid, redundant language that might have been lifted intact from one of his cease-and-desist orders, Price instructed Vickie to "quit completely, stop absolutely forever and ever stopping at Sonics and Dairy Queens, etc., for Cokes and ice cream." This was not only wasteful, but bad for the children, he felt.

Price's list of errors, with its passivity of tone—"We need a new deep freeze and a new lawnmower"—suggested a lack of enthusiasm for the task of self-criticism. He hinted at some possible overexuberance for controlling the purse strings, and promised to "try" to expand Vickie's budget or credit privileges. He pledged to make an effort to get a handle on his smoking habit (three packs a day). He conceded his penchant for continuous work, and expressed optimism that he could channel some of his energy into the child they were expecting.

Price apparently ran out of steam with admission number 11, but his "fault" column needed one more item to round out the dozen and thus match exactly in number his list of gripes. He decided to get in a little jab of his own. Echoing an earlier pledge to give his wife "more sex," Price wrote in his last item, "Even more sex. Remember her special cravings, wild desires, and constant needs."

In November 1979, partly in the spirit of this new effort to save the marriage and partly out of a desire to save money, Price moved his offices from a downtown building to a double-wide trailer north of town, not far from the turnoff that led to the family spread and his house.

The abandonment of his downtown headquarters signaled a redirection of his professional energies as well. Before his primary defeat, Price's real-estate dealings with David Parker and other partners had been mostly a diversion: something the workaholic Price used to fill time between politics and legal work. With the move up the road,

Price's Liberty Land Company sign was displayed more prominently than the certificates documenting his legal background. An even worse fate befell the mementos of political achievement that adorned his former office. They were boxed up and put away, save for a photo of Lyndon Johnson, and another of Jimmy and Rosalynn Carter—these, rather than being affixed to a wall in the new office, were left to reside in haphazard ignominy on the floor.

Price threw himself into real estate with a zeal that had been conspicuously missing from his political pursuits. Whereas even at the height of his political career, he had never been one to glad-hand the public, he now bestowed avid greetings upon everyone who came through the door of the trailer. Suddenly, he was a "natural" salesman. His enthusiasm for the properties he listed was infectious, even over the phone. In fact, it spawned a highly effective technique he would employ with prospective buyers. He'd call up someone he knew was interested in real-estate speculation and speak in glowing terms about a certain property he had taken as a listing. He'd suggest that he was interested in buying it for himself. The reason for the phone call, he explained, was simply that he "wanted to get somebody else's opinion before taking the next step." The sincerity in Price's voice, coupled with his reputation for knowing his stuff, investment-wise, usually got the other party thinking: Hey, if a sharp customer like Price Daniel, Jr., wants that property, then maybe *I* want that property. As often as not, the person he had "consulted" would show up at the office with an offer of his own.

The dramatic change in Price's demeanor led to much private speculation about whether he had ever been truly comfortable in politics. Political stardom had been forecast for him since he had first learned to tie his shoes, but he had never impressed people as being terribly happy with his life in Austin. Now, Price was his own man; he did not have to worry about following in his father's footsteps or measuring up.

Clearly, too, real estate was more suited to his personality. Price was a doer. When he got an idea—and he got them often—he became obsessed with putting it into action. That, however, was not how things worked in the legislature. You could invest years in attempting to bring about a certain change and still come up empty in the end. In real estate, on the other hand, a man had personal control of his destiny. And he could make things happen fast.

Price began spending much time in conference with partners assessing the resurgence of East Texas. Houston, in particular, was booming again. Already America's fifth-largest urban center, Houston would become, in 1981, the first city in U.S. history to spend $2 billion on total construction in one year. Suburban sprawl was reaching out and lifting the property values of all satellite towns, Liberty included. If Price could not be a political luminary of the first magnitude, at least he would be the land baron of Liberty County.

Toward that end, one of his first projects, after opening his new doors at 3802 North Main Street, was to find an assistant. His choice was intriguing.

Mary Cain was an old acquaintance, whose name was well known to the local citizenry. A feisty, chestnut-haired divorcée—tall, dark, lushly assembled—Mary had distinguished herself not merely through her self-reliant attitude but by an ability to hold a job. Not just a menial, make-ends-meet kind of job but one that provided a genuine breadwinner's salary.

As is so often the case with women of independent mind, men had reacted to Mary with feelings at once of loathing and desire.

Price had heard of Mary's interest in a real-estate career. Though she didn't yet have her agent's license, he persuaded her to start out by lending a hand at office work.

Her first secretarial efforts proved disastrous. But Price kept her on anyway, to the delight of gossips all over town. Somewhat less delighted was Vickie.

Like all who joined Price's employ, Mary Cain was quickly indoctrinated in Price's meticulous office routine. Her first morning was given over to learning the proper way of sharpening and stocking Price's formidable reserve of pencils. Each would have to be sharpened to the same length and rake as its neighbors and then aligned shoulder to shoulder in a pencil box with labels facing outward. (This, even though the pencils were stored behind cabinet doors.) No less painstaking, Mary learned, was the procedure for paying office bills. Price had instituted a system of checks and double-checks worthy of a $10 billion corporation.

On the other hand, Mary noticed that Price was phenomenally sensitive to his employees' mental states. If she had the smallest look of sadness on her face, he would pause on his way past her desk and talk to her. "Somethin' wrong, Mary? Well, let's just sit down and talk about this here." He was no less generous with the rest of those in his employ.

Mary, an analytical sort, knew it was partly a matter of the relationship between employee morale and productivity. "Price is a bottom-line person," she would tell friends, when asked to describe her enigmatic boss. "Unhappy employees don't produce as well as happier ones."

So it was with the lunchtime routine that developed. Because Price wanted the office continuously staffed he began having lunch with the group regularly. Special occasions—the closing of a particular deal or the birthday of one of the office workers—would warrant taking everybody to a local restaurant. But usually, either secretary Betty White or typist Pam Locke whipped up a light lunch in the trailer's own kitchen area.

Such togetherness only served to inflame the resentments that were tearing apart his marriage.

February 1980 witnessed the birth of Price and Vickie's second son. Vickie favored naming the boy Marion Price, to continue the tradition begun with Price's grandfather. Price was lukewarm. The pressure to perform was already strong enough in this family, he argued; you don't want to further burden the child by giving him a name to live up to. "You have no idea how hard it was for me to be a junior," he acknowledged. Nonetheless, when it came time to fill out the birth certificate, Vickie told the hospital people she had decided on Marion Price Daniel IV.

Most saw it as a tribute. Vickie herself said she hoped that naming the boy after his father might spur the acceptance she felt had been withheld in Franklin's case, for Price's favoritism toward Tom was steadily worsening.

Nonetheless, a story circulated that shed another possible light on her motivations in choosing the name.

For years, there had been some controversy in the family over whether Price senior was in fact deserving of the "senior," in that his father, also Marion Price Daniel, was alive at the time of Price junior's birth. Therefore, in reality, Price junior should have been Marion Price Daniel III. Which, in turn, meant that Price senior was actually Price junior. None of this would have mattered had there not been a feud of sorts between Price senior and his brother, Bill (Price junior's uncle). Bill took great pleasure in reminding folks that the real Price senior was actually *his* father, and not Governor Daniel himself.

Thus it was suggested that Vickie's purpose in naming the baby Marion Price Daniel IV—and making the "IV" a part of the boy's actual name, as she did—was to provide Price with a living reminder of the family feud. One witness even claimed to have heard Vickie gloat, after filling out the hospital form, "That's one for Uncle Bill!"

And yet it was Price who, typically, had the last word. A black youth, Robert "Bob" Broussard, was living with the family at the time, doing odd jobs for Price. There had been some tension between Broussard and Vickie. In addition, Price knew his wife had an Uncle Robert whom she didn't particularly like.

Price decided he would refer to his new baby as Bob.

To Vickie's chagrin, the name stuck.

Robert Broussard became Price Daniel's constant companion in the later months of 1979. The young man had been hired to do yard work and general cleaning, but he had quickly assumed a more important role. Price invited him to live in the guest room at the house, and he became a habitual presence. For example, Broussard accompanied Price when he came to pick Vickie up at the Del Ray after the TV Fight. And when Price visited Vickie in the hospital right after the birth of the baby, Robert Broussard was by his side. When Price came to take her home from the hospital, he actually handed Broussard the baby to carry out to the car. "Can you imagine that!" she told friends. "His brand-new baby, and yet rather than carry the child himself, he hands it off to Robert!" Because Vickie did not want a scene right then and there, she let Broussard carry the baby until they reached the elevators, at which point she thanked him for his help and politely took little Bob herself.

It grew perplexingly clear to Vickie that Broussard worshiped Price. Certainly, it couldn't have had anything to do with what the youth was being paid for his services.

Price did buy Robert gifts: clothes, a bike, this and that. It got to be a sore point, in that Vickie felt Price was lavishing more attention on Broussard than on her or the children.

One morning after Price left for work, Broussard came over to Vickie as she was doing dishes and asked if he could talk to her, maybe clear the air. Their conversation began cordially enough. But Vickie grew increasingly tense and vitriolic. Broussard made up his mind to move out as soon as possible.

Years later she recognized that the boy served the role of fawning admirer. "He needed someone to be in awe of him," she concluded, "and so he took Robert with him everywhere he went because Robert saw him that way."

But at the time, she was too jealous for such rationalizations. Deeply resentful of Price's attentions to Robert, Vickie wondered exactly what was the nature of the bond between the two men.

Around this time, Vickie began taking nursing courses. Price loyalists believed Vickie was attending school at her husband's urging; it was an example of Price's continuing efforts to encourage her to make the best of her limited potential. (Or, as one of Price's office workers put it, "to give the girl something to do.") To Vickie partisans, who believed (or had been led to believe) that Vickie made all the arrangements herself—and in secret, no less—it was an outgrowth of Vickie's desperate need to escape her stifling home environment.

Price also suggested that Vickie see a psychiatrist. Vickie, at first, was cynical. "*I* should see a psychiatrist," she snorted. "What about you? Aren't you part of this?"

Price prevailed anyway. In the spring of 1980, Vickie made an appointment with a Houston specialist. But she

· ·

came away from the experience feeling no better about things, and perhaps a bit worse.

During this time, it seemed to her that even the stars were conspiring against her. She read, in an astrology manual on Price's bookshelf, that Virgos like her and Geminis like Price made for a terrible marriage.

Chapter Six

That same spring, Vickie's "woman troubles" culminated in a hysterectomy.

For many couples, the operation, following an initial period of adjustment on the woman's part, signals the beginning of a new sexual freedom. For Price and Vickie, the operation had the opposite effect. It produced a coolness, a physical estrangement that lasted to the end.

Even prior to the operation, sex had become an ordeal for Vickie. Now Price moved out of their master bedroom and into a spare room down the hall. All four kids began sleeping with Vickie in the master suite. Thus, most of the rooms in the huge house remained unoccupied.

If the issue ever came up—why, in such a huge house, were all four kids crammed into a single bedroom?—Vickie would skirt it. Only after Price's death would she tell her version of the full story.

Out from under the pressures of politics, and perhaps also because of the increasing distance he put between himself and Vickie, Price Daniel began to relax in the final eight months of his life. And with this relaxation came an enormous change in his appearance and image.

The change had actually begun not long after the birth

of Bob, when he went out and bought a Ford pickup. Now Price put his self-reassessment into high gear. He forsook his three-piece suits, his sartorial staple since schooldays, for western attire: cowboy shirts, boots, and blue jeans. Designer jeans, to be sure, not Levis or Wranglers. But jeans nonetheless.

Price seemed committed to his new image. Now and then, in the middle of the workday, he would, without warning, simply swing his boots up onto his desk, turn up the volume on the office stereo, and issue an almost-sacrilegious edict calling for a slowdown in the tempo of office work. "Why are we all killin' ourselves over this stuff?" he would yell. "Let's take it easy for a while!" At a loss for words, his co-workers could only exchange stunned looks.

Nor were his employees the only ones who noticed. Price's efforts to adopt a new, western image left not a few people around town struggling hard to suppress belly laughs.

"Price didn't really have the western physique, to be honest with you," David Parker would recall. "And as far as being a 'cowboy,' home on the range and all that—heck, I doubt he had ever mowed his yard. None of 'em did. It just wasn't how they were brought up."

A second relative noted the designer labels on Price's jeans, and remarked, "I guess that's about as far as old Price could get himself to go."

Indeed, there were signs that Price's metamorphosis had come at a psychic cost. Mary Cain was among those who wondered if it was possible that the kind of man who agonized over his office pencils could so easily turn a new leaf?

As if to support such a hypothesis, Price's musical tastes became more melancholy and contemplative. At one point, he developed a fixation on the then-popular Stephen Sondheim song "Send in the Clowns," with its wistful, almost self-reproachful lyrics.

During this period, too, came the lone occasion when he cast off his outward reserve and gave vent to the hurt he must have felt over his living arrangements with Vickie. "How do you think it makes a man feel," he came up and asked her one night, "when his wife won't sleep in the same bedroom?"

Drink in hand, he walked off. To Vickie, the remark was not only out of character but a bit out of touch with the facts. As she recalled it, Price had been the one to initiate the move to separate quarters.

Price began to move even closer to his office staff. He recruited them for errands a husband might normally perform with his wife. For instance, Price would go grocery shopping with the women from his office. The items were shelved temporarily at the office trailer until Price went home at night, at which time he'd take a bag or two with him. (As with the pencils, the labels on each can would be turned outward and precisely centered.)

Vickie knew that Price was looking for every possible excuse to spend less time at the house. She especially resented the communal meals. "He has time for everybody but me," she fumed. It was no longer a question of saving the marriage but rather of avoiding humiliation.

On Vickie's birthday, September 12, she was invited to a buffet luncheon held more or less in her honor by a Liberty women's club. Not long after the festivities got under way, Price and his office retinue walked in on separate business. Price waved to Vickie and her tablemates, but only in passing. The perfunctory nature of his greeting did not surprise his co-workers; as Mary Cain put it, "Theirs was not a real romantic relationship." But to Vickie, it was an outright snub. "He cares about them more than he does me," she said to her friends, "and he's certainly a lot freer with money with them than he is with me!"

When it came to finances, Price's friends were of the opinion that Vickie was seeing things the wrong way; that she incorrectly ascribed Price's caution to tightfistedness. Price, they believed, was trying to protect Vickie from herself.

"He takes care of her the way you take care of kids," one of Price's workers told another during an after-hours conversation. "He knows it's kind of a put-down on his part, but it's necessary if she's not going to blow the whole week's budget in a couple of days. Vickie just has no idea of what to do with a dollar." Having never had much money previously, the co-worker pointed out, she had a tendency toward occasional impulsive spending. Then too, it was entirely possible that, given Price's background, Vickie thought the reservoir of money was endless. If so, she was badly out of sync with her husband's outlook. "His daddy's money is his daddy's money," Mary Cain understood. "Price wants to make it on his own."

In any case, Vickie couldn't help feeling slighted. As Vickie assessed things, Price was depriving his own children at the same time he was off playing Sir Galahad to the members of his office.

The main focus of Vickie's frustrations in this area was secretary Betty White. Early in 1980, White faced eviction. She had few resources and even fewer prospects; her husband had long since absconded without giving a thought to his support obligations. With nowhere for herself and her two children to go, she appealed to her boss for help. Which was only fitting, in a way, inasmuch as it was Price and Mary who had initiated Betty's quandary by selling to a doctor the modest house which she was renting.

"What am I going to do?" she asked Mary, almost in tears.

Mary reassured her co-worker and friend. "We've all got to think about this thing. But don't you worry, Betty. We'll call a meeting. We're gonna solve this."

"Yeah," Price agreed when Mary approached him. "Let's have lunch and think. We'll come up with something."

Before long, Price had hit upon a solution: Betty should buy a mobile home. One of Price's clients and business associates was Pat Chapman, who owned a slew of trailer parks in Liberty and Harris counties. The deal would be easy to arrange.

"How much can you afford?" he asked Betty.

"About two hundred a month," she replied.

A unanimous gulp reverberated around the office. Even in a trailer, two hundred a month wasn't going to cut it.

"Tell you what," said Price. "The only thing I can think of is, let's see if Pat has a repo. Something he's trying to unload. Maybe that'll work out."

In true family style, Price, associate Mark Morefield, Betty, Mary, and another secretary looked over potential trailer homes, found several that were not too far out of reach, and selected one with Betty's blessing. Since that still left the problem of getting credit approval, Price agreed to co-sign Betty's mortgage note. The trailer was moved behind the Main Street office, to a mobile-home community called Twin Oaks Park, which Price owned in partnership with Chapman.

Later that year, Betty complained with particular ferocity about her gas-guzzling clunker of an automobile. The repair bills showed signs of outstripping her salary. In typical style, she petitioned Price for a raise of $400 a month. Price had a counterproposal. He would give Betty a $100 raise, guarantee the car loan, and arrange to have the first installment delayed until the arrival of Betty's 1980 tax-refund check. Fair enough, said Betty. Once again the office staff went out, this time in search of a car. Within days, Betty was handed the keys to a new Ford Granada.

Early December found the office staff celebrating Betty's

birthday at a seafood restaurant, as Price's guests. Though Vickie attended as well, she did not feel very much like partying. She could not help but think of Betty's car, parked outside, and Betty's trailer, installed a few miles away.

Nor could she overlook the obvious contrast between the gala mood here at this party and the embarrassing spectacle at her own birthday fete just three months earlier.

Southern custom proscribes men from being the aggressor in a divorce action. Behind closed doors, a man may beat his wife; he may place her under the equivalent of house arrest; he may force her to toil under conditions most modern females (and males as well) would find intolerable. But he must not subject her to public humiliation by marking her as an "unwanted" woman. Ironically, the privilege of being the aggressor in a divorce action is one of the few prerogatives the woman is allowed. Further, men, in the ruggedly Spartan traditions of Texas, are expected to be able to bear almost any hardship with unflinching stoicism. For a man to be the one in a marriage to throw his hands up in defeat would be viewed as a sign of weakness.

Thus it fell to Vickie to sue for divorce. Which she did, finally, with the assistance of Baytown attorney Andrew Lannie, on December 31, 1980. Happy New Year.

Her legal strategy hadn't changed much in two years. She might have used the same petition, alleging once again that "the marriage has become insupportable because of discord or conflict of personalities." She requested child support and temporary control of the home and her car. A hearing on an order to restrain Price from selling or disposing of any property was subsequently set for Thursday, January 22, with both parties to be present.

The appointment would not be kept.

The filing caught Liberty off guard. True, Vickie had filed before, and the tensions in the marriage during Price's political campaign were common knowledge (even if the specific problems were not). But even the most ill-spirited gossips had assumed that things had been turned around by Price's determination to forsake public life in favor of becoming a local businessman.

Only Vickie had forseen the inevitability of a despairing finish, and the role she would play in it. As an addendum to her list of Del Ray demands, she had written, "To be really honest I'll have to tell you that I can't change. Miracles just don't happen like this. We're both too proud to give in."

Notwithstanding the divorce filing, Price and Vickie remained in the house on Governor's Road. Vickie didn't have much choice; she was without the funds to move elsewhere. Toward the latter part of 1980, she had worked for a short time as a cashier in a Baytown supermarket, but the money, she would insist, had been spent at Christmastime, to supplement Price's gift allowance.

Price, meanwhile, felt no particular compulsion to leave. The house, after all, was his—totally and incontestably his—a gift from his parents upon his marriage to Diane. Be that as it may, friends suggested that it would be prudent, under the circumstances, for him to move out at least temporarily. He could always return after Vickie had left. Price said he'd mull it over, but what undoubtedly troubled him as a lawyer was the old saw about possession being nine tenths of the law. He was not eager to have to come to grips with the potential problem of dislodging a recalcitrant Vickie from the premises at some future date. What harm could the arrangement possibly do in the short run?

The plan was to relocate Vickie in a place of her own

as soon as possible, but things did not move smoothly on that front. Price urged her to buy a trailer home (he promised to get her started), and in mid-January she found one to her liking. With its numerous frilly touches—its elevated bedroom, tinted bathroom windows, sheer curtains, and garden tub—it could not have differed more from the model selected by Betty White, or from what Price had envisioned.

In addition, Vickie was not happy about Price's plans concerning where to locate the trailer: behind his office at Twin Oaks. An awkward enough prospect considering that Betty lived there, and all the more uncomfortable because the plot would be clearly visible from the office. Price had a perfectly logical explanation for his choice of sites. He said he wanted the kids close at hand to facilitate visits. But Vickie suspected it had more to do with her than with Franklin and Bob; she just couldn't countenance her ex-husband keeping tabs on her.

"What about a house?" she proposed. "There must be something suitable on the market . . . ?"

Price and Mary Cain sat down to discuss this new proposition. Mary noticed right away how methodical her boss was. Even in the tensest situations he was still the same old super-organized, dispassionate Price. The rap session aimed at finding a suitable house for Vickie was in almost every sense a reprise of the brainstorming session that had been devoted to Betty White's housing problems. "Okay," Price would say, "now if Vickie gets a job, she's probably not going to make a lot of money, so we have to ascertain that what we come up with is within budget. . . ." He sounded like a tax adviser talking about a client, not a man talking about a woman who had been his wife for the past five years. Only in one respect was Price more sensitive. It seemed important to him to protect Vickie's sense of self-esteem, to send his wife off on the right foot, confidence-wise. He said to Mary, "Whatever we wind up with, it's got to be something she can feel good about. Something she can feel that she's doing herself, and that makes her feel worthwhile."

Soon, Vickie was presented with a list of comfortable (if not opulent) local properties. Still, she could not decide. Price began to question whether Vickie really wanted out. Every time he came up with a new alternative, she came up with a new obstacle.

Throughout all this, Price and Vickie continued with their daily routines. Price went to work; Vickie tended to functions at school, Scouts, whatever. Nighttime was spent working out the terms of their settlement. As usual, money was at the heart of things. Price felt Vickie should be able to tend to Franklin and Bob on a total of seven hundred dollars per month. Vickie took the figure as further evidence of Price's blatant favoritism toward Tom; Diane, after all, was receiving five hundred dollars in monthly support for one child. Price held firm, and as the days wore on, that issue remained up in the air.

In mid-January, with a new life just over the horizon, Price allowed the last barriers of ritual parsimony to come crumbling down. He suddenly abandoned the bizarre check-writing procedure at his office. From now on, he declared, Betty White would simply issue the checks. All members of the office staff were given raises. Trusted ally Mark Morefield was offered a partnership.

Excitedly, Price began talking about getting a new car—and not just a sedate, workmanlike vehicle like his pickup. No, he had in mind something flashy. Like a Riviera, his one indulgence in recklessness during his freewheeling, relatively untroubled college days.

On January 16, Jean Murph had a ninety-minute phone conversation with her brother and sister-in-law. The discussion concerned the deteriorated marriage and focused particularly on Vickie's perception of her husband's indifference to her needs and demands.

Nothing was resolved—Vickie kept claiming that Price was drunk and unreceptive to honest discussion—and Jean got off the phone feeling unnerved. The situation in the house sounded far too incendiary.

On the morning of Monday, January 19, a war-weary Price arrived at work clutching the latest communication from Vickie. In the angry note, which he showed to Betty White, Vickie had returned to one of her abiding peeves of the past few months:

"You raised Betty's salary so she could afford the new car you helped her get. Why can't you raise the children's child support for only 3 yrs., so they can have a place to stay? . . . You felt so sorry for Betty and found a way to get some extra money, why can't you do the same for your boys? If Betty is so special to you then maybe you had better start letting her do more for you . . . Let Betty feed you, don't ask me to ever wait on you again! She is getting paid and I'm not!"

Vickie's rage leaped up off the page at Betty. She remarked on how beleaguered her boss looked and noticed what appeared to be a small gash on the underside of his chin. She asked him if he was all right. Price told his secretary not to worry. In an aside, which was meant to be reassuring but took on ironic significance in light of events to follow, he told her, "Everything will be over before you know it."

Vickie, that day, phoned Judy Moore, Larry Moore's current wife, and chatted awhile about child support and related matters. During the afternoon, she buttonholed Susan Parker, whom she had run into at Franklin's preschool. Susan heard Vickie explain how petty Price was being about some of the items to be divided up; he had even asked for several things back he had given her as

· ·

gifts! Still later, Vickie was back on the line to the Moore residence, to solicit her first husband's assistance for her impending move to a Baytown apartment she had found the preceding weekend, in lieu of more permanent quarters. Affable Larry, as always, agreed.

Price left his office at approximately 6:30. It had been a thoroughly miserable day, one of unrelenting wetness and chill. As he drove home, what light remained began to recede. It appeared that at any moment, the sky might open up, and all hell would break loose.

Chapter Seven

O scar Cantu, a moon-faced, bespectacled emergency medical technician, was working the late afternoon shift at the Liberty Fire Department. In Liberty, as in many suburban towns across America, the fire department has responsibility for ambulance service. EMTs like Cantu are often the first people to reach the scene of a crisis.

Cantu had been on the job a year, but he considered himself a rookie nonetheless. Liberty was that kind of town: uneventful. There was an occasional cardiac arrest, or a drunk-driving mishap. But the victims were seldom dead as a result of intentional violence.

Cantu was at his downtown desk at about 7:30 P.M. on the night of January 19 when the call came from a deputy at the Liberty Sheriff's Department. An ambulance was needed at the junior Daniel's home out on Governor's Road. It was uncertain what the nature of the problem was or who was involved; whoever had initially phoned the hospital to report the emergency had dropped the receiver at one point and been understood to yell, "Price, get up!" But the female caller's voice had been unsteady and confused. She was, the hospital people felt, very probably close to the edge. So expect anything, Cantu was warned.

Technically, the Liberty rescue squad's jurisdiction ended at the town line, about half a mile southeast of the Daniel spread, but exceptions were routinely made for wealthy families who lived on the outskirts. Over the years, some of the locals had been irked by such favoritism. But Cantu just saw it as a fact of life. He ran out into the heavy air and took his place on the ambulance alongside his boss, David Bautsch, and co-worker John Anderson. Flying up Main Street toward FM 1011 with sirens blaring, they covered the distance, despite the fog and mist, in about ten minutes.

At the house, Cantu greeted the slender blond woman who stood at the door, clutching a washcloth, with a polite if somewhat apprehensive request for the nature of the emergency. Cantu took the woman to be the lady of the house, Mrs. Price Daniel, Jr. She seemed relatively lucid, but also struck him as being shaken and somehow just—not right. Especially around the eyes. A little like a trapped animal, he thought.

When she mumbled something unintelligible, Cantu repeated his question a second time, more firmly.

"He's *back there*," she said in reply, pointing with a stiff and jerky movement down the long center hallway.

By "back there," Cantu at first assumed Vickie was indicating the bedroom at the end of the hallway on the far left side of the one-story house. He ran in that direction with Anderson and Bautsch, passing, on the way, a descended pull-down attic stairway with a man's outer jacket hanging from it. However, there was no body in the bedroom, nor even a bed—just some toys, stuffed animals, and personal effects.

Cantu ran halfway back up the hall. The woman, who by this time had confirmed to one of the other EMTs that she was, indeed, Vickie Daniel, met him there. The two of them now peered at each other through the thin wood slats of the attic stairs. It was an odd confrontation that reminded Cantu of the familiar movie prison scene where the convict talks to a visitor through mesh screening.

There was also something about the situation that seemed to mock the affluence the residents of this house clearly enjoyed. Somewhere within its sumptuous seven-thousand-square-foot confines was a man who was desperately ill—perhaps dying, if the woman's grave and slightly off-center demeanor was any indication—and *they couldn't find the guy.*

"Where *is* he!" Cantu asked again, this time screaming at Vickie.

"He's *back there,*" Vickie repeated, almost hysterical by now. She seemed, as she said it, to be pointing not straight back, as Cantu and the others had originally thought, but more diagonally—toward the kitchen, which was off to the side of the bedroom.

On the tile floor in the kitchen, Cantu and Bautsch found a body: a male, in his mid-thirties, whom they took to be Vickie's husband, Price Daniel, Jr. Sprawled facedown next to a pantry, he was a few feet from a door that led out to a carport. The door was shut, but none of them noticed, at that point, whether it was locked—an issue that later would take on critical importance.

Daniel was ashen. A pool of blood spread out from under him, across the floor, and beneath a freezer about a foot from his head. The pool formed, roughly, the shape of an hourglass, largest around his midsection and his mouth.

Cantu rolled him over slightly to see if there were any obvious wounds that might need tending to, although all of his instincts—and the amount of blood he saw, now, bubbling from Price's nose and mouth—told him that help had come to late. Still, Cantu checked for vital signs, as did Bautsch. There was neither pulse nor respiration. As expected.

From out in the hall, the men heard Vickie's fragile voice:

"He's O.K., isn't he?" She said it more than once. There was a hopeful ring to it that sounded ludicrously out of touch.

Cantu ran back out, bypassing Vickie, got on the radio and sent word of what had been found. Bautsch, as the senior man on the call, stayed with the body to preserve the chain of custody until the proper authorities arrived.

Cantu then walked over to where Vickie was standing. He noted, off to the side, in the hallway, ice melting on the floor beside a spray of cigarette ashes and broken glass. Vickie hunched over slightly, her fingers extended, arms bent at the elbow. Not unlike a linebacker's stance, Cantu thought, except wilder and less disciplined. He approached her and started to talk. Caution seemed to be called for.

"What happened back there?" he asked tentatively.

In hollow tones, Vickie replied that she had shot Price. She then asked, "How is he?"

As Cantu began to form the words, Vickie suddenly sprang forward, grabbed his arms, and dug her nails into his jacket. She brayed wildly, angrily, spewing gibberish and spittle.

Cantu was astonished at her strength and ferocity. Quickly, he called Anderson for help. The three of them became a tangled mass of flailing arms and gnashing teeth, each one jockeying for position. Despite the fact that it was two grown men against one rather frail woman, as they fell to the floor in a heap, Cantu was genuinely concerned about whether or not they would be able to maintain the upper hand, and what might happen if they couldn't.

The night of January 19 found Bill Buchanan, owner of KPXE Radio in downtown Liberty, covering the local school-board meeting. It was the kind of mundane assign-

ment that in a larger market would have merited coverage only by a novice reporter. But at KPXE, Buchanan
served as the station's reporter as well as its investigative
journalist, anchorman, commentator, assignment editor,
program director, advertising sales rep, general manager,
and ambassador of goodwill.

"There are sixty-one radio stations that put perfect signals into this town," Buchanan liked to say. "We've got to
be able to offer something they don't." So in his four years
in Liberty, Buchanan had become a champion of local
news. Short and gaunt, with a certain knowing twinkle in
his eye that belied his farm-boy grin, Buchanan imbued
his repartee with a sophistication not typical in East Texas,
small-town radio.

Around the middle of the school-board session, Buchanan was distracted by the wail of sirens outside. At
first, he reacted with ambivalence. But, in one of those
borderline clairvoyances for which people are unable to
account forever afterward, he soon decided that these
particular sirens, on this particular night, meant something important was happening.

His mind raced. He went over to a phone and rang up
a friend who had always been a good source of late-break-
ing news.

"What, uh, just went out?" Buchanan asked.

There had been an accident at Price Daniel's place.

"Senior?" The elder Price was old enough so that health
would be a question.

"No, out at Price junior's."

"Is it serious or what?"

"I don't know, but I'm almost sure Price junior's
been shot."

Damn! thought Buchanan, who had grown to know and
like Price even before coming to Liberty. Their relationship dated back to the time when Price was a young leg-

islator sponsoring Texas's landmark Open Records Act. Buchanan, as a member of the Texas Association of Broadcasters, had served on an Austin committee that helped prepare the measure, which was patterned after sunshine laws passed in other states. Later, during Price's ill-fated attempts to get the new constitution passed, Buchanan had moderated three different question-and-answer periods with Price, which had been broadcast statewide. Still later, Price had announced his intention to run for attorney general on Buchanan's morning show, *Party Line.* After that election, Price had come back to do a half-hour postmortem and openly discussed what he'd done to "screw things up." Buchanan considered that a fairly courageous act for someone in public life and admired Price as "a pretty up-front guy." The two men had a rapport that was defined by a certain playfulness. For example, because Price was a couple of months older, Buchanan would call him "Dad."

Stunned by what he was now hearing, Buchanan thanked his source and returned to his seat at the rear of the meeting room. Buchanan's mind danced, considering the possibilities. Shot! Had there been a gun accident? A burglary that went awry? Something seamier? He turned to the woman next to him, who happened to be covering the meeting for a newspaper in which Price had a financial interest.

"You might want to check on your boss," Buchanan advised, making a determined effort to keep concern out of his voice. "There's been some kind of an accident out at the farm. I don't know for sure, but they just sent an ambulance."

With that, Buchanan placed his running cassette recorder on the table so as to have some semblance of a record of the events that would occur in his absence, and raced out the door.

Buchanan jumped into his car and squealed away from the hall. He bore down with his right foot on the accelerator, careening around Main Street's gentle turns as had Cantu, Bautsch, and Anderson moments earlier. He then cornered a hard left onto FM 1011. Wisps of white fog clung to the low spots in the road.

Pulling into the long driveway he recalled his many previous visits to the Daniel home under more congenial circumstances. He noted the presence of an ambulance and Houston Daniel's wife's late-model station wagon. He pulled the car alongside Houston's, on the grass, and leaped out, not bothering to close the door.

It occurred to Buchanan as he started up the sidewalk that in the course of his several visits to the home, he had never before used the front door. As a matter of fact, despite all those visits, Buchanan could not recall ever being in the front part of the house, which encompassed the main center hall, dining room, and living room. Later, he would think it strange that he had made his first walk through the front door on the occasion of Price's death.

The door stood slightly ajar, and as he got closer, he could hear a loud and angry commotion, consisting mostly of a woman's tortured screams. He figured the screams had to belong to Price's wife. . . . Odd, too, that while he had probably exchanged more words with her than with Price in recent years, he could not for the life of him remember her name.

Buchanan rushed in through the door. And stopped cold, aghast at what he saw.

Price's wife was writhing on the floor with two emergency medical technicians struggling to keep her down. The men, one of whom maintained a feeble headlock, looked genuinely terrified. With no real idea what was happening, Buchanan went over and hovered above the group for a brief moment. Below him, Price's wife growled and bit and scratched and sought to break free of her captors. In her frustration at their efforts to restrain her, she seemed bent on self-injury. She would slam her head against the floor with a vigor and fury that amazed Buchanan.

Finally, Buchanan decided to help by simply sitting on her and trying to pin her arms to the floor. As he did so, he remembered her name was Vickie. He began to talk to her, in as soft and soothing a voice as he could manage, given the situation. At the same time, the newsman in him tried to get some idea of what was going on. "Where's Price?" he asked a thoroughly rattled Oscar Cantu. Cantu, whose first priority was keeping Vickie's flailing arm away from him, gestured with his head toward the kitchen.

"In there," he told Buchanan. "David's out in the kitchen with him."

Buchanan, planted firmly across Vickie's chest, yelled for someone to get a pillow to place under the woman's head to prevent her from doing any real damage, and one of the EMTs complied. All the while, she was screaming, "Go help Price! Leave me alone! *Go help Price!*" Every now and then she would seem to fade. Her eyes would roll back up into her head, she would collapse back on the floor in exhaustion, and the men would think the worst was over. Then, in the blink of an eye, she'd catch her wind again. Her stamina was remarkable. Buchanan had always been skeptical of the stories about panic-stricken women lifting cars in order to save the lives of the children. Now, he believed.

It took perhaps ten minutes before the men got Vickie under enough control so that Buchanan felt comfortable about leaving the EMTs and going to check on Price. At this point, no one had yet mentioned Price's condition. Cantu's remark about Bautsch being "in the kitchen with him" had made it sound as if the two men were having some sort of discussion. Perhaps Price and Vickie had had a spat, and the arriving EMTs had directed them to separate quarters—standard operating procedure in cases of family disputes.

And so, despite Vickie's entreaties to "go help" her husband, and despite the foreboding news he had received ten minutes earlier from his source, Buchanan was shocked and horrified to find Price lying facedown in a river of blood. Buchanan's first thought was that it had been a case of suicide. True, people didn't usually commit suicide in the kitchen, seemingly on their way out the door. A family man, especially, would be unlikely to shoot himself in one of the most heavily traveled areas of the house. Nor had Buchanan been aware of any special despondency on Price's part. But the thought that Vickie might have harmed him didn't even cross his mind.

Out in the foyer, John Stapleton of the sheriff's office was on the scene and trying to get information from a now-stuporous Vickie regarding the whereabouts of the gun. Buchanan, his thoughts focused on suicide, was a bit surprised to hear Stapleton asking such questions of her.

As Vickie gradually surrendered herself to complete physical and mental exhaustion, the nature of her vocalizations was undergoing a dramatic change. The violent shrieks and threats had given way to an odd and unique private language. To Cantu, it sounded like garbled nonsense; she appeared to drift in and out of coherence. This woman, he thought, has gone off the deep end. But to Buchanan, there was a certain cadence to it that reminded him of childish cooing or baby talk. He couldn't quite make any of it out, at first, but it didn't sound altogether like nonsense.

Stapleton, meanwhile, just shook his head and shrugged. The young officer was struck by the improbability of it all. An everyday, business-as-usual feeling about the house denied the horrible scene in the kitchen—where, as a matter of fact (and most disquieting of all), green peas and spaghetti still simmered on the stove above Price's body.

Turning off the burner, Stapleton felt, in some vague sense, as though he were closing the book on a marriage and a life. An eerie chill climbed his back, took hold of the hairs at the nape of his neck and would not let go.

Chapter Eight

I f Hollywood were casting the role of small-town southern sheriff, it could not have found a better man for the part than Liberty's C. L. "Buck" Eckols—save, perhaps, for his height. But in every other respect—from his crusty demeanor to his imposing midriff, from his tart and vaguely malevolent sense of humor to his appraising eyes and sunbaked appearance, from his tendency to make analogies to the world of rodeo, his original stamping ground, to his characteristic southern fondness for prefacing everyone's name with the word "old" (as in, "So I said to old so-and-so")—Eckols was a natural.

Sheriff Eckols looked forward this January night to relaxing in a hot shower. More often than not, in Liberty law enforcement, when your workday ended, your workday ended. Oh, there'd be the occasional break-in, or some kid might toss a brick through the window of a liquor store—but nothing that couldn't wait till daybreak.

Hadn't always been that way for Eckols. In 1943, he had gone to work for the law-enforcement arm of the Texas & Southwestern Cattle Raisers' Association, for whom he hunted down modern-day cattle rustlers and other unsavory characters who skulked about in shadow on the periphery of the rodeo and cattle-raising scenes.

Shortly thereafter, however, the quickening pace of the war in Europe recalled Eckols to active duty. He got home in January three years later, only to find a letter from the association in his mail. His replacement had been killed. Would Eckols consider coming back on board?

Though the circumstances of this offer might have given another man pause, Eckols figured, what the hell. But he didn't want the job permanent-like. Well, they told him, just stay till we find somebody. Okay, he said. I'll just stay till you find somebody.

Twenty-nine years later, he took his pension. The excitement, he would explain, had gotten under his skin.

But now, at age sixty-three, Eckols had left all that behind him. Indeed, he would sometimes joke that he had "retired" to his post in Liberty.

As Eckols reached for the shower faucet, he listened absently to his scanner, which was on in the background. At perhaps 7:45 P.M. he heard the call go out for a justice of the peace at the Daniel ranch.

The reference to a J.P. was ominous, Eckols knew. People outside Texas might think justices of the peace exist solely to marry people. In truth, the office is an elective catchall whose most solemn responsibility is to function more or less as a coroner in cases where death is unattended by a physician. The justice of the peace cannot perform autopsies; that job, in the case of Liberty, is farmed out to neighboring jurisdictions that maintain a medical examiner's office. The J.P.'s task is merely to render a preliminary judgment on whether or not foul play may have been involved. So the call for a J.P. could mean but one thing: Someone at the Daniel household was either dead or dying.

Eckols immediately dressed and called Justice of the Peace I. B. Carrell with the news. The aging Carrell had a spinal disorder, which inhibited his head movement and made driving awkward, especially at night. The sheriff therefore offered to pick him up.

Conversation en route focused on the health of Price Daniel, Sr. Both men naturally assumed that something had happened to the elder Daniel, and not the son. Price senior's imposing colonial-style residence sat about a mile up FM 1011, just about midway between Price junior's house and Main Street. Upon reaching the house, Eckols and Carrell were puzzled by the apparent lack of activity. It was dark both outside and in. There was no sign of any ambulance or Sheriff's Department car.

The two men looked at each other, shrugged and decided to continue up the road to Price junior's house.

Buchanan and Stapleton were again querying Vickie on the whereabouts of the gun. In reply, she said, or Buchanan thought he heard her say, "Ith in de fwag woomb." Her voice was a high, lilting falsetto, like something you might expect from a Shari Lewis puppet character. She repeated the remark two or three times before Buchanan was able to decipher it. (To Cantu, in fact, her words remained unintelligible.) Inasmuch as neither Buchanan nor any of the other men yet understood her reference to a "frog room," they concluded that Vickie had, quite simply, flipped out.

Sheriff's Deputy John Stapleton had been rummaging through the house and had located two spent shell casings from what appeared to be a small-caliber weapon. They were lying about a foot apart in the main hallway, off to the right of the attic stairs on which the man's jacket still hung. He concentrated his search for the gun in a sitting room directly behind the foyer, because Vickie's head gestures suggested to Stapleton that that was the room she had in mind. But a meticulous search had yielded no weapon.

Only when Buchanan asked Vickie, yet again, to tell

them where the gun was, did she accompany her remark about the "fwag woomb" with a wave of an arm toward the far end of the hall. Stapleton, joined quickly by Buchanan, took off in that direction. In the corner where the main hallway turned left toward the kitchen, the pair discovered a "theme" room containing children's toys and dolls. The room's chief attraction was an informal display of frogs of all descriptions: big frogs, little frogs, ceramic frogs, stuffed frogs, pictures of frogs. Hence a "fwag woomb," as Vickie's own young children probably described it.

Lying in the middle of the floor in plain sight, about twenty-five feet from where Price had fallen dead, was a bolt-action .22 rifle. Stapleton noted that the bolt was in the extract position. A shell thus sat in the breech, waiting to be chambered. Seven more live .22 long-rifle rounds reposed in the clip.

A registered nurse named Nancy Bell lived up the road on what had once been Daniel land, and maintained a casual relationship with the family. She had been alerted to the unfolding drama by an acquaintance at the hospital where she worked, and she hurried to Price's house to see if she could help. As shocked as she was to find Price dead, she was even more taken aback by Vickie's condition; she had arrived to the spectacle of Vickie chewing on John Anderson's clothes in a rabid effort to get at his knee with her teeth. Bell's professional opinion was that Vickie Daniel was in an extremely fragile mental state and should be removed to a hospital as soon as possible. Bautsch had Cantu and Anderson tie Vickie to a stretcher with gauze and ambulance stretcher straps and cravats (normally used to stem extensive bleeding). The two men loaded her into the back of the vehicle and sped off towards Yettie Kersting Hospital.

Stapleton continued his workmanlike investigation of the premises. He noted that the door from the kitchen to the outside was locked, not just with one lock but with four. He noted that the jacket that had been a silent witness to the pandemonium in the hall was, in fact, a man's ski coat. He noted a key pouch on the floor, a short distance from the attic stairway, and glass and ashes off to one side, toward the dining room. He noted a legal pad on the carving island in the kitchen. It contained writing pertinent to a divorce settlement: It set forth a short "his-and-hers" description of property, and its brevity led him to believe that it had not been finished before whatever it was that happened, had happened. In a closet near the back door (the closet from which it would subsequently be determined Vickie had grabbed the gun with which Price was shot), Stapleton located a second weapon, a single-shot .410-caliber shotgun.

Figuring from the shell casings, the jacket, and other bits of evidence that the shooting had probably occurred in the immediate vicinity of the attic staircase, Stapleton set about the task of finding bullet holes. He wanted to begin to determine the trajectory of the shots.

Of all the crucial pieces of detective work done in the aftermath of a shooting, this is in some respects the most crucial. The trajectory of the bullets, in the context of a crime scene's layout and other information, can often pinpoint the location of the shooter and contradict whatever self-serving scenarios might later be offered up by clever defense attorneys.

Thwarted in his search for the bullets themselves by the darkness of the attic, Stapleton asked for Buchanan's help. But no sooner had Buchanan come to his assistance than Bautsch yelled from the kitchen, "Bill, come here a minute."

Buchanan turned and took a step or two toward the

kitchen before he heard Stapleton bark, "Look, Bill, are you gonna help *me* or not?"

Buchanan went into an ungainly pirouette and proceeded to step on one of the two .22 shell casings that lay on the floor. At once, he stopped, stiffened. Oh, shit, he chastised himself, the very thing I've been trying to avoid, I've done.

Aloud, to Stapleton, he said, "John, uh, come here."

Stapleton, whose head was in the attic, mumbled something Buchanan couldn't make out.

"Come here, dammit!"

The deputy backed down the steps and Buchanan outlined his predicament. He concluded by asking, "What do I do now?"

Not to worry, Stapleton assured him. He had already taken the necessary photographs that would "freeze" the crime scene for expert analysis. He had learned that you did those kinds of things first, because evidence had a way of moving around the crime scene—even disappearing entirely—once people started to arrive.

"Well," said Buchanan, "this bullet's not gonna be where it was when it comes to measuring."

"I've already measured, too," said Stapleton.

Buchanan felt better. Still, he was not eager to become the scapegoat if people later started complaining, as they typically did in such cases, that the crime scene had not been adequately secured. So he reached down under his foot, took the tip of a finger and brushed the empty cartridge away from the sole of his shoe onto the floor, reasonably certain it would fall where it had previously reposed.

After hearing the ambulances go by, a second neighbor, Laverne Capps, had phoned Daniel's brother Houston. Actually, Capps was more than just a neighbor. She was the personal secretary to Price senior. Her house, being slightly southeast of Price's on FM 1011, was a better vantage point from which to see traffic heading up the road than was Houston's. As soon as he received Laverne's anxious call, Houston Daniel immediately grabbed his wife, Charlotte, by the hand, led her quickly to her station wagon, and drove to his brother's place, diagonally across the street. He had arrived about midway in time between the ambulance and Buchanan.

Confusion and contradiction would forever mark attempts to reconstruct the exact behavior of Price's brother Houston that evening. But his role apparently began with a simple (if highly improbable) misunderstanding and went on from there.

Upon his appearance at the front door Houston was informed by Bautsch, in measured tones, that Price was "gone." Houston unaccountably took this to mean that his brother was simply not at home. His failure to question this bit of information—coming, as it did from an ambulance attendant who had just responded to an emergency call—would inspire much disbelief. Bautsch next asked Houston to "go look after the children." They were huddled in the bedroom, yelling and screaming. Over the course of the next fifteen or twenty minutes, Houston was to be seen popping up here and there around the house. The precise nature of his activities led to much speculation later.

Eventually, Houston reappeared in the front hallway and headed toward the kitchen, where he was intercepted by Buchanan and nurse Nancy Bell.

"Houston, you don't need to go back there," said Bell. She assumed that he already knew of his brother's death; by her remark, she simply meant that there was no constructive purpose to be served by his going back there to confront the horror of it all. Seeming dumbstruck and confused, Houston again nodded slightly, following along as Bell and Buchanan each took an arm and guided him toward the front door. Just before reaching the door, Houston stopped.

He spoke with stammering urgency. "W-well, have they taken him to the hospital? I-I mean—how *is* Price?"

The nurse and the newsman exchanged a quizzical look. Had Houston, too, gone off the deep end? He'd been in the house as long as they. The presence of his car in the driveway as Buchanan arrived testified to that. How could he not know what, by this time, a half-dozen strangers knew?

Buchanan and Bell continued nudging him out the door.

Bell spoke: "There's just no sense puttin' this off. Price is dead. There's not anything anyone can do for him."

Houston's scream seemed to cut the mist with its intensity.

Buchanan and Bell each held one of Houston's arms and led him away from the door, out into the night. He continued to sob and wail. After a few steps, the nurse said, "Bill, you gonna stay with him?" Buchanan replied, "Yeah, I'll stay with him, we'll be OK." With that, Bell went back inside the house.

Houston and Buchanan walked aimlessly across the front of the rambling house, past the growing fleet of cars haphazardly abandoned on the driveway and lawn. As they turned the corner toward the carport, Buchanan for the first time saw the pickup truck, with its door standing open and the dome light on inside.

Buchanan looked briefly into the truck, but neither man made a move to inspect it more closely at this time. They just walked around its rear bumper toward the back of the house. Only once, Buchanan noted, did his companion shoot a quick, uneasy glance toward the carport door, on the other side of which lay his dead brother. Bu-

chanan recalled that earlier he had seen Houston standing directly outside that same door and staring in with a
vacant expression. (This was after Houston, unbeknownst
to Buchanan, had been dispatched by Bautsch to look after
the children.) At this time, it had seemed to the newsman
that Houston deliberately had avoided looking down at
the floor. As if he knew what he would see and didn't
want to see it. It was one of the reasons Buchanan had
concluded that Houston already knew the sad news.

Now, as they reached the back of the house, Buchanan
still held Houston's arm as though he were leading a blind
man. And, in fact, the two men had plunged into the total
darkness of an overcast, moonless night. Buchanan stepped
gingerly. He knew that there was a lake back here somewhere, and he didn't care to find it by accident. Despite
himself, Buchanan was suddenly amused at the idea of
his acting as a guide for someone who was doubtless much
more familiar with the terrain than he was.

After traversing the entire back of the house, they came
upon a small concrete landing, a mini-patio outside the
door to the large bedroom suite that had once been Vickie
and Price's. Houston stepped up and opened the door.
Buchanan began to follow, but checked himself when he
saw Houston's wife, Charlotte, and the three children who
were living with Price and Vickie.* Up to that point, it
had not occurred to him that kids were in the house.
Buchanan retreated out onto the step.

He asked Houston if he was going to be all right.

Houston said yes, thank you.

Buchanan closed the door, and stood there mulling
things over for a moment. What should he do? Stay with
Houston . . . ?

From inside, Buchanan heard a terrific thud. Instantly,

*Jonathan was living with Larry Moore at this time.

87

he wheeled around, flung open the door to the bedroom, and took a step inside.

Charlotte put forward an admonishing hand.

"It's OK," she said. "He's all right, Bill . . . he's just pounding on the wall."

Buchanan looked around. Houston was nowhere to be seen. Charlotte gestured toward the master bath, from which direction there now came another sound, not as loud.

"You all right?" Buchanan asked Charlotte softly.

"I'm fine," she said.

Buchanan left and continued around the house but found it even darker there than where he'd just come from. So he retraced his steps, going the long way back. This time, he stopped and indulged his newsman's curiosity by taking a peek inside the truck.

But he kept his hands in his pockets so as not to touch anything.

From the moment of his arrival, Sheriff Buck Eckols acted as though he had it in for Bill Buchanan. Perhaps he felt it was wrong, just plain insensitive, to have a newsman around to chronicle every aspect of the Daniels' grief. Then, too, perhaps he felt Buchanan's presence at this critical stage of the investigation was procedurally inappropriate. It was like making him a *part* of the case.

Going back through the years, the two men had never really had words, but it was also safe to say Buchanan was not too fond of the Liberty sheriff either. Some of this problem could be ascribed to the traditional tensions between law enforcement and the media. Aside from that, though, it was a fact that on this night Buchanan had some honest doubts about Eckols's methodology.

Buchanan noticed, for example, that Eckols, in the process of walking around the house, had been picking things up and examining them. True, suspicion thus far had naturally settled on Vickie. In the presence of Anderson and Cantu, she had even admitted doing the shooting. But this early in the case, the involvement of outside parties in some sense or another could not be altogether ruled out.

At one point the sheriff strolled over and lifted a white Styrofoam cup that sat atop the freezer in the kitchen, near Price's body. He smelled the contents, took a sampling taste, then, as if seized by the awareness that there was a traitor among the ranks, jerked his head up. Eckols's voice was gruff and accusatory.

"Buchanan, this yours?"

"No, Sheriff, sure not. I believe it may have been Price's or else somebody who was here in the house." The clear implication was, this could be part of the evidence, Sheriff, and here you've got your hand wrapped all around it.

Grumbling, the sheriff put the cup back down, but he continued to eye Buchanan with disapproval.

Moments later, Eckols conferred by phone with Houston, who had now taken the children back to his house. Their discussion was brief and pointed. The two men shared a common concern over the carnival atmosphere and agreed that something needed to be done to reestablish order. Eckols got off the phone and made an announcement on behalf of Houston Daniel. Buchanan would recall the words as "I want everybody out of the house who has no authority to be here—and start with Buchanan!"

The edict was directed, too, at the burgeoning troop of reporters and photographers beginning to arrive from around the county (to be followed, in due course, by reporters from around the state and the nation). Eckols, vowed to put up barricades and threatened to arrest anyone who trespassed. We can't, Eckols was saying, have people trampling all over the evidence in this case! Got to conduct a thorough, skillful investigation. Buchanan could not suppress a wry smile as he left.

Chapter Nine

O scar Cantu was in the back of the ambulance, keeping an eye on Vickie, as the vehicle sped back down Governor's Road, onto Main Street, toward Yettie Kersting Hospital. The farther they got from the ranch, the calmer and more clear-headed Vickie became. About midway in the six-mile trip, she looked up at Cantu and offered a brief and ram-bling—but coherent—recap of the shooting:

"We had an argument and he went upstairs to get some pot and I went to get a gun to scare him and Price said, 'Oh, no,' and it must have gone off and . . ."

Her voice trailed away, and she said nothing further about the events of the evening. Oscar did not press her for more.

In town, Vickie was transferred to hospital custody, se-dated, and taken quickly to a private room. Cantu found that word about "something happening at the Daniel place" had spread quickly through the hospital, and emergency-room attendants were eager for news. Protocol prevented Oscar from pronouncing anyone dead in advance of the J.P.'s official ruling, so he simply said that Price Daniel, Jr., was not too healthy right now.

Meanwhile, Stapleton's workmanlike investigation had moved outside to the carport. In a scene worthy of Hitchcock, the parking area was bathed in the hazy glow of the carport light, a thoroughly spooky kind of illumination that ebbed and flowed as weblike wisps of mist drifted slowly by. One of the deputies compared the scene to "the English moors, something out of *The Hound of the Baskervilles.*"

Stapleton took note of Price's pickup, with the passenger door flung open and the dome light on. Inside the pickup were a few shirts on hangers, some other clothes, and the box from an order of custom letterhead. Inside the box were some personal documents and a fifth of what some would recall as Cutty Sark Scotch, others Jim Beam bourbon.

Meanwhile, inside the house, Marvin Powell, the Sheriff's Department's criminal investigator, had arrived. Fingerprints were lifted from the rifle, from the plastic drinking cups (one of which Eckols himself had handled), from the settlement agreement Stapleton had found in the kitchen. In a curious omission, however, no fingerprints were taken from Daniel's body. Vickie, having already been whisked to Yettie Kersting Hospital, was unavailable for fingerprinting. Although that situation would be remedied the following day, Powell was annoyed that his examination of the premises would have to begin minus the principal player.

Back in the kitchen, Justice of the Peace I. B. Carrell felt safe in pronouncing Price Daniel's death to be of non-natural causes. At the same time, he decreed that it was probably not accidental. One careless shot was plausible, but a tremendous leap of faith would have been required to accept two such shots. Carrell ordered an autopsy, to be performed with all due speed by the well-known Houston medical examiner, Dr. Joseph Jachimczyk.

Now that the crime scene was left to the professionals, Buck Eckols had a chance to step back and take stock of things. In his many years in law enforcement, Eckols had shot others, had been shot at himself at close range. Nonetheless, he found it hard to appraise all that he saw before him with customary detachment. The sheriff had a long-standing friendship with the Daniel family; had even gone to "the old man's" wedding. Not that he had really socialized with Price junior all that much. He could recall a few Elks Club functions where he had run into Price and his first wife, Diane, whom he considered a very fine woman. And he had, of course, stopped to chat with Price from time to time, outside Liberty's courtrooms, on Liberty's streets.

Still, Eckols held Price in the highest esteem and described him as "one of the finest men I've ever known." Nor was this loose talk. Pictures of Eckols and Price, Eckols and Price senior, Eckols and Price and other Liberty officials, adorned the sheriff's den wall, and were among his proudest possessions. Which is why he could not look at this as just another crime scene. People like Price Daniel, Jr., were simply not gunned down in their homes.

Every detail Eckols noted seemed to reinforce his preliminary notion of what had happened. Had the altercation occurred in the kitchen, and had Vickie reached around behind her and grabbed a knife or something, well, that might've been different. *But she actually went and got the gun!* The evidence said to Eckols that Price had been shot, probably ambush style, as he descended the attic steps; the location of the shell casings, together with the fallen key pouch and the jacket wedged between the springs of the retractable staircase, were all consistent with this scenario.

Eckols visualized a mortally wounded Price stumbling toward the back door in an effort to escape to his pickup, only to find the door had been locked—his assailant having cut off his escape route. It was even possible to assume from where the gun was found that Vickie had followed him a few steps down the hall, perhaps with the intention of shooting him again if he hadn't collapsed. The rifle, after all, had been cocked for a third shot.

The keys Price had evidently dropped as he was shot— keys that didn't fit anywhere in this house (Eckols had tried them all)—told the sheriff that Price was through arguing when it happened. He simply *wanted out,* and was on his way to somewhere else.

By the time he left the house that night, Eckols's opinion of the case had formed, and hardened. He knew it was no accident, and he knew at whose feet to lay the blame.

Dr. Joseph Jachimczyk had handled thousands of deaths since becoming Harris County's chief medical examiner in 1960 but had probably achieved his greatest notoriety to date as a central figure in the Joan Robinson Hill case, the subject of Thomas Thompson's best-selling book, *Blood and Money.*

Jachimczyk began his autopsy on the body of Price Daniel, Jr., at about 7:30 A.M., some twelve hours after the time Vickie had called for assistance.

The Harris County M.E. found that Price had been shot once in the stomach. The gunshot wound was just below and to the right of Price's navel. The bullet had traveled about 20 degrees upward and 15 degrees from right to left. It had passed cleanly through the intestines before severing the aorta and lodging in Price's second lumbar vertebra, where Jachimczyk now recovered it. The M.E. calculated that Price bled to death in ten to fifteen minutes after his aorta had been punctured. That meant that Price had died just as the three EMTs were arriving. Jachimczyk also noted that the small calliber of the weapon and the area of entry were such that if the aorta had not been injured, the wound would not, in and of itself, have been fatal. It was bad luck, as much as anything, that had killed Price Daniel.

Jachimczyk fixed the time of the shooting at about 7:30 P.M. the preceding night. Vickie's call for assistance had thus been prompt.

During his examination of the body, the M.E. found a number of bruises and abrasions similar to those he had found on the bodies of thousands of people known to have been involved in fights during the last moments of their lives. The five-foot-eight-inch, 153-pound Price had a two-inch scratch on his chest, a cut on his shin that was an inch long and almost a quarter inch at its widest, and half-inch abrasions on the bridge of his nose and his chin. Also: a one-and-a-half-inch bruise under his left nipple and a small bruise on his left wrist. A trace-metal test revealed a pattern on Price's right hand.

A test for heavy drug use was negative, and analysis of Price's spinal fluid revealed a .03 alcohol content—what would normally be expected in someone who had consumed about one and a half ounces of alcohol just before death. Jachimczyk did not consider this a particularly significant amount of alcohol; certainly it was below legal intoxication.

In the bizarre terminology of the medical examiner, Price was otherwise "healthy," save for a dozen kidney stones and noticeable blackening of his lungs and lymph nodes as a result of his heavy smoking.

In every respect, Jachimczyk had performed his disagreeable task in a thorough, competent manner. Except that once again, no fingerprints were taken.

Throughout much of Texas, the shooting easily upstaged Ronald Reagan's inauguration as America's fortieth president and shared the front page of Houston's *Chronicle* and *Post* with the details of ex-President Carter's deal for the release of Americans who had spent 443 days as hostages in Iran. The story received prominent play in the national press and network newscasts as well. Print accounts tended to focus on the political angle and examined the parallel careers of father and son. Most of the broadcast stories leaned heavily on the curious relationship between the high-born politician and the girl from the neighborhood Dairy Queen.

As is so frequently the case, the very early reports were replete with errors. Price was described in the *Chronicle* and elsewhere as having been shot "possibly twice." His wounds were reported to be in "the chest or the stomach." One radio report, doubtless relying on third-hand descriptions of the blood encrusting Price's face, announced that he had been shot in the head. The weapon was variously identified as a shotgun, a pistol, and a "gun of unspecified caliber."

Vickie was described as having been "in hysterics," but otherwise uninjured, a characterization with which her attorney would soon take issue.

When Vickie had filed for divorce the second time, on New Year's Eve, she had chosen as her attorney Andrew Lannie of Baytown. Lannie was a likable fellow with a respectable local reputation; what's more his practice wasn't based in Liberty, where the Daniels' sphere of influence was greatest. The day after the shooting, with the divorce action clearly academic, Lannie assumed Vickie's criminal defense. Two of his first acts were to contend that Vickie had been battered that night—the bruises, he said, were just beginning to show—and that one of the shots fired— the slug officers had thus far been unable to recover— had been a warning shot.

Eckols wanted very much to discuss all of this with Vickie, but Lannie refused. His client, still under sedation at the

hospital, was in no condition to submit to any such interrogation. Vickie's family physician of more than a decade,
Dr. J. E. Bunce, would back Lannie up on that. Bunce
had first seen Vickie in the emergency room about an hour
after the shooting, and like everyone else that night, he
was astonished at how truly out of control she appeared
to be. Though Vickie was no longer physically bound to
her bed (the straps had been released for the first time
Tuesday morning so that deputies could perform trace-
metal tests), she remained in shock and largely unres-
ponsive.

Eckols was disconsolate over this. He had a way of staring people down that, in the past, had produced its share
of spontaneous confessions. Once, some years earlier, a
rapist had menaced Liberty. There was little to go on except the victim's rather sketchy description. On a hunch,
Eckols arrested a fellow. He hoped he would find, in the
suspect's past, a history of sex offenses or something that
might, at least circumstantially, tie him to the crime at
hand. But when the check came back, the man had a pris-
tine record. "Better than mine," Eckols would later joke.
Then the lawman noticed the man's thumb. He recalled
that in her statement to police, the victim had mentioned
trying to bite her attacker on the hand. The fellow Eckols
now had in custody sported a draining sore on the tip of
his thumb. A few days before, when fresh, Eckols figured,
it must have been quite an ugly, ragged gash.

The sheriff pursed his lips, looked his prisoner straight
in the eye, and said, "Damn, you sure got a bad spot on
your finger, don't you, fella?"

The man's eyes went like a shot to his injured thumb,
and then, slowly, crept back up to meet Eckols's. "You
know all about it, don't you, Sheriff?" A confession followed forthwith.

Eckols dreamed of having the chance to bring some of

97

the same down-home, window-to-your-soul powers of persuasion to bear on Vickie.

In his statements to the press, Eckols began to stray further and further from the official line established on Tuesday, by Liberty District Attorney Carroll Wilborn. Wilborn, a man known for his fairness and restraint, had publicly confirmed that the rifle shot was fired by Vickie Daniel, but was otherwise noncommittal.

Eckols, however, characterized Price's death as a "homicide," and left the impression that action against Vickie was only a matter of time.

On Tuesday, prior to adjourning for a day so that legislators could attend Price's funeral on Wednesday, the Texas House passed a unanimous resolution calling him "a positive influence in the lives of many Texans and in the operation of State government." The former speaker, said the resolution, "leaves a legacy of exceptional legislative achievement . . . exemplified by utmost integrity and dedication." Bill Clayton, who had succeeded Daniel as House speaker, said, "History will be kind to Price Daniel junior. . . ."

Meanwhile, dribs and drabs of what presumably would evolve into Vickie's defense had begun drifting back to Buck Eckols. Around the office, he ticked off some of the elements that would have to be addressed in any attempt to defend her.

First and foremost, she had already admitted firing the gun, and trace-metal tests taken at the hospital were positive. True, the test could not be absolutely conclusive—trace-metal deposits could also come from such innocent sources as doorknobs, key chains, and kitchen utensils. But the trace-metal patterns on her hands and palm could be compared with the manner in which a gun and trigger are held.

Second, she had claimed that Price was on his way up

to the attic to get his "pot." But the simple fact was, no drugs of any kind had been discovered—a specially trained police dog had shown no interest whatsoever.

Third, there was the "his-and-hers" document on the counter. And a search of Price's office had turned up a check for $1,250 made payable to Vickie. More evidence, Eckols felt, of the fact that a once-and-for-all split between the two of them was about to occur. Eckols figured Vickie didn't like the terms Price was offering and decided to supplement her bargaining position with a rifle.

Lannie kept talking about Vickie's state of mind, harping on the degree of her hysteria the night of the shooting. Maybe he was gearing up for a plea of temporary insanity. Wasn't it interesting, though, that she waited for the ambulance crew to arrive—even had the presence of mind to ask about Price's condition—before suddenly going bananas? Once the EMTs got there, and she was sure he was dead, that's when she up and "threw a fit." Either she was acting all along, Eckols suspected, or the insanity didn't set in until after Price was dead. Whichever it was, she had no defense for the shooting itself.

Word had filtered back to the sheriff that Lannie would insist his client hadn't locked the back door; on the contrary, he was saying, she had not been able to *un*lock the door after Price had kicked and beat her. But how did one reconcile the fact that the door was locked when Vickie tried to flee with the fact that Price had evidently been loading stuff into his pickup just moments earlier?

To Eckols, the door was the key to the whole affair.

That the carport light was on, the pickup's front door was open, and clothes and other personal effects were found in the pickup suggested Price had already made one or more trips from the house to the truck.

Eckols began to play devil's advocate with himself, but try as he might, he could not imagine a scenario in which Price had locked the door. Perhaps, if he had loaded the car sometime earlier, it might have made sense for him to lock the carport door. But then why would he have left the pickup door open? Did it make sense to be so obsessively concerned about locking the door to the kitchen— *every single lock* had been locked—and at the same time leave the pickup door wide open?

Maybe, someone else suggested, Price had unlocked and relocked the door each time between trips to the pickup?

Eckols couldn't swallow that. Even with Price's notorious attention to detail, he wouldn't do that under the extreme circumstances of January 19.

All right, but did the fact that Price couldn't have done it mean automatically that Vickie did it? Couldn't someone else have been responsible?

The top candidate for "someone else" was Houston Daniel, and Eckols knew that the possibility could not be simply dismissed. Houston had arrived at the scene quite early, right after the ambulance crew. He had apparently been poking around, conducting his own informal investigation both inside and out, for some time before the official investigators began to arrive. Perhaps he was just trying to get things straight in his own mind—or perhaps, like a good brother, he sought to do what he could to protect his slain brother's memory. Either way, it was a fact that Buchanan had first noticed the carport light when Houston tried to gain entry to the kitchen through the locked door. A clever defense attorney could make something of that.

A clever defense attorney might even argue that Houston had staged much of the scene: locking the door, putting the clothes in the car, dropping the keys in a strategic place. But that was an awful lot of plotting to expect from a man who had to work covertly, in only a few minutes' time. And in what had to be a grievously unsettled state of mind.

No matter how Eckols approached it, it always came up the same way. Vickie had locked Price in, confronted him, shot him where he stood. That was the way he would pursue the case, and nothing would change his mind.

Early on Tuesday, Bill Buchanan cornered Marvin Agnew, pastor of the First United Methodist Church of Liberty. Buchanan asked Agnew what he intended to do about the crowd expected at the Daniel funeral services to be held the following day.

"Oh, we'll just put 'em out in the foyer," said the minister.

Buchanan did a double-take. "No, no, I don't think you understand, Marvin. This isn't just a funeral we're talkin' about here. It's gonna to be an event. *A happening.* You're going to have people here not only from all over the state, but the country! You're going to need every seat in the chapel, every seat in the fellowship hall. We're gonna have to block off the street. . . ."

Agnew blanched, his eyes rolled up into his head. When Buchanan had finished reciting his vision of the proceedings, the minister asked, "Bill, will you help me?"

Buchanan laid out plans for organizing the flow of people and offered to act as an usher and recruit others to do likewise. Also under Buchanan's supervision, church personnel rigged up a sound system. It would be nice, after all, if these important people who'd come from far and wide to pay their respects had some idea of what was going on. Finally, arrangements were made with the Daniel family to broadcast the funeral, live, over radio station KPXE, Liberty. Afterward, the tape of the sorrowful event would take its place in the Sam Houston Regional Library, just up the road from Price senior's house and Price junior's burial plot.

On Wednesday, January 21, better than a thousand

mourners convened at the First United Methodist Church on Main Street. Buchanan had been right; the list of dignitaries was long and distinguished, including state legislators past and present, senators (from Washington as well as Austin), former governors (of Texas and several other states), the current governor, and Mark White, who had defeated Price for attorney general. Rounding out the throng were scores of members of the Daniel extended family and hundreds of curiosity seekers. In anticipation, four blocks of Main Street had been cordoned off.

In addition to the hundreds who had been expected, there was one mourner who might not have been. Vickie had made up her mind to attend the service, although there were several good reasons for her not to. Dr. Bunce had warned of the grave psychological risks. Friends had warned of possible objections to her presence on the part of the immediate family; it was not the time for an ugly scene. Eckols, meantime, had threatened to arrest her if she showed up; he felt it was the least he could do to protect the feelings of Price senior. Undaunted, Vickie came anyway. She was accompanied by Lannie, who planned to run interference in the event Eckols decided to make good on his threat. Subdued and weeping, hands clasped in front of her demure blue suit, she arrived moments before Price senior and Mrs. Daniel took their seats in the church.

Eckols, not wishing to make the scene any more circus-like, restrained himself and did not arrest her. But he couldn't resist ordering the driver of the blue Cadillac that had transported her to "move that car." It was parked in a space reserved for family members.

If a celebrity funeral brought out the people, Buchanan discovered, it also brought out the worst in people. There was, in particular, one overly zealous reporter from a Dallas newspaper. Buchanan had grown accustomed to hard-nosed reporting—had done a not inconsiderable amount of it himself—but the Dallas dynamo was too much. Every time Buchanan turned around, he was trying to back somebody up against the wall, get into their ear. The guy didn't even have the decency to respect the privacy of those who had been closest to Price. So strong was Buchanan's distaste for what he saw that even years later, the memory would make the veins in his neck stand out, angry and red.

Vickie was whisked away from the church by Lannie, who took a moment with reporters to express his hope that her improving mental condition would permit her release from the hospital by the end of the week. The immediate family returned to the ranch for a private service at the graveside, beneath the shade of the massive library devoted to Price's famous great-great-great-grandfather, in an enclosed area just a few yards away from the street. Reporters kept a respectful distance, coming by to inspect the site only after the mourners had gone.

In lieu of flowers, the family had requested donations to the Price Daniel, Jr., Memorial Fund for Development of a Children's Area of Liberty Municipal Park. But the reporters saw that the flowers had been sent anyway, dozens upon dozens of them of every color and description. Also noted was one ironic detail: At a far corner of the plot nearest the roadway lay a crumpled cup from Dairy Queen.

Chapter Ten

n Thursday, Ann Rogers received an uncharacteristic early-morning call from Charlotte Daniel. Ann had slept badly, and she was in no mood for what Houston's wife had to say.

"Um, I just wanted to call and tell you that, um, Price is dead now, and there's no point saying anything derogatory that would tarnish his memory," Charlotte began. She explained that during a family discussion among Jean and the elder Daniels and others after the funeral, the subject had turned to the ugly rumors about Price that were beginning to surface in town.

"We wanted you to know," Charlotte continued, "that Houston and I think the world of you and Pat. And we know you wouldn't go repeatin' anything of that nature about Price because if you did, we would have to take offense."

Those last few words brought Ann up short. It suddenly occurred to her that Charlotte might not be talking about casual gossip but rather about testimony in an upcoming trial. Ann had not really figured on having to take sides in court. Suddenly her mind rewound to some of what she had seen and heard over the years.

"Charlotte, I'm gonna tell you something," she said. "If I'm asked anything, I'm gonna tell the truth. Because I feel like, you know, I'm gonna have to live with myself after." A woman's life was at stake here, thought Ann. The Daniel family had had its favorite son up on that pedestal too long to begin with.

For a moment, Charlotte was silent. "Well," she said then, "we just love you and Pat so much, and Houston just wanted you to know that we'd have to take personal offense to it if you did that."

"I'm sorry," said Ann, "but the way I feel is, if it ever comes to trial, I'm just gonna have to tell the truth."

On that sour note, the phone call ended.

That same day, Ann buttonholed Bill Buchanan. Like many others, she was puzzled by some of what had transpired on January 19. There'd seemed to be a lot of loose ends, notably where Houston was concerned. Charlotte's admonishment had served only to increase her suspicion that something funny was going on.

"Hey, Bill?" she began. "How'd you come around the house that night?"

He told her he first entered through the front door.

"You mean, you didn't go past the truck?"

"No, matter of fact, I didn't," said the newsman.

"Well, did anybody go 'round that way?"

Buchanan shrugged.

"So you're telling me that in, say, thirty minutes, nobody went back to that truck, and yet Houston had been there all that time . . . ? You don't think that if I had a sister and something happened to her, and I saw something I thought was not—favorable—that I wouldn't do a little shiftin' and shufflin'?" With a laugh that was more of a snort, Ann shook her head. She pictured Houston opening the door, reaching into the pickup, removing some embarrassing or incriminating evidence—something that might have bolstered Vickie's defense. "I'd do it myself," she told Buchanan, "for my own family."

106

Buchanan scratched his bony chin. He had to admit that the truck, in law-enforcement parlance, had remained "unsecured" for quite a while as these things go. During that time, Buchanan himself had seen Houston at the carport door, in the hallway, and elsewhere in the house.

"You might have a point there," he told Ann Rogers.

Thursday afternoon, the tributes continued to pour in. Daniel was praised lavishly by Senator Carlos Truan, who had occupied the seat next to Price during his tenure in the House, and by Senator Carl Parker, who focused mostly on Price's image as a reformer. Parker concluded, "It's fitting that we pause to remember a man who did leave his mark on the state."

At about the same time Austin legislators were delivering encomiums on behalf of Price Daniel, Jr., a sensational murder trial was in progress in Houston. Kathleen Sandiford stood accused of killing her heart-surgeon husband, Frank. The couple had lived in River Oaks, one of Houston's most exclusive neighborhoods and the scene of a number of celebrated murder cases. Prosecutors alleged that Mrs. Sandiford had been furious over her husband's affair with another woman. Mrs. Sandiford claimed her husband came at her with a tennis racket—the culmination of many years of mental and verbal abuse—and she shot him in self-defense. In any case, she left nothing to chance, shooting him five times with a .357 Magnum. The killing took place just days after she had failed in a bid to commit suicide.

It was a complicated trial of tangled plots and subplots focusing on Frank Sandiford's maniacal dedication to achievement, and his brutality. ("Sex," his wife testified at one point, "was not a reciprocal thing. It was sort of like being beaten.") Mrs. Sandiford's attorney, Marion Rosen, portrayed her client as "a woman who loved and feared a man. We're not denying the shooting did occur. But not every shooting is a murder."

In an office in downtown Houston, a lawyer with a colorful name and a reputation to match watched the Sandiford developments with an eye to predicting the outcome for Vickie Daniel.

On Friday, after spending four days in a locked room, Vickie herself prepared to leave the hospital. As she did so, Sheriff Buck Eckols was ready to arrest her.

The evidence, thought Eckols, was overwhelming. Though investigator Marvin Powell did not quite share the sheriff's enthusiasm, in the judgment of D.A. Carroll Wilborn, the case against Vickie was clear. Eckols and his deputies still hadn't turned up the missing slug from the supposed "warning shot." Nor had the issue of the locks on the kitchen door been resolved to Wilborn's satisfaction. Generally, the timing and circumstances of the shooting seemed inconsistent with self-defense. Wilborn felt confident about getting an indictment from the grand jury, which was scheduled for the following Wednesday, and although he himself had originally planned to wait to file charges until after the grand jury's findings, Eckols just couldn't abide the idea of Vickie being out on the street. So Wilborn gave the go-ahead.

On his way to the hospital with the warrant, Eckols ran into Price senior and Mrs. Daniel, who were on their way to see Vickie for the first time since the shooting. The elder Daniel asked if Eckols would mind waiting till after they'd finished their chat with her, and Eckols naturally agreed. During the visit, however, Vickie was unable to carry on any kind of coherent conversation. When the Daniels asked about her health, she stammered, then became hysterical. The Daniels subsequently reported the incident to Eckols, who decided to back off. He was not eager for a chaotic scene. Instead, he phoned Lannie, telling him he'd "appreciate it" if the attorney would surrender his client the following day.

Lannie agreed, then promptly went before the press. "Until I view the inside of the house and compare it with the statement that my client has made, I won't have a clear idea of exactly what happened," he said. In an effort to counter the emerging notion that Vickie had simply picked Price off as he strolled across the hall, he added, "I want to look for that bullet!"—a reference to the warning shot.

Vickie surrendered to sheriff's deputies at a little after 5:30 P.M. on Saturday, was fingerprinted, photographed, and booked on suspicion of homicide. To Eckols, Vickie seemed "cool, calm, collected." He had the impression that she was a consummate actress performing the role of her career. It was nothing he could quite put his finger on, just lawman's intuition.

Within hours, she had been released on $50,000 bond, with Lannie telling reporters he was still undecided about his plea. The bail bond was guaranteed by Jean Murph— improbable to begin with, and even more so in light of subsequent developments.

Late on Saturday, Eckols finally acknowledged that Marvin Powell's investigation team had turned up evidence that one shot went through the roof "and God knows where." Nevertheless, Eckols steadfastly refused to accept Vickie's characterization of the errant bullet as a warning shot.

The Sandiford case continued to make front-page headlines. Kathleen Sandiford claimed her late husband had planned to rub out Denton Cooley, his rather more famous colleague at the medical center, in order to further his own career. (Ironically, it was Cooley who pronounced Frank Sandiford dead.) The plot attributed to the late physician, bizarre in almost any other context, nonetheless typified the East Texas consciousness. This was a place where rifles bobbed proudly in the backs of pickups, and family and professional disputes—disputes of all kinds—tended to be settled the old-fashioned way: with bullets.

There were those—many of them—who felt that occasional gunplay was just part of Texas's heritge, and vengeance every Texan's birthright. The state had been conceived in vengeance, at the battle of San Jacinto, and now, one hundred and forty-five years later, the legacy was still an active one.

Price Daniel's East Texas contemporaries knew they lived in a place where little was left unsaid, few other cheeks got turned, and few challenges went unaccepted. Even by women. In the life-style section of the *Chronicle* on Super Bowl Sunday, January 25, was a feature article on the increasing number of Houston women who owned and shot firearms. "You don't shoot to play," the article quoted one housewife, "you shoot to kill."

And kill they did—women, men, everyone. Minor traffic mishaps that, anywhere else, would result in little more than an exchange of licenses and insurance cards resulted instead in the exchange of gunfire. People were gunned down for sitting on other folks' cars, or less. A few words muttered in the dim light of a bar inevitably escalated into a fight, which spilled out onto the street and culminated in a shootout. On a single day, January 27, the week after Price Daniel was killed: a man shot another man after a routine traffic accident; a woman was found shot dead in her car; a woman was shot by a man she was arguing with in her home; an argument outside an apartment building led to a shooting; and a woman fired a shot at her lover's wife—in the Harris County Courthouse, no less. None of these incidents appeared to involve any motive other than simple retribution.

The fascination with violence cut across all social strata, and seemingly reached out to the youngest citizens. In mid-February, around the same time that two men were shot to death in parking lots on opposite ends of the city of Houston, a four-year-old boy shot his mother four times with a .22 caliber revolver—once in the face as she arrived home, three more times as she fled in confusion and fear. The twenty-nine-year-old woman had kept the gun loaded and near her bed. She survived the attack and could fathom no motive for any hostility on the part of her son. Tellingly, the boy was described by neighbors as "just an average kid."

Meanwhile, Texas lawmen, in 1981, were coming off a banner year in their war against crime. Between them, policemen in Houston and Dallas gunned down some twenty-five people in 1980. On a per capita basis, no other state had two leading cities whose enforcement agencies could boast of such marksmanship.

The end result was that the people of East Texas had become inured to killing, in all its forms, official and otherwise. More than anything else, their benign tolerance kept the mayhem going on and on, from day to day, from generation to generation, almost as though it were a genetic condition.

Chapter Eleven

T he grand jury that convened on Wednesday, January 28, heard D.A. Carroll Wilborn tell them that their mandate was clear: "The evidence indicates murder. The case does not fit any justifiable-manslaughter charges." He went on to say the state would contend that Vickie killed her husband after a disagreement over dividing property in the pending divorce action. Which was not to imply he viewed the crime as one that had occurred on a moment's impulse. There was evidence, he said, that pointed toward premeditation.

Of the nineteen people called by Wilborn to appear at the grand-jury hearing, only one—Vickie's daughter, Kimberly—had been in the house that Monday night. In a soft, shaky voice that became softer and shakier as she went along, Kimberly told the jury that she saw an argument but neither she nor her two younger brothers witnessed the actual shooting. Toward the end of her twenty-five minutes on the stand she began to falter badly, and was escorted from the courthouse by her father, Larry Moore.

Many people felt that the most graphic testimony came from Bill Buchanan. The KPXE owner's recollection of Vickie's behavior on that fateful night might have described a cornered animal: "She tried to hit her head on the floor, clawing herself and grabbing an EMT's coat by the teeth, growling and snarling. She was not in her right mind." He told the grand jurors about her regression to baby talk, and the discovery of the gun in the "frog room," where Vickie had said it would be. He said he noted no signs of struggle, save for the broken glass ashtray. However, Buchanan softened the impact of his testimony by adding that "Vickie's whole concern was for Price. She told us to leave her alone and help him."

Technically speaking, no one outside the proceedings was supposed to know what Buchanan or Wilborn or any of the others had said. Courts, ideally, like to try cases before a "virgin jury." Publicizing grand-jury testimony ordinarily diminishes the likelihood of finding jurors who haven't already heard all the details and tried the case in their minds. Further, rules of evidence in grand-jury proceedings are more liberal than in open court. Because of such concerns, testimony in the grand-jury room was ordered sealed. Which, of course, only served to fortify the press's resolve to find sources. By late afternoon, the media had some fair idea of the testimony of most of the people who would come to play leading roles in the trial.

Given the nature of the proceedings, much of the information that was leaked was highly unfavorable to Vickie. Lannie went before the press in an effort to set the record straight. Blithely, he denounced the state's case. "With regard to premeditation, that's absurd. She was at the time of the incident tending to two children who had flu symptoms. She was also in the process of cooking the family dinner." Lannie supported his point by noting that medicine was found in the kitchen, near the simmering spaghetti and peas. The lawyer also informed the press that Kim had observed a fight in which Price hit Vickie and "the little girl had to help pull him off.

"Mrs. Daniel, according to her doctor, was bruised. She had a red mark on her forehead that was so sensitive that it could hardly be touched with a washcloth, and a mark on her arm." He pointed out that Vickie herself had not appeared before the grand jury because she continued to suffer from severe shock.

Eckols, who had been first to testify that day and had articulated the state's evidence with gusto, was having none of it. He suggested that Vickie was bruised when, some time after the shooting, "three grown men" had to subdue her, ultimately wrestling her to the ground—and perhaps the mark on her forehead was self-inflicted while she was banging her head on the tile floor. Privately, Eckols suspected that Vickie's head-banging episode was a calculated effort to provide her with precisely the kind of defense Lannie was now raising.

Looking to clarify the discrepancy, reporters sought out Buchanan, whose testimony court sources had praised for its attention to detail. Said the radio personality, feeling rather odd to be spending so much time of late on the opposite side of the mike, "If there were any bruises, they weren't obvious. But those sorts of things usually don't appear until later.

"We tried to make her comfortable. Nothing that we did could have bruised her."

It became clear to reporters that this particular issue, like so many others surrounding the case, would have to wait for open court to be resolved.

After ten hours of discussions, the Liberty grand jury handed up an indictment. Characteristic of Texas jurisprudence, the document was as succinct as proper legal form would allow, accusing Vickie Daniel of "intentionally and knowingly causing the death of an individual, Price Daniel, Jr., by shooting him with a gun."

* * *

On Thursday, January 29, a three-page will, dated May 23, 1980, was filed with Liberty County Clerk Lela Mae Catchings. In accordance with Price's request, his sister, Jean Daniel Murph, was named executrix. Price's property, described merely as being "in excess of $10,000," was divided equally among Price's three children. Their inheritance would be held in trust for them until their twenty-first birthdays by Jean, who was given power of attorney over the estate. The simple will lumped all assets together, making no explicit provision for the distribution of property.

No provision at all was made for Vickie.

(A preliminary inventory filed by Jean three months later would list some $691,022.43 in personal assets, including more than a quarter of a million in real estate and about $350,000 in assorted stocks and bonds. Vickie, however, would have been entitled only to her share of the *community* property acquired since the marriage, amounting to just $41,375.17. Further, the community property was encumbered by some $26,000 in liabilities, so Vickie stood to gain about $16,000 free and clear.)

The fact that the will was dated fully seven months before Vickie's second divorce action seemingly confirmed that Price had been planning to cut Vickie out of his life for some time.

Vickie issued no statement in response, and Jean Murph refused to comment on whether Vickie was aware beforehand that she had been omitted from her husband's will. Lannie, however, just shrugged and said, "To my knowledge, Vickie knew nothing about it."

Still, in the context of this new and provocative document, many speculated that Price's death had resulted from Vickie's fears of being left penniless. This particular assessment did not necessarily imply premeditation. Vickie

116

hadn't really reasoned it all out. Had she done so, she would have quickly realized that the state tends to frown upon attempts by women who have murdered their husbands to collect from the deceased's estate. Rather, she acted impulsively, in the heat of the moment, as a last-ditch effort to get the money she felt she was owed. Perhaps, the theory went, she hadn't even planned on shooting Price, just scaring him, but something went awry. Perhaps Price had even taunted her, provoked her, driven her to do it.

Yet the image that stuck was the one of Vickie staring Price down with a gun in her hands, demanding her due.

The case began to inspire bizarre humor: When, some weeks later, the county decided to hire a coordinator to direct a campaign to collect unpaid fines, someone suggested they hire Vickie. "She'll get the old boys to pay up," said the jokester. "She'll make 'em an offer they can't refuse."

The same day as the will filing, an article appeared in the *Chronicle* questioning the professional credentials of the man who had done the Daniel autopsy, Houston medical examiner Joe Jachimczyk. Reading the story, Eckols and Wilborn could only shake their heads. The timing could not have been worse.

On Tuesday, February 3, amid the coldest wintertime temperatures ever recorded in East Texas, Vickie appeared before District Judge "Dub" Woods and pleaded innocent to the charge of "intentionally and knowingly" shooting her husband. Afterward, she repeated her in-court statement—"I did not intentionally shoot my husband"—for the benefit of the press. A pretrial hearing was set for March 20.

Two days later, Kathleen Sandiford was convicted of voluntary manslaughter in the shooting death of her husband. The jury had received a set of instructions that struck many observers as strange and unusually pointed. The following day, Mrs. Sandiford was sentenced to ten years' probation and a $10,000 fine. The sentence—considered very light—drew cheers from a contingent of nattily dressed housewives representing the leisure-class enclave where the Sandifords had lived. The implications of the slap-on-the-wrist verdict for the Vickie Daniel case could hardly be missed.

As Kathleen Sandiford was crying tears of relief, Jean Daniel Murph and her newly retained attorney, Zeke Zbranek, were en route to a local district court to file an action requesting temporary custody of her brother's children by Vickie Daniel. To Jean, the matter was cut and dried. Vickie, she argued, was in no condition to care for kids, given her mental state in recent weeks; and if it were to develop that she had, in fact, murdered her husband in cold blood . . . well, what then? Jean thought she should have the kids at least until after the matter of Vickie's guilt or innocence was resolved.

Hearing about it later in the day, Lannie fumed: first the will and now this. He had figured the family might file such a suit at some point, and it struck Lannie there was a good chance a judge would indeed award temporary custody to someone other than Vickie, given her technical status as an accused murderer. Unfortunately, later on, even if his client was cleared, she might have a tough time wresting control back from the Daniels.

On Thursday, February 12, with East Texas plunged into a deep freeze and everyone on the lookout for tornadoes, Lannie filed a motion asking Judge Woods to appoint a "temporary managing conservator" to protect the children's interests in the legal action. The lawyer considered it an excellent strategic countermove. The children's attorney would start from the premise that the kids' interests were best served by having them with their natural mother; he would have to be convinced otherwise. This seemed to weight the scales of justice in Vickie's favor. Woods complied with the request, and named Liberty attorney Don Taylor.

Resolving another of the small, bitter legal skirmishes between the two factions, Woods also dismissed an earlier suit requiring Vickie to surrender property she had taken from a small, self-storage warehouse that she and Price maintained in nearby Dayton. The property under contention—principally two hundred letters written by and to Vickie during the marriage, but also such commonplace items as birth certificates, school records, photos, cosmetics, stockings, bank statements, and even clothes hangers—were originally taken when Lannie and Vickie went to the warehouse and broke the lock. (Eckols had taken Vickie's keys as potential evidence.) Jean Murph had gone promptly to Judge Dempsie Henley, who was overseeing the administration of Price's estate, and demanded that Vickie return the goods. Lannie was reluctant to comply. He claimed that the letters were "vital to Vickie's defense," and should not be allowed to fall into Jean's hands. In the end, he had prevailed.

The wrangling over the letters gave them an aura of mystery that dramatically heightened public interest in the case. What could these letters possibly say? Who were they from? Lovers? Foes of the Daniel family? People who knew some terrible secret about Price, or Vickie, or the problems at the house on Governor's Road?

The media, especially, licked its lips in anticipation. It would make one helluva trial.

. . . .

Chapter Twelve

Enter Richard "Racehorse" Haynes.

For some time, it had been clear that this was a Racehorse Haynes case; all that remained was for the celebrated Houston criminal defense lawyer to turn up to claim it. Which he did, finally, late on the afternoon of Friday the thirteenth.

The announcement came from Andrew Lannie: Haynes had agreed to lead the defense team after a phone call earlier that day. The Houston attorney had been observing the case from afar with interest. Haynes would charge a reduced fee—considerably below his customary $250 per hour—because Vickie's funds were tied up in probate court. Her family would help her some as well. Lannie, who would stay on along with Harlan Friend, added that he was pleased at Haynes's involvement.

The Houston lawyer's appearance elevated the case to a new plateau. Haynes had tried the famous *Blood and Money* case. He was then Texas's most celebrated criminal lawyer and was spoken of with the same awe that, not so long ago, people used when referring to Percy Foreman. As one who customarily defends accused murdererers— at least some of whom, the currency went, had to be guilty—Haynes was not universally revered among law-enforcement officials. There was a flamboyancy to Haynes, a cockiness and bend-the-rules expediency that the purists and corporate-law types found irritating and sometimes embarrassing. Thus, he was more celebrated than honored. Or perhaps he was honored as John McEnroe was honored—grudgingly, and despite himself.

Daniel family members were especially disheartened by the news of Haynes's involvement. They knew all too well that his cases tended to get blown out of all reasonable proportion. Invariably, the prosecution was made to feel as if it were on trial, and not even the dead were exempt. Casting doubt was Haynes's job, but casting aspersions was his métier.

Naturally, the press loved him. Haynes was, simply, good copy, and not just because of his courtroom antics (he once planned literally to nail himself to the defense table in order to make a point). Haynes was as quotable a man as there was in public life, ever ready with the pithy phrase, the sardonic putdown, the spontaneous one-liner that places things in perspective. Another attorney might go before the press and state dryly that the prosecution's indictment made little sense. Haynes would hold the document before him at arm's length, regard it with curious fascination, cock his head, screw up his impish features into a zany mask of complete puzzlement, turn the page upside down, and say, "It reads just as intelligently this was as it does right side up." Haynes's courtroom presence was large in a way that belied his small stature.

What relatively few people knew at the time, however, was that Lannie had rather oversimplified the circumstances of his illustrious colleague's entry into the case. Haynes's appearance was no accident. It was very much a product of, and once again underscored, the fact that the Daniel house was divided by antipathy and distrust into two distinct camps.

* * *

Price Daniel, Sr., was not the only son of Marion Price Daniel, nor even the only one to embark on a career in politics. There was a younger brother, Bill Daniel. Bill Daniel also lived in Liberty, and it was the mark of the man that his large spread had been converted into an ersatz western town—not just the semblance of a town, mind you, but an actual western town in miniature. There was even a book about Bill Daniel, called *Mr. Texas*. Some said Bill wrote it himself. One acquaintance was fond of saying that Bill "was the fellow for whom the word 'ostentatious' was invented."

Although the brothers had experienced the inevitable comparisons and jealousies since their earliest days, sibling tensions first exploded following the death of their father. At the time, Bill was a law student at Baylor, while Price had already established a law practice in Liberty. Nonetheless, the father unaccountably named Bill as executor of his considerable estate.

The relationship survived that incident, as well as other unpleasantnesses later. But the breaking point came when Bill, as a state legislator, approached Price, then governor, for support in his attempt to become speaker of the House.

Price declined. Just wouldn't be right politically, he said.

Bill felt snubbed. Over the years, minor frictions between the two of them notwithstanding, he had devoted no small amount of time and enthusiasm to supporting his brother.

Once, during a speech on Price's behalf in a hayseed town, he had happened to notice three jets flying far overhead in triangle formation. "See that jet up there, leadin' the way?" Bill roared, his voice brimming with evangelical fervor. "Well, that jet's my brother, Price Daniel, out in front, leadin' the way for Texas! Watch him, just *watch him*—watch him lead the way for us all!" While

123

pointing to the sky, Bill got so caught up in the moment that he lost his footing and fell off the flatbed tractor that had been his impromptu stage. It was an outrageous performance, but still it won friends for Price Daniel and his doting, if slightly zany, brother, Bill.

Bill reminded Price of such incidents when he spoke of withholding his endorsement.

"Bill, this isn't the same thing," Price rebutted. "You weren't in state government when you were helping me. But here I am, the gosh-darn *governor*! It would look terrible! Like we're trying to set up our own private little government here!"

The day of the vote, Price came out in favor of someone else. Brother Bill, no doubt feeling foolish, immediately withdrew, and was never again able to mount much momentum in his quest for elective office. The apex of Bill's political career was his appointment by President John Kennedy as provincial governor of Guam. It was largely an honorary appointment, and not long after, Guam converted to an electoral system, so Bill's career as a head of state, such as it was, came to an abrupt end.

Price, noted for his peacemaking skills, tried to make it up to his brother. Once, when Bill Buchanan was preparing a story involving the two men, Price asked if Buchanan would mention Bill's name first. "I know it sounds peculiar," said Price, "but sometimes those things are important to him."

As he got on in years, Bill compensated for his relative lack of political achievement through ever more grandiose gestures. He gave millions of dollars to charities, and made sure people knew from whence the largesse had come.

Bill was never a man to hide his light under a bushel. For church services, he would arrive early, stroll in the front door up by the pulpit, politely seat his wife, remove his big white hat, and spend the next few moments giving an informal audience of sorts, smiling and waving at the crowd. It was as if he were still running for office. Price senior, on the other hand, made every effort to avoid being noticed. He and his wife would wait outside in the car and then, just as the services were to get under way, would all but sneak into the back of the hall. Observed Buchanan, "If you took a stranger and sat him down in the church and let him watch all this, and then you asked him to pick which one of the two men had been a three-term governor of Texas and which hadn't, there's no way they'd pick the right man."

In more recent years, there had come a certain mellowing between the brothers, yet the old grudges were passed along to the new generation, and seemed to crystallize in the person of Price Daniel, Jr. To those on Price senior's side, Price junior could do no wrong. To brother Bill, his family, and their sympathizers, Little Price did little right.

Price's death laid bare the tensions among Daniel family members. David and Susan Parker—Susan being one of Bill's daughters—came down staunchly in favor of Vickie. Besides the family feud he had married into, Parker had his own reasons for disliking Price. Back at the time when Price was in the process of divorcing Diane, Parker and he were partners in an embryonic banking venture, Southeast Savings & Loan. Price used company funds to make frequent trips to Austin, ostensibly to see the Savings & Loan Commission for approval of the new bank's charter. But Parker checked with the commission on one such occasion, only to discover that Price hadn't even shown his face.

Parker felt that Price's mishandling of the application procedure also made it necessary for him to resign his job at another local bank: This occurred when a form that

Price had assured Parker would remain confidential turned out not to be.

After Price's death, Parker grew concerned about Vickie's defense.

"She's not going to get any representation in Liberty County," he remarked. "It'll be a railroad job. They'll run over Friend like a train." Parker needed only point to the 1977 divorce business as proof.

An outsider was needed. Someone whose very presence would shift the balance of power, or at least neutralize the Daniel family's inherent edge.

Under cover of darkness, the Parkers walked to Friend's office, where they outlined their worries. (Preferring their efforts on Vickie's behalf to remain anonymous, they had purposely left the car at home, lest someone should recognize it in front of Harlan's office.) Yes, they told Friend, they had confidence in him—but he was still part of the local fraternity, and frankly, did not enjoy a high enough profile to accomplish what the Parkers felt needed accomplishing. Who, they asked, might he suggest to fill the bill? Harlan ticked off a couple of names, ending with that of Racehorse Haynes. The Parkers jumped at the suggestion. Friend volunteered to phone and find out if Haynes would be available.

Nor would this be the only action that Price senior's side would have regarded as traitorous. Several weeks later, the Parkers and Friend once again convened in secrecy, to pore over a list of prospective jurors. They sought to identify those who might be sympathetic to Vickie, or, alternately, those who might have potentially compromising relationships with the family of Price junior.

The trial thus became a civil war of sorts, further dividing a house already divided. Most of the salvos were to come (if in sub rosa fashion) from the Bill Daniel side. Whether out of honest compassion for Vickie, a woman whom they felt stood to be unjustly victimized, or merely to bring Price's side of the family down a peg or two, remained moot.

February 20 saw Vickie's attorneys go to court seeking a new venue for the custody trial. Vickie had recently been living in Tyler, in nearby Smith County, with her sister, Patsy Denman.

"Vickie and the children were residents of Smith County at the time the suit was filed," Lannie explained to Judge Woods.

Zbranek wasn't about to let that slip by. He noted that in order for Tyler to have been Vickie's legal residence, she would have to have lived there for a minimum of six months prior to the action. He pointed out that in her divorce petition of just six weeks earlier, Vickie listed her address as Liberty.

Well then, at the very least, Lannie wanted a new venue for the criminal trial. "Price junior was a lawyer and represented many clients in that locality," he argued. "By the same token, he may have represented cases against folks, too. It might be to the best interests of both the defense and the prosecution to seek a change of venue." The request was denied by Woods. Both trials would take place in Liberty.

Zbranek was exultant. Score one for us, he thought.

The day of the pretrial hearing, the temperature hovered at a balmy 80, portending an early spring. Inside, the testimony was already generating midsummer heat, as Jean Murph took the stand and disclosed the abortion Vickie had had toward the middle of her marriage to Price.

Racehorse Haynes, just getting his feet wet, implied that Price had "compelled" her to do it.

Nonsense, rebutted Jean. The abortion had very much upset her brother. "She told me this summer that she had

had an abortion and that it had killed Price . . . but that she'd been in such a deep depression that she could not think of having another child at this time." Haynes deftly countered by suggesting that Vickie's funk was the aftermath, not the cause, of her abortion.

Haynes suggested that the timing of the custody suit was intended to "enhance the prosecution of my client."

"That's not true," said Jean evenly. "I still love Vickie. But my primary concern here has to be the welfare and safety of the children."

Jean went on to voice her opinion that the children were seriously in need of psychiatric evaluation—they had been through a terrible tragedy. Then there was the question of how much they knew, and whose version they were hearing. "Franklin told his grandmother that he had heard his mother hurt his daddy," she said. "It is very important that whatever is told to him is done in a correct way. That someone determine his emotional state."

The two boys were ordered to have psychiatric examinations, to be performed by a pair of Houston specialists, Dr. Kenneth Wetcher and Dr. Michael Brandon. Woods ordered that no drugs or hypnosis were to be used in examining the children. (Regression hypnosis, wherein the subject is actually taken back mentally to the event in question, is revealing but can be dangerous.)

Vickie, too, would have an examination. There was some evidence—apart from the obvious—to suggest that she might have recurring psychiatric problems germane to the custody issue. Zbranek noted that Vickie had received psychiatric care during March and April of the previous year. No, she hadn't just gone to appease Price, Zbranek said. On the contrary, Jean had told him that Vickie, at the time, acknowledged her need for such help.

Zeke lobbied hard for the psychiatric testing, even knowing that, where Vickie was concerned, it was a calculated risk. If Vickie were to be found unaccountable for her actions, Jean might get the kids now, but the state's ability to successfully prosecute her in the upcoming criminal trial would be seriously impaired. It would be like giving Haynes a gift-wrapped insanity plea.

Having failed to get the venue switched to Tyler, Haynes went for a continuance. He wanted to postpone the custody action until after the murder trial.

This, he told all who would listen, is unprecedented, an outrage! How can you penalize a woman—and what greater penalty could there be than taking her children?—before she's even had her day in court?

Having the ear of the press, he took the opportunity to reprise what had quickly become one of his favorite themes: the possibility of impropriety resulting from the wide reach of the Daniel dynasty. This time, Haynes had something specific in mind. One of the psychiatrists involved in the case had been represented by attorney Ron Krist. Krist's law partner happened to be Richard Morrison of Liberty, who also happened to be one of Jean Murph's lawyers. Not only that, but Morrison had formerly been Price's partner. On that basis alone, Haynes felt it was only proper that the psychiatric report be permanently sealed.

Eventually, the request would be denied, as Zbranek revealed that the psychiatrist—apparently a very busy man—also had dealings with one of Haynes's partners.

Vickie herself kept an extremely low profile. After missing the grand jury, she had not kept an appointment for a deposition with Zbranek the following week, nor had she attended either session of the pretrial hearing—although she was spotted within two blocks of the courthouse one afternoon. Her lawyers explained that she was afraid of being placed on the stand and asked questions that violated her constitutional right against self-incrimination.

Patsy Denman told the court, and later reporters, she was worried that the children would be harassed if she disclosed their whereabouts; the Daniels would try to get them "any way they can." Why, just the other day, Price senior himself had told her he didn't think Vickie should be allowed to keep the kids.

She remembered the conversation especially well for its ominous undercurrent. "See that Jeannie or I take the children," the elder Daniel had said after sidling up to her during a break. Then, eyes narrowing, he added, "*Something* is going to happen or I'm going to intervene."

Gathering steam, she segued into a harsh criticism of Jean Murph's candor in explaining the circumstances of Price's death to young Franklin.

It had happened over the previous weekend. Vickie had agreed to let Jean take the kids for a visit. When Denman and Vickie went to retrieve them, the first words out of Franklin's mouth were "Mommy, why did you kill my daddy?"

The two women were aghast. Patsy Denman now added, "I wouldn't ever want to tell a child something that would affect him that way. That's cruel."

She seemed to be saying, so much for Jean's concerns about the boys' psychological well-being.

Chapter Thirteen

P rice senior began to grow restive. The news accounts anticipating the trial were unsettling. Somehow, the emphasis had shifted. The trial now promised to be a protracted examination of an alleged darker side of his dead son's character. As one who was used to life in the limelight, the Governor knew that to a certain extent, this was to be expected. Give the media a silver lining, they started looking for the cloud. Still, he couldn't help asking himself, Dear Lord, who's on trial here?

All week at the pretrial hearing, he listened in despair as Racehorse Haynes intentionally tipped his hand to rally public sentiment behind his client; Haynes dropped vague hints that such issues as homosexuality, child abuse, wife beating, and drug usage would play a prominent role in the defense.

Feeling increasingly estranged from his grandsons—whom he had seen just once, briefly, since the shooting—and realizing that the chances for even the most uneasy rapprochement with Vickie were worsening daily, Price senior, on Thursday the twenty-sixth, broke his silence on the case.

"I have tried to say nothing," he complained to the *Chronicle*'s Cindy Horswell, in obvious exasperation, "but

I got dragged in it yesterday. . . . This case should be tried in court and not in the newspapers, like Mr. Haynes is doing. When the evidence is in, it will be shown that *Racehorse Haynes is dealing in lies.*"

Vickie for the first time attended the pretrial hearing on Friday. It was an appearance that shed little light on the mounting controversy, however. Citing her Fifth Amendment rights against self-incrimination, she refused to answer questions about the events leading to the crime.

She was less reticent on the subject of her sister-in-law.

With an edge to her voice, she testified that she felt the children might be emotionally endangered if Jean Murph got custody. She based her opinion on the manner in which Franklin had been told by Jean of the killing.

Asked how *she* might have phrased it, Vickie began to sob. "I would have given an explanation that I loved their father. It was a sad situation. I would have let them know there was some feeling there."

After the court session, word came that Larry Moore had filed for permanent custody of Kim. The suit alleged that Larry, too, was worried about his ex-wife's mental state. He claimed that Vickie had threatened to physically remove Kim from his home, and asked in his petition that Vickie be stopped from "interfering in any way" with his possession of the girl.

"Oh, that's just wonderful," snorted Racehorse Haynes.

In effect, Larry Moore had enjoyed custody of Kim since the night of the shooting. On that night, Charlotte Daniel phoned to say it was "urgent" that Larry collect Kim at Laverne Capps's house. Thus began what Larry would come to view as a puzzling intrigue involving his daughter.

On the day of the funeral, Patsy Denman called to say she needed to pick up Kimberly. Lannie had requested an interview with the child at his Baytown office. Larry consented, on the condition that the child be back within a couple of hours. Kim was picked up promptly at four by Denman and Alvis Lee Steadman, the husband of another of Vickie's sisters. She would not return until 9:00 P.M.

In the intervening hours, it turned out, she had been not just to Lannie's office but to the hospital to see her mother as well. In the course of trying to track his daughter down, Larry reached Vickie by telephone at the hospital. She instructed him not to let the girl talk to anyone or sign any kind of statement.

No sooner had Kim gotten home than Larry noticed some subtle changes in her recollection of the events of two days earlier. Whereas the girl had previously said something about Price slapping her mother with an open hand, she now had the two of them exchanging blows with closed fists. Larry found it an interesting coincidence that this revision should come so close on the heels of seeing her mother and Lannie.

Around the end of the month, Larry told Vickie he needed to have some type of legal control over the child; inasmuch as it looked as if Vickie would have her hands full for a while, he wanted to register Kim in his neighborhood Dayton school. Vickie acquiesced, and an agreement was worked out between Lannie and Bruce Stratton, Moore's lawyer, whereby Larry would receive power of attorney over Kim.

A few weeks later, Vickie called and again asked if she could see the children. When she returned, as Larry would later remember, she took him aside and spent a fair amount of time trying to get him to color any statements he might be called upon to make under oath. Larry told Vickie he had already given sworn statements to Eckols and to Marvin Powell, and it made no sense for him to change anything now. Besides, his primary concern was for Kimberly; he was worried that she was being pressured to remember the events of the evening in a certain way. He didn't want the girl caught in the middle of his ex-wife's legal problems, and that's why he'd been considering a custody suit of his own. Kim herself had expressed a desire to stay with him, he told Vickie. She wanted to remain in the Dayton school rather than move to Tyler, where Vickie was living with Patsy Denman. The mood was tense as the two parted company.

Larry now decided to resolve the issue. Relieved to have an ally of sorts in Jean Murph, he made up his mind to go to court.

After the hearing on Friday, Larry and his wife walked down to Howard's on Main Street to buy a birthday present for a relative. In hot pursuit were Denman and Vickie, the latter determined to change Larry's mind about the custody action. She stressed that it made her look bad at the worst possible time.

"If you keep this up," Larry would remember her words, "you'll be sending me to the pen."

As the four of them stood arguing on the sidewalk, the conversation got louder, and Larry became self-conscious.

"Look," he said, "I really don't want to be standing out in the parkin' lot talkin' about this. Can't we meet someplace private where we wouldn't be disturbed?"

By mutual agreement, Larry picked up Vickie at her sister Rita's house the following morning. They drove from there back to Larry's house, where Vickie insisted on asking Kim directly whether she'd like to come up to Tyler and live with her. The girl said no. Vickie then asked if she'd like to come up just for the weekend, to visit. Another no. Kim explained that Larry and Judy were planning on taking them to the San Jacinto monument and Battleship *Texas*, and she was looking forward to the trip.

No doubt feeling defeated, Vickie left in something of a huff.

Early the following week, the furor over the Daniels' immense political influence took its first casualties. Judges Dub Woods and Clarence Cain (Cain had been slated to hear the suit by Larry Moore) bowed out of the case. Woods merely cited a crowded docket. Cain, however, admitted, "It is my sincere and studied opinion that this case should be tried by a judge other than one holding office in this district." He noted that the Daniel family was "prominent in the community," and some felt that Cain was alluding not only to the specter of impropriety but also possible repercussions to anyone placed in the position of deciding against the Daniels.

Thus the baton was passed to Judge Sam Emison of Houston. Emison was an expert in family law, which the case demanded, and more important, he was not a member of the local political club.

Haynes went before the press to say he was still less than thrilled. If Vickie continued to take the Fifth during the trial, the judge had the legal prerogative of awarding temporary custody to Jean. This, after all, was a civil proceeding; the judge did not need to be convinced of Vickie's guilt "beyond a reasonable doubt" in order to deem her a risk to her children. Allegations presented by Jean Murph et al., if left unchallenged by Vickie, might look sufficiently damning to warrant the granting of temporary custody to Jean, pending the outcome of the criminal trial. If, on the other hand, Vickie took the stand in her own defense, the custody trial could become a murder trial. Vickie would doubtless be grilled extensively about the circumstances of the shooting, and the information could only bolster the prosecution's case—giving it, in effect, a dry run, and subjecting Vickie to the effective equivalent of "double jeopardy."

Haynes went on, further, to theorize that the Daniel family, working in cahoots with the D.A.'s office, had planned it this way. The idea was to force Vickie into a corner—either reveal details of the shooting or risk losing the kids.

Zbranek dismissed Haynes's complaints with a sneer. He stuck to his contention that "the best interest of the children" was the sole reason for the suit.

On Tuesday, March 3, the legal teams went behind closed doors for a marathon six-hour session aimed at resolving the ground rules of the impending hearing. Haynes outlined his concerns for the new arrival, Judge Emison, and an ingenious compromise was worked out.

Vickie agreed to waive her Fifth Amendment protections. She would, as Lannie put it, answer "any and all questions" during the March 12 hearing. In exchange, she would receive, rather than a temporary-custody award, a permanent decree to be decided by a jury.

It took a bit for Zeke to realize it, but he had been outmaneuvered. For a few brief moments, he experienced a certain giddiness at the prospect of having Vickie up on the stand, at his disposal. Then the reality of what had happened set in. A jury of Vickie's peers, in contrast to a judge, would be unlikely to deprive the woman of her children before a verdict had been rendered in the criminal trial. A judge would be more dispassionate, would decide the case solely on the principles and objectives of family law. A jury, on the other hand, would be guided in no small part by emotional considerations extraneous to the facts in the case.

Zbranek's concerns became more serious when Don Taylor stepped out of the case and his duties on behalf of the kids were assumed by Haynes. Taylor said his legal fees, estimated at $12,000, would have been a burden to both parties in the suit. Vickie, especially, had no reliable source of income at the moment. Zbranek was skeptical. How could Haynes simultaneously—and, more to the point, impartially—look after the kids' and also the mother's interests?

Over the next few days, the principals, amid batteries of attorneys on both sides, gave lengthy depositions behind closed doors at the Liberty County Courthouse. Jean's turn lasted for six hours. Vickie began her testimony on Wednesday, March 11. She was still there the following Wednesday. Depositions would be sealed until the start of the custody hearing, and the lawyers were refusing comment. But, as always, there were the rumors, fanned by Liberty's many town gossips, and seemingly confirmed by press leaks from "informed sources."

The word was that Vickie would claim she shot her husband after he became violent because she flushed away a stash of marijuana. The two were arguing bitterly that night. At one point, Price was supposedly on top of Vickie on the floor, and when Kim tried to pull him off, he struck the girl.

Pressed for a reaction to Vickie's statement, Zbranek chose his words with care. "I don't want to say anything ugly about her," he replied. "I don't want to say anything that might harm or prejudice a jury against her." It was a coy way of saying what he wanted to say without actually saying it.

While the hearing was going on, in another part of the courthouse, Emison was wading through the letters and other bits of correspondence that Vickie and Lannie had taken from the self-storage warehouse. Jean was suing to get hold of them, and eventually, she would get her look. But the letters, it would turn out, were much ado about nothing.

"Uh, Jonathan, just tell me your name."
"Jonathan Moore."
As Zbranek saw it, things were getting seamier and

137

seamier. Price was being portrayed as everything from a sex fiend to a drug pusher. Zbranek was taking a deposition of his own in an effort to get to the bottom of things.

"Let me ask you this—you lived with Price Daniel and your mother, Vickie, after they got married, for, well, about half the time that they were married, right?"

"Yes, sir."

"Can you tell me, say, the dates or the years that you came first to live with your father, and then moved back, and those things?"

"Well—no, sir."

"You just remember they happened."

"Yes, sir."

"All right, now let me ask you this. During the time that your mother was married to Price Daniel and that you were there in the home and observed them, uh, how did Price Daniel treat you?"

"He was—nice."

"All right, did you help with the chores around the house?"

"Yes, sir."

"And would he pay you for that?"

"Yes, sir. When the black boys weren't there he would let me work more, and he'd pay me for it."

"Did Price ever take you anywhere?"

"Yes, sir."

"Tell me about all those things, what would happen, give me some of the examples."

"Well, he'd take us to the ball games—he took us to the football games, the baseball games, and hockey games, and soccer games. Sometimes he'd take us to the movies."

"All right, now, by us—who was us, Jonathan?"

"Everybody. Mom, Tom, Bob, Frank, me, him."

"Who was Tom?"

"His son."

"All right, now how old was Tom?"

"He was my age."

"And, uh, how often did Tom come down?"

"Holidays, and when he was out of school."

"All right, now, Jonathan, did you all have any other events or things going on out there that Price would take you to?"

"He would take us to the [inaudible], he would take us fishing, and he would take us to the roundup, every summer."

"To the what?"

"Roundup. In August."

"All right, in August. Well, what was the roundup?"

"We would go out and, if we could rope a calf, we could keep it. And we had to take it out to Grandpa, and he would keep it for us."

"OK. Well, uh, when you say you went to the roundup, what was the part that you children played, just trying to rope a calf?"

"We roped a calf, and we rode horses."

"And where was this done?"

"Over at the ranch. By Price's house, my grandpa's house."

"That's your grandpa Daniel's house?"

"Yes, sir."

"OK, now let me ask you this. Jonathan, did Price ever, uh, whip you?"

"Yes, sir."

"All right, how many times?"

"Once."

"And how did that happen?"

"I don't remember what happened."

"Well, did he whip you with his hand, or with a paddle, or what?"

"With a belt."

"OK, and where did he hit you?"

"On the rear."

"OK—strapped you close to the butt, huh?"

"Yes, sir."

"Do you remember how many licks he hit you?"

"One."

"OK. Uh, and that was the only time?"

"Yes, sir."

"Well, I guess during this time your mother had to whip you some, didn't she?"

"Yes, sir."

"OK. Now, during the time that you and, uh—that you lived in the home with Price and your mother, did you ever see 'em have a fight where they actually hit each other?"

"Yes, sir."

"How many times?"

"Once."

"Can you tell me how that happened?"

"Well, there's three TVs. Kim's and my TV and two other color TVs, one in their room, and one in the playroom. He was watching a program in the playroom, and walking all through the house, and he turned the program on those TVs, both the color TVs. He'd be in the playroom, and Mom would turn it on in the other room, and he would come in the room and find out that she was watching something in the other room, and he told her to go and watch it on Kim's black-and-white TV. And she went in the playroom and turned her show on, and he came in there to use the second one, and turned it back to his program. He was watching a baseball game. And we were watching some other special. We went back to his room, to their bedroom. And when he got through reading he'd come in there, and he started rappin' at her, and tellin' her to go watch it on Kim's TV. And he started rappin', and they started fightin'."

"Did they actually strike each other?"

"Yes, sir."

"Did you see him hit your mother?"

"Yes, sir."

"Did your mother hit him?"

"Yes, sir."

"Did you see who hit the first lick?"

"No, sir."

"Well, what did—did Kim try to do something to intervene?"

"Yes, sir."

"OK. Uh, what did he do to—well just tell me what happened, Jonathan."

"Well, when, you know, after they had started fussin' and fightin' and everything, we came in there and we saw, and—and then Kim really went in there and tried to help Mom, and Price pushed her away. And then she tried again, and Price pushed her away again. And—Frank was trying to go in, I was keepin' him out, and he started cryin', and I took him to a different room."

"What room were they in when they had this fight?"

"The bedroom."

"Their bedroom?"

"Their bedroom."

"All right, and did, uh, did, uh, you see Price, uh, did he hit her—slap her, hit her with his fist, or what?"

"Hit her with his fist."

"And where did he hit her?"

"In the stomach."

"And, uh, did she—did she hit him with her fist or slap him?"

"Slapped him."

"All right. And is there anything else about that fight that I hadn't asked you about that you ought to tell, Jonathan?"

"Well, he did—he did push her and then she got up and slapped him and then he hit her."

"When he pushed her, did she fall down?"

141

. . . .

"He pushed her off balance . . ."

"OK, she just—"

". . . before she had Bob . . ."

"OK."

". . . when she was pregnant."

A small but unmistakable tinge of rancor in the child's voice said he understood the full significance of what he had just told the lawyer.

"And—and she slapped him."

"Yes, sir."

"And then—is that when Kim got into it to try to help your mother?"

"Yes, sir."

"And, uh—OK. Now did, finally, the fight stop?"

"Yes, sir."

"All right. Did they get along all right then?"

"Yes, sir."

"Did they fuss from time to time in addition to that one fight?"

"No, sir."

"Seemed to get along all right?"

"Yes, sir."

"All right. Now, on the—as far as you saw—not what you heard someone say or anything—as far as you saw, is this the only physical fighting contact that you observed?"

"Yes, sir. It was the only one that they had when I was there."

"All right. Now, after that fight, did your mother leave Price?"

"Yes, sir."

"Now who did she take with her?"

"She took me, Kim, and Franklin."

"All right. And, uh, well, let me ask you this—was she bruised up or beat up about the face or anything like that?"

"Not that I saw."

"All right. Then you all came to stay with who?"

"We went to stay with our grandmother. We stayed there two nights, and it was so hot there that we went to stay at a motel, the Del Ray motel, over there on the highway. And then, I stayed there a night and she brought me over here."

"Over here, you mean to your daddy's?"

"Yes, sir."

"Now was that—did you ever move back and live with him after that?"

"Mmmmmm—no, sir."

"That's when you came to live with your daddy the last time, and from that time you stayed over here?"

"Yes, sir."

"And of course you know that your mother went back to Price, right?"

"Yes, sir." Jonathan's voice seemed to crack slightly at this point, and Zbranek decided to move momentarily to a lighter topic.

"All right, now, Jonathan, did Price ever buy you anything?"

"Yes, sir."

"Buy you toys?"

"Yes, sir."

"Do you remember anything else that he bought you?"

"We all went to a hockey game, he bought us a hockey puck. And one time when we went to a soccer game, he bought us a pennant."

"Well, look, I didn't ask you this question. I know I forgot to ask you this question. . . . There's been some talk about Price molestin' little boys, or foolin' with their private parts—do you understand what I'm talkin' about?"

"Yes, sir."

"Did he ever do that to you?"

"No, sir."

143

"Did you ever see him do it to anybody else?"

"No, sir."

"So as far as you know, from what you saw, you never saw anything like that."

"No, sir."

Haynes was in Nevada on a previous commitment, a pretrial hearing for an extortion and kidnapping case, but Emison refused to hold up jury selection in his absence. The case already showed signs of stretching beyond all reasonable expectations for a custody lawsuit.

In his stead, Racehorse had left his associate Margaret Covington. She would act as a consultant to Friend and especially Lannie, who did the main questioning of prospective jurors. Covington, a clinical psychologist, had helped Haynes on a number of previous occasions by invoking what came to be known as her "secret formula" juror profile. The formula assigned values to specific background features or perceived character traits, as an insurance company might assign values to various factors in rating an applicant motorist. Much was made of this emphasis on psychological factors—which were considered exotic in a town where people were judged mostly at face value, on their word and deed. But though Covington admitted her formula considered "a lot of variables," she also maintained that her ultimate objective was simple: She wanted to find twelve jurors who understood the common problems people faced in their daily lives.

"And given who she's defending, the more common the better," joked one reporter who sometimes wrote for his newspaper's society page.

No doubt feeling the pressure of Racehorse and his retinue of experts, Zbranek, too, availed himself of the services of a pair of well-known psychologists, Dr. Curt Wills of Beaumont and Dr. Jerry Landrum of Tyler. For Zbranek, a man not normally given to psychological games-manship—he was, in many respects, Buck Eckols in a suit and tie—it was a step unprecedented in his twenty-five-year legal career. He said he found their services valuable, especially when it came to deciding on his "strikes." But a number of onlookers privately chuckled and shook their heads, convinced that Zbranek's heart wasn't really in it. Zeke had spent a mere sixty minutes questioning the final selections, while Lannie devoted five and a half hours to interrogating those same candidates. Lannie and Friend understandably wanted the jury to be at least half female, and a few blacks wouldn't hurt either. They knew what it was like to be underdogs in a small town like Liberty.

The fact that not a stitch of evidence had been formally presented as yet did not deter reporters from regarding those jurors not selected as a random sampling of public opinion. The consensus held that Vickie should not have to give up her kids in advance of a verdict in the criminal trial.

Three juror rejects, from a trio of nearby townships, spoke for the majority:

Mike Presswood of Cleveland: "Why should an aunt have the kids, instead of the mother? I can't see it."

John Wilson Vail, Jr., of Hull: "I don't think they should take her kids away unless she's in the pen or something like that."

Georgia Fragia of Moss Hill: "I just felt a mother should have her kids with her until proven guilty." Alluding to possible extenuating circumstances, she added, "I've heard quite a bit of gossip in the case."

All of the prospective jurors were aware at least of the shooting, and—an uncomfortable sign for Judge Emison—many said they had gotten the bulk of their information from "talk around town."

By later afternoon on Friday, March 13, twelve jurors—

145

nine men and three women—had been chosen. This, over the continuing objections of Vickie's team, who wanted the proceedings delayed until Haynes's return from Las Vegas. Judge Emison was unmoved. Vickie, he noted, had not designated a lead lawyer. The judge also seemed, in his rebuttals, to be subtly goading Friend and Lannie, as if to say, What's wrong with *you* fellows? Don't you feel you're up to it?

Zeke beamed over the selection of nine men. "We intend to prove she has a histrionic personality defect, which means an overreaction to stress situations that finally culminated in her shooting her husband," he told the jurors, who turned their heads to see the defendant sitting quietly, showing little if any emotion.

Barely drawing a breath, he informed the jury that doctors who had examined Vickie would testify that subsequent explosions could be even more violent. Now that she was facing "the most stressful situation of her life"— the pending murder indictment—she could be a threat to the children.

"That," Zbranek continued smartly, "is why you're being asked to 'act now,' instead of waiting for the murder trial."

He stressed there were no ulterior or vindictive motives behind this lawsuit—waiting till after the murder trial just didn't make sense. You couldn't protect the children retroactively.

Lannie, refusing to get caught up in the issue of Vickie's guilt or innocence of murder charges, reminded everybody once again that the natural mother is always the preferred custodian except in the most unusual of circumstances. Setting the tone for the defense's conduct throughout the custody case, the lawyer urged everyone to remember that Vickie's criminal liability was, strictly speaking, irrelevant to the matter at hand. "We intend to ascertain that this action focuses only on her parenting ability."

In subsequent days, newspaper accounts broke the jury down by race, age, sex, employment, and educational background (as well as noting other less relevant characteristics—one radio station reported that the jury seemed exceptionally tall). It was pointed out that seven of the men were blue-collar workers and all three women were housewives. The range in age was from twenty-three to fifty-eight. One was a teacher and one a church choir director. Most were high-school graduates, although the jury was not a particularly literate one. All but one said they seldom read the newspaper; they got their news of the case from TV or radio. On balance, they formed a pretty accurate microcosm of the public-at-large in Liberty.

"Ideally, we would have wanted more women with children at home, who would have that instinct of motherhood," said Covington after the jury was empaneled. And she wished, again, that Haynes had been present. (In fact, this was a first for Racehorse. Never before had he failed to have a hand in the selection of a jury in a case involving one of his clients.) But overall, and the preponderance of males notwithstanding, Covington said she was pleased with the final selections, that they "seemed to be a fair and impartial group of people."

"We were looking for people who would be objective about what is in the best interest of the child," Zbranek began, sounding egalitarian enough. However, he then went on to add, "Without being overly emotional about what it would do to the mama. We wanted somebody flexible, not a rigid fundamentalist."

The assessments continued, late into the night and through the weekend. Only on Sunday evening did the mood among the principal players change from labored analysis to quiet expectancy. The time for speculation had ended. The custody trial began in the morning.

Chapter Fourteen

The Liberty Courthouse, set amid cannons and monuments at the corner of Main Street and San Jacinto, had witnessed half a century's worth of human discord. It also housed, on its third floor, the largest county courtroom in the state, with 276 seats—every one of which was needed (and then some) as Liberty turned out en masse to hear Vickie Daniel tell what promised to be a riveting story of skeletons in the Daniel family closet.

The townsfolk were not disappointed. From the time Vickie took the stand at 8:37 A.M., she answered Zbranek's questions directly and with feeling. Occasionally her composure would falter, and she would need a moment or two; Zeke, gentlemanly almost to the point of deference, obliged. But Vickie seemed to hold nothing back—especially in characterizing her late husband. To the horror of Jean Murph and the other Daniel partisans present, Vickie painted the portrait of a volatile loner who abused his wife and kids, drank excessively, and smoked dope. When the subject turned to sex, she made Price out to be a shameless exhibitionist whose true sexual orientation was in doubt. Heightening the impact of the accusations themselves was Vickie's vaguely apologetic delivery. Her implicit message was: I hate to have to say these kinds of things about *anyone*, but I have no choice. . . .

The litany of alleged offenses was long and graphic. Typical was her testimony about the abuses heaped by Price upon Jonathan, now ten years old. Price would, she said, "get Jonathan to sit on his hand," and sometimes "put his hand up under Jonathan's seat." She testified that on many a morning Price would amuse himself by pulling down his pants and underwear around the boys because "he wanted everyone to look at his behind."

That wasn't all. To hear Vickie tell it, when Price wasn't fondling or making sexual advances toward the boy, he was goading ranch hirelings to "beat up on him." Vickie would have to rouse her husband from his drunken sleep to get him to stop the beatings. Sometimes, she said, Price did things that were truly malicious, almost sadistic. She claimed he often made Jonathan burn trash in a barrel, using gasoline for fuel. When the youngster lit the fire, it blew up in his face. Once, Jonathan's nose had in fact been singed. Because of all this, she explained, she ultimately permitted her former husband, Larry Moore, to have permanent custody of the boy.

Vickie's account of Price's treatment of her was no less ugly. She recalled being kicked in the stomach while she was pregnant. She claimed that during the course of the marriage, Price had thrown chairs, ice, glasses, and pieces of wood at her, poured drinks on her head, smacked her squarely in the mouth. She did not see a doctor to have the resulting wounds tended to—it was "too embarrassing"—but she did tell her ex-husband, Jean, and Charlotte about the recurring abuse, and in fact had left Price several times, temporarily: "He would hurt me and I would leave."

The question was on everyone's lips, and Zbranek asked it: Why, in light of all this, did she stay married to the man as long as she did?

"I loved him," she replied simply, and without hesitation. "And I believe in marriage."

Zbranek's next line of inquiry gave the audience what it had really come for. Deliberately at first, and then with growing speed and emotion, Vickie brought the jurors back to the night of January 19:

After a typically long day at the office, Price got home a little before seven. The atmosphere he found there was tense and unpleasant, as it almost always was in recent months. The marriage had so deteriorated by this time that few words passed between husband and wife that did not concern either the necessities of day-to-day living or the impending divorce.

Price had brought a divorce settlement home with him. It contained an accounting of their assets and a formula for their distribution. He was intent upon her signing it. Vickie was equally insistent about not signing it. She told Price she had to talk to Lannie first to protect her interests. Price glowered at this remark, and they argued for a while. As she threw the document down on the dining-room table in a gesture of finality, she spilled Price's drink. Whereupon he exploded, leaped at her, took her by the neck and shook her violently. She managed to get away, but presently he caught up with her again, grabbed her roughly by the shoulders, and knocked her to the floor.

Having heard the commotion from her bedroom, Kim came to Vickie's defense, jumping on Price's back and trying to pull him off her mother. Price, completely out of control, wheeled around and lashed out at the girl. Only Vickie's desperate grab prevented her from landing hard on the floor.

Price narrowed his eyes on the girl. His words were chilling. "Get her out of here," he growled at Vickie, "before I do something to her." Vickie bade Kim return to her room, and she complied.

Price's fury was still clear to see, but this turn of events seemed to bring about a sudden change in him, as if he were feeling chastened by having gone so far as to strike Kim. He calmed down long enough to let Vickie up. Composing herself as well as she could, she straightened her clothes and told him she was going to the kitchen to fix supper; she would, she said, be expecting him to leave the house, under the circumstances. Things were bad enough—the boys were sick and had been to the doctor earlier in the day.

Walking away, she prayed he would listen. Their relationship had been volatile for some time, and she had always worried about what Price might be capable of—but this evening's upheaval was worse than usual. Never before had she been more fearful of what he might do to her or her children.

Vickie felt some relief when, at first, Price went to his bedroom and gathered up some belongings. She next heard him pull down the attic steps, a short distance away in the main hall, and figured he was getting some other last-minute things before leaving. But the path to the truck brought him through the kitchen, where Vickie was preparing supper.

He paused to ask her where "his stuff" was.

"I flushed it," she said, referring to the marijuana that she had disposed of, in a fit of pique, eight months earlier. The news upset Price all over again, even though it was not, strictly speaking, news: Vickie recalled taunting him with the revelation when she had first done it.

Enraged anew, Price headed for the attic steps, presumably to look for his stash himself. Vickie trailed close behind to keep an eye on him. But when she started coming up the steps after him, he kicked her in the forehead, then jumped down on top of her and began pummeling her again. She broke free and ran toward the back door, seeking to escape, only to find all of the locks fastened. She was unable to undo them.

She was, by now, hysterical, terrified. More afraid than she could ever remember being, she reached inside the closet near the back door and withdrew a bolt action .22 rifle. She checked it to make sure the clip was loaded, and headed back to the hallway.

Price had returned to the top of the staircase, where he was peering into the attic.

"Please leave," she said, hoping to sound firm, struggling to keep her voice from giving her away. "I want you to *leave.*"

He held his ground, glaring down at her. She repeated her demand.

He shouted, "I'm going to stick that gun up your ass!"

She fired a warning shot over his head.

"I'm gonna kill you!" He came charging down the steps toward her.

Vickie closed her eyes and backed away. And then, without even being aware of aiming the rifle or pulling the trigger, she heard an odd sound, like a stone hitting water.

When she opened her eyes again, Price had walked past her, on his way to the same door from which she had tried to escape moments earlier.

Unaware that he had even been shot, let alone mortally wounded, she ran into the "frog room." She stood there, by a bed, in the dark, until she heard something at the back door. Assuming Price had left, she tiptoed into the hallway, then the kitchen, where she saw him lying near the carport door. . . .

At this point in her testimony, Vickie broke into deep sobs, unable to continue. Judge Emison summoned both sides to the bench, and it was mutually decided that a recess would be in order.

. . . .

* * *

A pretty good yarn, Zbranek had to admit. Vickie had covered all the bases. And the tears were convincing. But Zeke felt she had slipped up on certain points.

For starters, he could not fully understand why a woman who was so fearful of her husband—who had just seen her husband pummel her daughter, and who had been *very nearly strangled* herself—would go looking for trouble the way Vickie had. He was thinking in particular of the events immediately preceding the second fight, when, she had testified, she actually followed Price to the attic steps and began to go up after him. Now why on earth would she have gone and done *that*? If, indeed, her story about having flushed "his stuff" was true, she knew he would find nothing. If Price was surly going up, he was sure to be even surlier when he got back down, his search having been in vain.

Nor was this the only detail that bothered Zeke.

"I remember seeing something gold in it," Vickie had said, when asked whether she knew the rifle was loaded. The remark projected a certain naïveté that was inconsistent with what Zbranek understood to be her considerable familiarity with firearms. Would someone who shot regularly—someone who had hunted rabbits and squirrels, and knew guns uncommonly well for a woman—would someone like that refer to a round merely as "something gold?" As though she were insufficiently conversant with guns to know what the actual term was? That had stuck in his mind.

Too, there was her description of the supposed warning shot. The notion of having enough skill and presence of mind to "intentionally miss," as Vickie had put it, did not jibe with the rather incoherent state of mind described in her testimony. Could someone be aware enough to "intentionally miss" one moment and then *not even be aware of firing the weapon* a second later?

154

In addition, there had been, occasionally, a hint of sarcasm in her replies to his questions about the shooting itself that hit Zbranek as out of step with the general tone of her narrative. Zeke had in mind especially her response when he asked if she recalled ejecting the first round and chambering the second. "I must have done it, there was no one else around," she had said, a bit snippily, he thought. But then, with the next breath, she had plunged right back into character, resuming the sobbing narrative she'd undoubtedly gone over again and again with her attorneys.

That was why, he realized, it was vitally important to keep her off guard, off balance. As Zbranek saw it, the more he could prevent her from spinning, uninterrupted, her rehearsed tale, the better his chances of coaxing the real Vickie out from under Haynes's carefully coached veneer.

As could be expected, the reaction to the day's testimony was mixed, and divided along predictable lines. Overall, Racehorse was encouraged; he felt the day had gone well, and thought he had read, on the faces of the jurors, a certain sympathy for Vickie, despite the serious crime of which she stood accused. Nor had she stumbled, as witnesses sometimes did in the hands of a skillful attorney, or been thrown seriously off guard. And make no mistake about it, there was, Haynes noticed, a deceptive "edge" to many of his counterpart's questions, a caginess or savvy that belied Zbranek's superficial courtesy.

Jean Murph, on the other hand, was devastated. Clearly, she had not expected the depth and breadth of Vickie's attack on her brother, and did not quite know what to say about it all. The trial, as she understood it, was supposed to focus on Vickie's character, specifically her suitability for safely raising the children.

It got her to thinking about the upcoming murder trial.

True, even if the evidence deemed Price to be something less than the ideal husband and father (a reality she was by no means prepared to accept), that was no justification for killing a man. But then, juries had been known to cast aside strict textbook interpretations when it was felt there were extenuating circumstances.

To the press, afterward, Jean poured out her anger and frustration. She quite naturally denied the allegations with great vehemence, promising that subsequent testimony would vindicate her brother. But she also betrayed a certain defensiveness.

Another relative was troubled that day, if for a different reason. The trial testimony had rekindled a disturbing memory of an incident that had bothered this relative at the time, but to which no lasting significance had been attached. Now, the event seemed less innocent.

It had happened during one of the family's August roundups, a year or so back. Price, with a singularly mischievous grin on his face, had trotted out Franklin, then a toddler, into the room where the festivities were concentrated for the moment. Positioning the boy in full view of the entire group—which included his very proper spinsterish aunts, Mim Partlow and Ellen Virginia Daniel, and even his mother—Price pulled down the child's pants and underwear and, smiling broadly, had him urinate for the benefit of his audience.

Mim, the family elder, pretended not to notice. Others suppressed embarrassed laughter, and dismissed the incident as an incredibly juvenile prank. Price, after all, always had a sense of humor that was a little—different. Within moments, the party was back in full swing, though it was clear, later, that Vickie had not shared Price's enthusiasm for the gross display. Looking back, now, this one relative just couldn't get over the sheer outrageousness of the act, and—more than that—the way in which Price had stood there with this odd gleam in his eye.

* * *

Vickie's assault continued on Tuesday. She produced a cassette tape, made in the bedroom of her house, which, she alleged, revealed Price in the act of playing illicit games with three-year-old Franklin and ten-year-old Tom, his son by his first wife. The tape was of poor quality, and most of the sounds all but indecipherable. About the only thing that could be determined with any certainty was that whoever was involved was having fun. Still, despite a heavy dose of Zbranek skepticism, Vickie stuck to her story about what the recording signified.

As the day progressed, Vickie turned to her late husband's financial and domestic habits, and the stories were no less grim. An unremittingly sordid picture was painted of trying to make ends meet on a meager budget. The terms and conditions of the couple's financial arrangements, even during the better years of their life together, appeared to be intolerable. Sounding fragile and wounded at times, Vickie told of Price's condescending habit of giving her lists with explicit instructions of what to buy, where to buy it, what it should cost. She told of how he constantly chastised her for impulse shopping at convenience stores, where, he observed (and correctly so, as Zbranek later pointed out), prices were 20 to 40 percent higher. Going even a small amount over budget, she explained, would invite one of Price's tirades.

It was getting harder and harder for the jurors to take. Not in the sense of credibility, for Vickie sounded nothing if not believable. Rather, it was the apparent contradiction between Price's public face—what they knew of his political career—and his private life that shocked, as well as titillated. As the testimony progressed, many of the jurors shifted restlessly. From time to time, they glanced over at the members of the family, possibly wondering if all this was as new to *them*. Price Daniel, Jr., was being described as a man who had few if any redeeming quali-

157

ties. Even Hitler, the jurors' faces seemed to say, was nice to his dogs.

Haynes had started to grow impatient with Zeke. Two days had gone by, and so far, from the questions and testimony, nobody would have known this was a custody trial. To be sure, Vickie was doing fine, but Zbranek was, for all intents and purposes, trying a murder case. Under normal circumstances, in a criminal case, the prosecution would not have an opportunity to probe the defense strategy until "game time," as Racehorse liked to put it. Zbranek was laying it all bare, here and now.

Despite this, in another corner of his brain, euphoria was slowly building. He saw something happening here, something wonderful and unexpected, something that overcame his original reservations about holding the trial in Liberty. As Vickie poured out her grief on the stand, Haynes began to sense a genuine communion between his client and the jurors, a spiritual bond. It went deeper than any political or family influence ever could. It reached down into the gut and stirred certain emotions—in particular, hatred for people who worry about things like what kinds of tax shelters to buy into next year. This, Haynes realized, was not Houston, where everyone aspired to wealth and power. Here were the simple, rural townfolk empathizing with a poor little girl—one of their own—caught up in the whims and vicissitudes of a formidable political dynasty.

Looking on, Eckols felt the powerful empathy at work, too. But his lawman's analysis was rather less sophisticated than the celebrated defense attorney's.

"Everybody *believes* her," thought Eckols, shaking his head in despair.

Chapter Fifteen

Z eke Zbranek returned to his office to review the deposition Larry Moore had given on March 2. Moore's sworn statement posed striking contradictions to Vickie's testimony, and Zbranek felt he could use it to impeach many of Vickie's more damaging allegations. The lawyer now wanted to fix in his mind the precise approach he would take with this most important witness.

Zeke listened to the tape once again:

"OK, now what is your name?"

"Larry Moore."

"And what is your address?"

"Route 1, Box 616, Dayton."

"You were married to Vickie Daniel at one time, right?"

"Yes."

"Do you remember the date of your marriage?"

"We were married October the second of 1967."

"Now, did y'all have any children?"

"We had two."

"All right, now what was their name and date of birth?"

"Kimberly was born September the eighth of 1967."

"What—you mean a month before you were married?"

"No, uh, sixty-eight. I'm sorry."

Zbranek grimaced. Throughout the interview, Larry had

shown a disconcerting tendency to become confused about details, especially dates. In the eyes of the jury, such imprecision over details would often cast in doubt the witness's testimony on more substantive matters. Haynes could doubtless make a witness like Larry sound hopelessly flustered and unsure of himself. Zeke would have to work with Larry on that.

"Now what about Jonathan?"

"Jonathan was born August the sixth of 1970."

"All right. About—less than a year later."

"Mmmmm—almost two years apart."

"So that would be '71, then. . . . No that's right, '70, sure, '68 to '70, that's right, OK."

Zbranek shook his head—apparently the confusion was catching.

"Now let me ask you this. Did you—uh, during your marriage—well, just describe your marriage to Vickie in terms of how y'all got along."

"Uh, it was pretty much a back and forth marriage. One time you're gettin' along real good and another time you're fightin' like cats and dogs."

"When she got mad was she violent?"

"*Extremely.*" There was a certain awe in Larry's voice that would go over well with a jury.

"Did she ever attack you?"

"Yes."

"How did this happen?"

"Uh—we may be havin' a heated conversation, and a lot of times I would rather just drop it and turn around and walk off, and I'd get the back of my neck scratched with her fingernails for the effort."

"Mm-hmm. And did this happen—several times? That is, more than one time?"

"Yes, yes."

"And, uh—well, what would you say about her temper?"

"She had a very hot temper."

"Uh, there was some incident about when somebody came to your house and she took a twelve-gauge shotgun and run him off or something like that when y'all lived on Cornell Street?"

"Right."

"OK. Tell me about that."

"Well . . . her brother's wife was off somewhere else with someone else. They were supposed to have been at the drive-in theater here in Liberty. And he asked us to drive him up there so he could pick up his wife. We went up there and located her in the car with another man. And he went over and drugged her out of the car and put her in our car. And we left the show. And uh, the next day, her mother and father came over to the house— one of her brothers was with 'em—"

"You mean Vickie's mother and father?"

"No, no, no, the other girl's. Uh, her name was Edna, and her mother, father, and brother came over to the house."

"In other words, Edna was your sister-in-law."

"Uh, no, she would've been Vickie's sister-in-law."

"OK."

"She was married to Vickie's brother."

"What was his name?"

"Uh, Benny."

"OK, go ahead. So who came now? Edna's . . . ?"

"Edna's mother, father, and brother."

Zbranek made a mental note to try to avoid getting bogged down in these kinds of excursions into the family tree. It was too hard to follow.

"Mmm-hmm. OK, go ahead."

"We were out in the front yard, talkin'. They were a little aggravated about us interfering with what her daughter did, and actually we were just more or less takin' Benny up to the show to find his wife, which—I didn't

161

really see anything wrong with, myself; we didn't get involved in the argument. And uh, they hadn't used any violence nor threatened to, on me or the family, but, uh, Vickie got mad, went back in the house and came out with a twelve-gauge shotgun. I tried to take it away from her and she jerked back away from me so that I couldn't reach the gun, and said something about she was gonna shoot one of 'em if they didn't leave. The people got scared and left. I finally took the gun away from her and put it back in the house. I don't remember if the gun was or was not loaded, but on occasions I did keep it loaded around the house on the fact that we had suspicions of prowlers around off and on."

"Did she make any threats against these people?"

"Uh, yes, she made the threats directed to the people."

"What did she tell?"

"She told 'em she was gonna shoot one of 'em if they didn't leave!"

"And you tried to dissuade her from that."

"Yes, it scared me that she had come out in the front yard with a shotgun like that."

"So the people left?"

"Yes, they did."

"And you got the gun away from her."

"Yes."

"Was she mad on that occasion?"

"She was."

The lawyer skipped ahead in the tape to the subject of Jonathan.

"All right, now let me ask you this. Do you remember approximately when you first got Jonathan?"

"Uh, I don't remember the exact date, it was something like around August, and I can't even be sure of the year. I think '78 or '79. . . . And he went to school with me for about—lived in the house and went to school in Day-

162

ton for roughly six to seven months. . . . Uh, I took complete legal custody of him August the sixteenth of 1979. So it would have been '77 or '78 that he lived with me the first time."

"All right. Now after he lived with you that first time for a period of time, uh, how long was it after that—how long did he go back and stay with Vickie and Price?"

"It would've been over a year, or around a year."

"So that would've been—"

"Should've been '78."

"That you would've gotten him the first time."

"Mmm-hmm. It was shortly after Judy and I were married. We were married June '77. July, August"—Larry had ticked off the months as though counting, mentally—"maybe it was '77, three months after we were married."

"OK. So that—"

"He was livin' with us the first time in '77, and then I got legal custody of him August sixteenth of '79, and he's been livin' with me ever since."

"What reason did she give for lettin' you have him the first time?"

"Uh—she just thought he would be better off livin' with me. He was to her opinion uncontrollable."

Zeke smiled. No black boys beating up on Jonathan; no fires blowing up in his face; no probing hands in the dark being slipped underneath his rear end. The boy was just giving his mom a hard time, was all.

"All right. Now, uh, how come she took him back?"

"She wasn't gettin' her way with me for some reason, and I wouldn't do something that she wanted me to do, I don't remember what it was, and she got mad and ran out and took Jonathan back."

"Did she on this occasion tell you anything about the fact that Price was mistreatin' the boy or doin' anything—?"

163

"She told me that he was doing, uh, some unusual things as far as—uh—she said something about he knocked the glass off the icebox one time and blamed it on Jonathan and got mad. That's about the only thing I can remember specifically, she said that he was just mistreating Jonathan. I've questioned Jonathan on those matters and he denies ever being mistreated by Price. He prefers to lean in the other direction that he liked Price to a good deal of an extent."

"All right. Now, the second time that she gave him to you, did she tell you anything about mistreatment or anything like that?"

"She didn't say anything about Price mistreating Jonathan, no."

"OK, the second time that you got him, and you finally got custody, tell me how that happened."

"Well, I was constantly trying to get custody of Jonathan, anyway. I thought it would be best for him to live out there with me. She wasn't sending him to his school and everything correctly, to my opinion. Then I asked for custody and we finally made agreements to where I had Bruce Stratton make out papers for both of us to sign an agreement for a change of custody."

"All right, now let me ask you this. Did she ever tell you this time that Price was having any type of homosexual acts of conduct with Jonathan?"

"*No.*" Larry's voice could not have been more emphatic. "I have never heard anything like that from any of the kids or from Vickie or anyone."

"OK. And, uh, when was the first time that anything like that was said to you?"

"Vickie said something to me about it Wednesday of this week, and she also said something about it Saturday of this week."

"That would be Wednesday of last week, right? This is—"

"OK, this is Monday."

"Yes. This is Monday, March the second. So that would've been the twenty-fifth of February and the twenty-eighth of February."

"Right."

Right. In other words, thought Zbranek, after Racehorse and her lawyers had had a chance to sit down with her for a chat.

"All right. Now I want to get back to that conversation a little later, but let me ask you, uh, another question. During your marriage to Vickie, did you notice whether or not she would lie?"

A smile had come into Larry's voice. "She's very good at it."

"What would she lie about?"

"Oh, likely anything."

"What was her general stability, that is, was she a stable person, was she solid, well-grounded, the reliable type, or, uh—how would you describe that?"

"Uh, I didn't realize until after we'd gotten divorced exactly how much she had been pullin' the wool over my eyes. But I found out that there were a good many things that she had lied to me about. Anything in general that was to her advantage."

"And, uh, do you know anything about the fact she's supposed to have had an abortion in between times of the two boys she's got?"

"She told us something about—that she had had an abortion. It surprised me. I didn't think that Price could let something like that happen."

"Well, did she give any kind of explanation? As to why?"

"She said then, the way she felt and everything, she just couldn't handle another child. I think it was during the time that she was seeing the psychiatrist, or shortly before or something. But she said she couldn't handle another child at that time."

"Did she say anything that Price made her do it?"

"No."

Zbranek nodded as he listened. He was going to be able to get a lot of mileage out of Larry Moore.

After Vickie had testified for almost fifteen hours on Monday and Tuesday, Zeke began on Wednesday, March 18, what he would characterize as a "brick by brick" attempt to dismantle her sordid accusations against Price.

Each of four witnesses—Charlotte Daniel; Howard and Stephana Oldham (one of Price's business partners and his wife); and Price's bookkeeper, Betty White—described Price as a loving father, an industrious businessman, and a gentle person who neither smoked marijuana, drank to excess, chased other women, nor mistreated his children in any way.

One by one, under Zbranek's skillful guidance, they expressed outrage over Vickie's charges and her attempts to twist and distort the facts. Charlotte, in particular, was incredulous about the tape Vickie had introduced Tuesday as evidence of sexual play between Price and the kids. Nonsense, said Charlotte. She explained that Vickie had originally described the recording as nothing more than a harmless bit of silliness in which Price and the kids were laughing about "toots," their word for flatulence. She insisted she had seen the children often, and had detected no fear of their father.

Further, it was her sense that Vickie tended to overreact to things. She offered an illustration. In May of 1979, she said, Kimberly and Jonathan ran to her home asking for help for their mother, who was supposedly involved in a knock-down, drag-out fight with Price. Yet when Vickie came over to retrieve the kids, she appeared unharmed in any way. Granted, later that same day, Vickie phoned

Charlotte from the Del Ray Motel, and claimed Price had locked her out of the house. But that had nothing to do with Vickie's allegations of physical brutality. (Houston would later testify, of the same incident, that he had gone over to the house right after the children showed up and found things pretty quiet. If anything, his brother Price—sporting a big red mark on the side of his face—could have used some assistance in fending off Vickie.)

Zbranek's witnesses also strongly implied that Vickie imagined some things altogether. Stephana Oldham's testimony was typical. She told the court her friendship with the defendant had ended when Vickie implied that Price and her husband, Howard, used the trailer park they co-owned as a kind of personal harem, restocking their inventory with fresh faces from time to time.

Similarly, Vickie's complaints about lack of money were made by Zbranek's witnesses to sound shrewish, melodramatic, and exaggerated.

What about extramarital affairs? Zeke asked.

No, each of them testified in turn, they had no first-hand knowledge of any affairs Price was having. Yes, he did have a tendency to bury himself in his work and lose track of time. Perhaps that had been misconstrued. And, of course, he was a politician. Politicians always have to make the rounds and cultivate friendships that can later be put to advantageous use. But as a matter of fact, the taciturn Price was, if anything, less inclined to that kind of behavior than most.

On cross-examination, Racehorse took the opportunity to reprise one of his favorite techniques.

Although Haynes, like any good criminal attorney, would use sympathetic witnesses to refute harmful testimony put forward by the other side, he preferred to turn the tables on the opposition's own witnesses. It was an approach he had honed during the trials of John Hill, T. Cullen Davis, and other celebrated clients. Sympathetic information could just have as easily been provided by witnesses friendly to Haynes's cause, but he knew that it had more weight coming from those people who were sponsored by his adversary.

The Oldhams acknowledged that they were once upset with Price for giving them a marijuana-cigarette-rolling kit as a Christmas present.

Why was that? Haynes inquired.

"I thought it was in poor taste," Oldham said.

"Did you send it back?" Haynes asked.

"No, sir."

Thus, through one of Zbranek's own witnesses, Haynes established that Price was, at the very least, less than a total stranger to marijuana. In the bargain, he had also raised questions about Price's judgment, as well as about Oldham's own personal habits.

But Haynes's biggest coup on this third day of testimony was an admission wrested from Charlotte and Mrs. Oldham. The two women conceded that not only could they not testify to a single incident showing Vickie as an unfit mother but they had, on several occasions, left their own children with her. What, Racehorse felt, could possibly be more central to a custody case?

Having extracted this testimony, he looked to the jury and pursed his lips, as if to say, Well, I guess that about settles it, doesn't it?

No sooner had Haynes begun scoring points than Zbranek's witnesses began having memory lapses.

Earlier, Charlotte had testified that she and Vickie would on occasion discuss their sex lives. As Charlotte told it, Vickie had expressed no particular dissatisfaction with Price's bedroom performance. Haynes presently asked if she recalled a specific conversation, during the summer of 1977, in which Vickie reported she had gotten "venereal warts" from Price.

Charlotte said, "I don't remember," a phrase that became a favorite of the witnesses who followed.

Charlotte was equally hazy when Racehorse turned to the subject of her own telephone campaign to protect Price's memory. Haynes wanted to know, Had she called Ann Rogers with the intention of getting her to agree not to say anything derogatory about Price? After a moment of grudging silence, Charlotte conceded that she "may have." Taking that as a "yes," Haynes proceeded to ask Charlotte what, specifically, she had told Ann Rogers. "That Price is dead, and let him rest in peace," said Charlotte. Racehorse still wasn't satisfied. He wanted to know, *verbatim*, what Charlotte had asked Ann Rogers not to talk about.

"I can't remember," Charlotte said.

The memory-lapse syndrome spread to Howard Oldham, who had testified in some detail that Vickie complained about Price's having affairs with secretaries, and about the constant shortage of household money. In general, Howard had said, Vickie struck him as being paranoid where her husband was concerned. Her attitude had even undermined their friendship.

Haynes asked Oldham simply to recount Vickie's complaints in narrative fashion and let the jury draw its own conclusions about her "paranoid" state of mind. Tell us what was said between the two of you, Haynes asked. Tell us about the last time you spoke with Vickie, and about your overall relationship with her, and about your business dealings with Price.

To most of these questions, Oldham now had the same answer: "I don't remember."

By the end of the cross-examination, the phrase had been entered into the record so many times that Racehorse went before the press and said he felt more like a dentist than a lawyer. Spent the whole day pulling teeth, he mused. Of Howard Oldham, he added, "He reminds

me of a guy who went to memory school but can't remember where or when."

Betty White, Price's young, divorced bookkeeper, and
the object of a considerable amount of Price Daniel's gen-
erosity in the last year of his life, was the recipient of
the last phone call out of the Daniel home prior to the
shooting.

At about 7:10 P.M., roughly midway between the time
Price arrived home and the time he would be killed, Vickie
called to ask Betty to apologize for accusing her of steal-
ing scratch paper, mustard, and ketchup from Price's law
office. She was upset about the petty accusations, which
apparently had been relayed to her by her husband.

"She asked me if I was going to apologize," Betty told
the packed courtroom. "I told her no."

Betty testified that Vickie then accused her of having a
romantic relationship with her husband. Such suspicions
had flourished among the local gossips ever since Price
had begun helping Betty by co-signing her car note and
providing a solution to her housing predicament. Betty
herself had made light of the rumors, and friends claimed
Price wasn't even her type.

Betty had insisted as much during the telephone exchange with Vickie on January 19. After she hung up the
phone, she felt proud of the way she had handled herself.
It never crossed her mind that the husband of the woman
she had just told off might be dead in less than half
an hour.

Chapter Sixteen

O n Thursday, March 19, Larry Moore took the stand.

Vickie, said Larry, had "come to visit" him four or five times during the first seven months of her marriage to Price. When she and Price had "fussed," Vickie, with their two kids in tow, would set up housekeeping at his place for short periods of time.

"Did she stay in the same bed with you?" Zbranek asked.

"Yes, she did."

"Where were the children?" Zbranek wanted to know.

"In their bedroom."

"Was she pregnant?"

"Yes," said Larry, but he'd only discovered this during Vickie's next to last such visit. And no, the baby wasn't his.

"Did you have any record of Vickie's visits?" Haynes asked on cross-examination.

"I didn't keep records of my sexual activities," Larry shot back.

"Do you keep records now?" Racehorse asked smartly.

Chortles spread through the gallery and the jury, and even Zbranek had to grin. Haynes had not lost his sense of humor, but there was a certain tartness to his queries. Clearly, he was less than thrilled with this sudden assault on his client's morals.

171

Zeke thought that was pretty funny, under the circumstances.

In impressive detail, Larry Moore testified that he had seen Vickie angry "many times" during their marriage, and that her anger had often erupted into hand-to-hand combat between them. On and on Larry went about their domestic upheaval, Zbranek carefully leading the way.

"Now, uh, let's see, during the time that y'all were married, did Vickie ever take a weapon of any kind to you?"

"A butcher knife, one time."

"And were you able to take that away from her?"

"Yes. I was holding her arms when she turned around and swung at me with it. I grabbed her arms and was holdin' 'em and she was still trying to cut the inside of my wrist with the knife while she had it in her hand. And I reached up and slapped her upside the head, apparently pretty hard. I, uh, managed to get the knife away from her and hold her down and keep her from trying anything else until she could cool down awhile."

"Now the other occasions when she would jump on you and scratch you, what did you do to protect yourself on those occasions?"

"Usually I would try to catch her hands and hold her, and usually in the scuffle she would wind up on the floor and I would be holdin' her arms. Really that was the only way you could hold her to keep her from just continuing to scratch you."

"You had these difficulties—"

"Pretty frequent."

Larry told about the time he had to hold Vickie down and cut off her fingernails. A member of Wilborn's staff, thinking of the autopsy report and the scratch marks on Price's neck and chest, nodded knowingly.

Zbranek also felt it would be helpful to establish that even if Price *had* hit Vickie that night, it might not have taken a particularly fearsome blow to cause the marks noticed by her doctor and others in the days following the shooting. And so:

"Did you have a chance to observe, during your marriage to her, whether she would bruise easily?"

"Definitely. That specific time that she had the butcher knife and I slapped her, she had a bruise for over a week. It was something like a week and a half, two weeks before the bruise went away."

"You did slap her pretty hard that time."

"Yes. But it was an open-hand slap."

Then Vickie's ex-husband dropped a bombshell. On two occasions since their divorce, said Larry, Vickie had discussed shooting someone. One time, she had even identified her intended victim: her husband, Price Daniel, Jr. In late 1979 or early 1980, as Larry remembered it—he was still having trouble with dates—Vickie and he were having one of their end-of-the-weekend, drop-off-the-kids conversations. His ex-wife was telling him about some troubles she was having at home working out the terms of a divorce settlement with Price. "And," Larry testified, "she said that she would shoot the SOB before she would let him have her kids."

"Did she ever," asked Zbranek, "have a conversation with you about the type of gun to use to shoot someone?"

"Yes. We were sittin' at the end of the sidewalk again—another one of the weekend conversations—and she had asked me what type of gun I would use to shoot someone. And I told her that if it came to the point that she had to shoot someone, I myself would use a shotgun. And she asked me why. And I told her, you know, close range, a shotgun was very effective, and she asked about range and effects . . . uh, we talked about it and she came up and asked, as part of the subject, asked me, wouldn't a twenty-two do just as well? And I told her, well, it probably would

173

if you was to shoot him in the right spot. It would stop him."

Zeke also made sure the jury understood that Vickie was no stranger to firearms.

Zeke: "OK. Now during the time y'all were married, did y'all ever hunt?"

Larry: "Oh, yeah."

Zeke: "Did she know how to use a gun?"

Larry: "Very well."

Zeke: "What kind of guns did she—"

Larry: "Her favorite was a twenty-two automatic." (Price had been shot with a .22 rifle.) Also, Vickie "had experience with a shotgun."

Zeke: "OK, so she was able to load 'em, unload 'em—"

Larry: "Oh, yes. She knew how to load the guns, fire 'em, the whole bit."

Zeke: "At a later date, did she ever show you any kind of weapon?"

Larry: "Yes . . . Seemed like it was around November or December. I was at her house and I had gotten to the door and rang the doorbell—"

Zeke: "This was last November or December?"

·Larry: "Yes, of 1980."

Zeke: "OK."

Larry: "And uh, I was standing at the door talkin' to her, while Kimberly was gettin' her clothes bag and everything together to go spend the weekend, and I noticed the shotgun hangin' on the rack. And she mentioned the fact that it was a shotgun that she had just bought for Price."

Here again, Zeke smiled at the uncomfortable irony. True, Price had been shot with the .22, not the shotgun. But if Vickie had, indeed, used those words—that she'd "bought the shotgun for Price"—it was, as things turned out, almost as much of a wry pun as the old gag about the cannibals—the one where they meet an explorer in the jungle and say, "Why don't you come with us, we'd love to have you for lunch!"

Gratifying as it was to get such evidence of forethought into the trial record, Zbranek wished the jury could have heard Larry's testimony on that point. That would not be the case, since Racehorse had argued that the testimony might be prejudicial. Larry Moore's problems with his ex-wife had terminated with their divorce, four years ago. "The present state of Vickie Daniel is what's relevant," Haynes had concluded.

Never one to pussyfoot around, Haynes also backed up his argument with a threat. He raised the specter of an interminable trial by saying he could not allow Larry's testimony to go unchallenged in front of a jury; there are two sides to marital problems, said Racehorse, and he would be forced to cross-examine Larry on every fight the couple ever had. By Larry's own reckoning, this would amount to some two hundred fights.

Since testimony by ex-husbands against their ex-wives or vice versa is a gray area of the law to begin with, it was Judge Emison's judgment that Larry Moore's testimony about his physical confrontations with Vickie be given outside the presence of the jury.

Zbranek was upset. "I have a right to show what her condition was!" he pleaded, but to no avail. He was able to wrest from Emison nothing more than a promise to allow Larry Moore to be recalled to repeat his testimony for the jury's benefit if a psychological report could be produced showing that Vickie's past marital behavior had some direct bearing on the charges at hand.

Looking to poke holes in Larry Moore's testimony, or to dull the impact of its more sensational points, Racehorse cross-examined Larry for an exhaustive four and a half hours. Haynes specifically attacked Larry's assertion that Vickie said she would shoot Price junior—or, as Larry had quoted her, "the SOB"—before she'd let him take the children in a divorce settlement.

Under what circumstances had the remark been made? asked Haynes.

How did he mean? Larry replied.

Well, what, if anything, had precipitated it?

Said Larry, "I was sittin' in a pickup in her driveway and she had come out to the end of the sidewalk, and set on the brick wall there at the end of the sidewalk, talkin' about that her and Price were havin' trouble. She was tryin' to get a certain amount of money out of him and he wouldn't pay that much, and they were havin' trouble with it. And she was determined that she was gonna have her way in the matter. I mentioned the fact that if she pressured it too much, he might just decide to keep the children and not pay her anything." And that, said Larry, was when the remark was made.

This considerably softened the impact of Haynes's client's statement about shooting Price. Lacking any context, the words had sounded as if Vickie had made her threat out of the blue.

On a roll, Haynes pursued the issue of how much Larry knew about the shooting itself. To Zbranek's dismay, Larry responded with information that supported Racehorse's portrait of an unintentional shooting. He said that shortly after Price was killed, on February 28 to be exact, while he and Vickie were alone in a car, he took the opportunity to ask her, "What the heck happened?" Vickie told him the weapon discharged accidentally, when she lost her footing in the process of backing away from Price. "She said, 'You'll never believe me, but I tripped and fell,' " Larry testified.

In spite of such acknowledgments, the tensions between Vickie's former husband and his interrogator, established a day earlier during Haynes's questions about Larry's sex life, continued unabated. Each did his best to needle, frustrate, and out-quip the other, providing more than a few moments of comic relief in the midst of the more sober testimony.

Larry had said he knew that Franklin, Vickie's first son with Price, could not possibly be his because he'd had a vasectomy in September 1972. He had thus been sterile for several years. Racehorse mused aloud about whether such information could be quickly verified without doing tests or going back to the operating physician.

"No, I don't carry a certificate," Larry snapped, once again delighting the courtroom faithful.

Jean Murph was feeling buoyed by the latest testimony as the first week of the trial drew to a close. Finally, mercifully, the attention had shifted away from Price and was now focusing more on Vickie's own worth or worthlessness as a mother. In that connection, Jean sought out the press and made her lengthiest statement to date.

She began by taking a swipe at the allegations of Price's brutality. Margaret Covington, Haynes's psychological sidekick, had stressed that Vickie's marriage to Price Daniel epitomized the battered-wife syndrome. Jean now pointed out that recent testimony made Vickie's marital track record look more like two instances of "battered *husband* syndrome."

She used that observation as a springboard to her general views on the conduct of the trial thus far:

"I feel sad that so many people have to be hurt and an attempt made to destroy so many people's character in order to defend herself. But I feel we are beginning to see the real Price Daniel junior and we will see more as the truth comes out."

177

Jean continued, "We're beginning to see a lot about Vickie also. To be a mother is a lot more than changing diapers and feeding children. There must be characteristics of reliability, stability, and dependability. Those are not strong characteristics in Vickie Daniel. . . . The way the children's father could be denigrated in such a manner this last week is another example of parentage skills."

Jean Murph was not the only one who had sought out the press to offer some early returns. For his part, Haynes was shaking his head over the seemingly endless stream of "outsiders" recruited by the other side to testify against his client. Zbranek had originally said he planned to call "twenty or so" witnesses, but now the scope of the trial's inquiry seemed to be widening to include issues the defense team considered largely irrelevant to the task at hand. In typical fashion, Haynes deadpanned, "Pretty soon we're going to open the telephone book and tell the sheriff to bring them all in. This thing will never end. It's a cast of thousands.

"I don't know what happened to the presumption of innocence," he complained, segueing to the utter injustice of it all. "Just because someone has been charged with a crime, including murder, does not rob that individual of all their treasures, including children." He then added, in a patented bit of mock oratory, "Take heart, every time I drive into town I see its name—and it is *Liberty!*"

Off-camera, another relative had been observing the various performances. Jean's a little too involved in this, thought David Parker, the cousin who had engineered Haynes's entry into the case, and it's hurting her chances. Parker had watched as Jean sat there, shoulder to shoulder with Zbranek. Her eyes were riveted on Vickie, and she was scribbling furious notes. He wondered how all that intensity was coming across to the jury. Did she seem too angry? Were they beginning to suspect that the whole thing had just been a mammoth act of spitefulness?

Chapter Seventeen

Nineteen-year-old Pamela Locke found herself in an uncomfortable position common to Zbranek's female witnesses: She had to deny to Racehorse Haynes that she had had an affair with her former boss, Price Daniel, Jr.

But if the questions were intimidating, the young woman had firm and ready answers. With clear voice, Locke implied that Vickie had an irrational obsession with her husband's possible infidelities. For example, Locke told of how Vickie had seized upon the unlikely occasion of the opening of Price's Main Street office in November 1979—with all its overtones of hope and rebirth—to broach the subject of whether or not Locke and Price were lovers.

"Vickie had come right out and asked me if Price and I were having an affair," she stated. "She said Price liked young girls with blond hair." At the time, Vickie was seven months pregnant with Bob. "I was shocked at the question," the young woman added, sounding every bit as indignant as she claimed to have felt at the time. With equal vigor, Locke recounted Vickie's meddling in office matters, and corroborated testimony given earlier by Betty White regarding a piece of skin that had been missing from Price's chin on the morning of January 19.

Perhaps sensing the young woman's testimony was having an impact on the jury, Haynes during cross-examination changed the subject to another Daniel employee, Mary Cain. Did you, Racehorse asked, tell "anybody in the world" that Price Daniel, Jr., and Mary Cain had had an affair?

"I don't know," Pam Locke answered. She sounded suddenly more equivocal than before. "I don't think so."

Locke did say that Vickie once asked her to keep an eye on Cain's home and to tell her when Price visited. She explained to Haynes that she did not take issue with Vickie at the time of that particular conversation, but neither did she comply with the request, which she viewed as bizarre.

Mary Cain took the stand.

Haynes began his questioning, innocently enough, by asking about Cain's office responsibilities, her rate of pay and so forth—the sorts of minor details that tend to put witnesses at ease.

Mary replied that she had been hired at three dollars an hour and had received a raise to six dollars an hour early in 1980. Haynes paused a moment to let that sink in. Interesting, he seemed to be saying. A doubling in pay, over a relatively short period of employment, at the same time Vickie was trying to get Price to spring for a few extra bucks around the house.

Haynes then questioned Mary about a trip she and Price made to Houston about a week before his death, when she picked up a new Oldsmobile Toronado at a car dealership. How was it that the two of them happened to make this jaunt together?

Mary explained that it was not at all uncommon for the two of them to be out and about together. It was part of the job. If they weren't checking on a property, they were meeting a client in order to discuss a property. Indeed, it was she who'd accompanied Price throughout the legwork involved in checking out likely places for Vickie to relocate.

On the day in question, Price had planned to go to the Astrodome to pick up some baseball tickets. Hearing that Mary needed to go near there to pick up a car, he offered to drive her. That, she claimed, was all there was to it.

Haynes asked if they hugged and kissed at the dealership.

Mary said no, whatever gave him that idea?

Racehorse followed up by asking whether Mary had ever had an affair with Price Daniel, Jr.

In an even tone of voice, Mary denied it.

They sparred like that for a while. Haynes would approach the subject from different angles, and Mary would reiterate her denial with just as much determination. (Among friends, Mary would insist that Price wasn't even the type of person to flirt. If you wanted to tempt Price Daniel, Mary explained, you couldn't do it with women. Now *money*, on the other hand—that was a horse of a different color. Money was what turned Price Daniel on.)

Sometime after she left the stand that day, Mary found out Vickie had said she once saw Price kissing her at the Main Street office. Even years later, Mary Cain would insist that the incident had been fabricated by Vickie—perhaps even fantasized—just to have something with which to confront Price to get some of the attention she so badly craved.

The next few days saw the convulsive melodrama that had followed the shooting replayed in court.

The three EMTs, David Bautsch, John Anderson, and Oscar Cantu, all testified.

The EMTs described Vickie's mental state. All agreed that upon their arrival, Vickie was not yet hysterical, but appeared frightened. The chaotic tempo of things was such that the men could not, at that point, determine whether Vickie had been injured, or even whether her hair was out of place. Anderson and Cantu recounted the frenzied

181

melee in the front hallway, both men agreeing that Vickie kept screaming for them to "go help Price." Anderson told of her efforts to gnaw at his leg. Cantu spoke of what Vickie had told him in the ambulance about having shot Price by accident: "They had an argument and he went upstairs to get some 'pot' and she went to get a gun to scare him and Price had said, 'Oh, no,' and it must have gone off." At this first independent version of Vickie's "confession," reporters ran off to telephone their bureaus. (Newsmen for some reason discounted Cantu's testimony that Vickie's remarks to him had consisted exclusively of the three dozen words he repeated; afterward, they harassed him for elaboration, and over the next few weeks, when the phone rang at the firehouse, it was often as not for him.) Jim Stapleton then testified about finding the .22-caliber rifle in the "frog room," where Vickie, while still battling the two EMTs and Buchanan, had instructed him to look for it.

Haynes, during cross-examination of the EMTs, once again put his much-ballyhooed cleverness on display.

He twice assumed the role of Vickie: with Cantu, who demonstrated how she huddled in the corner waiting to spring, and with Anderson, who demonstrated how Cantu rolled to the floor on top of Vickie. In the course of the reenactment, Racehorse himself ended up on his back, eliciting laughter from the gallery and driving jurors out of their seats to see if he had really subjected his spiffy pinstripe suit to the indignity of the courtroom floor.

Racehorse offered the scenario in the interest of presenting more clearly Vickie's behavior on that crucial night. But with the brief bit of slapstick, he had also succeeded in breaking the darkness of the retelling of the events of January 19.

Chapter Eighteen

T|he day after Price was killed, Tuesday, January 20, Liberty criminal investigator Marvin Powell had gone to the house with a specific mission in mind. Liberty stationer Howard Oldham, later one of Zbranek's "character witnesses" for Price, had come forward with some information pertinent to Vickie's defense. The information concerned her allegations that Price had been searching the attic for pot. (That Oldham already knew of the "pot" story, less than twenty-four hours after the shooting, was a testament of Liberty's vast and efficient grapevine.) "Price," Oldham reported, "once told me that he and his first wife, Diane, tried a couple of marijuana cigarettes and didn't care for them." He added that, to the best of his knowledge, Price still kept the box containing those cigarettes hidden in his home. And so, with Oldham offering to play tour guide, Powell, Eckols, and Chief Deputy Clay Autery headed out to the ranch for one of many visits the three lawmen had made, either individually or together, since eight the preceding evening.

In one of three attics in the home—not the attic Price had been searching just before he was shot—Oldham pointed out a locked trunk and nodded. Autery rummaged around in Price's study, found some keys, and was

183

able to open the trunk with one of them. Oldham's eyes then settled on a wooden box about the size of a handgun case. "That's the box," he told the three men. Lifting its lid, Powell found, inside, small pieces of a green substance.

Now, under cross-examination from Haynes, Powell testified to a series of lapses that marked the Sheriff's Department's handling of the box after its discovery. He conceded that the box was not photographed as it was opened. Nor, for that matter, was it sent off to a Beaumont crime lab for analysis until early in March, some six weeks after the shooting. In fact, such was local law enforcement's lack of interest in pursuing this lead that the box was not exposed to the sensitive snout of the department's pot-sniffing dog at any time during its lengthy residence at the sheriff's office.

This last, especially, supported Haynes's growing conviction of bias on the part of Buck Eckols. Eckols had gone out of his way to publicize the fact that the same dog had pronounced as "clean" the attic Price was searching before his death. It was clear to the Houston lawyer that Eckols was being more than a tad selective in his use of the dog.

Marvin Powell's testimony continued to veer unsteadily between puzzling answers and unsatisfying answers. Nor was there any shortage of non-answers. When asked, for example, whether he had questioned Houston Daniel about whether Price kept marijuana in the house, Powell replied, "I don't remember." It struck many as odd that Powell would have either neglected to ask the question or forgotten Houston's answer.

Having broken ground on the marijuana front, Haynes decided to be more adventuresome.

"Did you find any white powdery substance to send to the lab for analysis," he asked Powell.

"Not that I recall, sir," Powell said.

"Did anybody remove any white powdery substance?" pressed Racehorse.

"Not that I recall, sir."

There was a striking evasiveness to Powell's tone. *Not that I recall?* Why not simply no? Or yes? This, after all, was *the investigator in charge of the case.* Hadn't he written anything down? At least one or two of the jurors were shaking their heads in disbelief. Judge Emison shared their impatience. Later, in an agitated voice, he instructed Powell to review his reports overnight so that he could provide Racehorse Haynes with some forthright answers on Thursday.

Meanwhile, over at Jean Murph's table, Zbranek could only sigh. He had hoped for a better fifty-first birthday. His discomfiture grew when he tried unsuccessfully to introduce a diagram showing the trajectory of the warning shot. Zeke felt the diagram might tend to cast some doubt on whether or not it was actually meant to warn Price, inasmuch as, the way Zbranek saw it, the trajectory of the first shot wasn't all that different from the trajectory of the second, and fatal, one. But Judge Emison rebuffed him again, this time because the diagram was not to scale and was, in the judge's view, confusing. Like so much of what had been heard that day.

For Jean Murph partisans, it went downhill from there. Marvin Powell did his homework, as ordered by Judge Emison. Still, the C.I.'s second full day on the stand went as badly as his first. Once again, he made the Liberty Sheriff's Department look dumb and lackadaisical, as Haynes used his cross-examination skills to assemble a veritable catalog of investigative oversights.

He brought out—or, more precisely, had Powell bring out—the following facts:

• The home was not properly sealed after the shooting; thus, there was no way of knowing how much of the damage or dislocation of personal property was done during the fight between Price and Vickie and how much was done after the fact by careless investigators and others (such as Bill Buchanan) who had no genuine authority to be at large on the premises.

• No fingerprints were taken from the items around the house, making it more difficult to refute or confirm testimony through physical evidence.

• No log was kept of when photographs were taken, thwarting efforts to reconstruct a chronology of events.

• No reasoning was provided for *why* the individual photos were taken, once again raising the possibility of bias on the investigator's part. How was it that some items were photographed two and three times and others not at all? Where, for instance, were the pictures of the fifty bottles of liquor Price Daniel had in his house on January 19?

• Evidence in ashtrays was blithely discarded. How, Haynes mused, could investigators who had gone to the residence in a supposed effort to find contraband blithely discard evidence from ashtrays?

• In making a search of three motor vehicles found at the Daniel residence, investigators somehow neglected to look behind the seats or in the trunks. Nor was an official report made of the search or the results it had yielded.

• The ejection characteristics of the .22-caliber rifle had not been studied. Because of this oversight—even assuming the shells hadn't been trampled (and one had to think of poor Bill Buchanan, again)—the location from which each shot was fired could not be accurately fixed.

• A jacket Price had laid aside that night could have been torn not during one of Vickie's supposed outbursts but by Powell himself, when he later dislodged it from the folding staircase.

• There were no identifiable fingerprints found on the

rifle with which Price had been shot, meaning that it would have been *physically* impossible to tie Vickie to the weapon had she not renounced her Fifth Amendment rights and admitted firing it. This was a point the significance of which would loom large during arguments before the criminal case.

Powell admitted that Zbranek had asked him to bring all the photographs from the murder investigation to the civil trial. Further, Zeke had specifically asked him *not* to bring the accompanying twenty-three-page report of the investigation—the report being far less dramatic, and far less conclusive in tone, than the photos. Once more, the legal reach of the Daniel family had been underscored. Would the D.A. have been so eager to cooperate with Vickie's heirs, had the tables been turned?

Such lapses, taken by themselves, might have been trivial or unimportant—the absence of photos of the liquor fell into this category—but the overall picture started to worry Haynes. Was it possible that the entire prosecution of this case was being orchestrated by a higher authority? Perhaps Price senior?

These were the kinds of questions Racehorse wanted to keep uppermost in the jury's mind.

The lead paragraph of the *Post*'s trial coverage of March 27 pretty well summed things up:

"While jurors hearing the child custody suit against Vickie Daniel have learned little during the past three days about her parental skills, her lead lawyer, Richard 'Racehorse' Haynes of Houston, used cross-examination of a sheriff's deputy to reveal a good portion of the evidence in the Jan. 19 shooting death of her husband, former Texas House Speaker Price Daniel, Jr."

And indeed, Haynes, particularly with Powell in recent

days, had been continually testing the waters, looking for the hidden pitfalls or inconsistencies that he could use to attack the state's case come the fall. In addition to factual evidence, it gave him a chance to divine the state's strategy. With a gusto evident to all observers, he took full advantage of the more liberal discovery privileges of the civil circuit. And why not! How often was a defense attorney presented with the chance for *a dry run,* to put his opposition under oath and grill them in glorious detail about tactics and investigative procedures. Haynes milked it for all it was worth. Why, between Tuesday and Wednesday alone, he had the case's chief investigator on the stand for more than eleven hours.

To those who stood on the periphery of the case, it began to appear that Jean Murph and her supporters had made a grave tactical error in bringing the custody suit at this time.

"It's just plain dumb," muttered one of Price's ex-partners. "They're givin' away the goldang store."

After Price senior's bitter outburst to the newspapers, his feelings had been soothed somewhat when the lawyers worked out an agreement allowing Franklin and Bob to visit with their paternal grandparents at the Daniel ranch between Wednesday and Saturday. On Wednesday night, Jean Murph went to the home of Vickie's sister, Rita Steadham, of Beach City, a lackluster Baytown suburb, to pick up the boys.

Also en route to the Steadham home that night, though unbeknownst to Jean, were reporters from two local television stations. At about 5:45 P.M., Elma Barrera of KTRK and Bob Nicholas of KPRC arrived independently and uninvited (or so they would maintain) outside Steadham's home, where they set up their minicams. While they waited, they were told by Vickie that the children loved the elderly Daniels and always enjoyed visiting with them.

Shortly thereafter, Jean Murph arrived to take the children, whereupon the fireworks commenced. In full view of the camera, the children began screaming they didn't want to go. Jean was filmed trying to take a yelping Franklin by the hand, then letting go of the boy and leaving the house. Presently, she returned with Mark Morefield, the one-time mobile-home salesman who had subsequently become Price's law partner. With Morefield lending moral support (and keeping a vigilant legal eye on the proceedings), Jean began a second determined effort to take the boys; just as determinedly, they continued to resist. They clung to each other and to their mother, their tiny hands at one point becoming enmeshed in her hair.

Vickie carried the children outside in the hopes of facilitating the transfer. Still they would not let go of her—all of this was being captured on film—and she soon found herself in the car with her sister-in-law. The improbable twosome made a tense circumnavigation of the block, exchanging unpleasantries as they drove. Finally, Vickie was let off up the street from her sister's house—offstage, as it were—and Jean, Mark Morefield, and the two boys drove off.

Later that night, the whole melodrama was replayed for the benefit of the Houston viewing audience. Clearly audible were Franklin's screams: "I don't want to go, Mama! I don't want to go!" (One of the reporters, Barrera, would defend the broadcast against those who found it intrusive and distasteful, saying that the tape had actually been edited to soften the impact of the scene. According to the KTRK reporter, the upheaval outside the Steadham house "was ten times worse, but we didn't use it.")

In court on Thursday, Zbranek was livid. He suggested the event had all the earmarks of a Racehorse Haynes setup. Morefield was even less restrained, plainly stating that the event had been staged. The idea was to make Jean look bad in the context of the custody suit. "She played the scene for all it was worth," Morefield seethed, denying Vickie's own claims that he threatened her while they were all in the car. The charges and countercharges flew back and forth for the balance of the day. Jean's lawyers demanded that the TV crews and unedited tapes be subpoenaed, and mistrial rumors began leaking out from a closed-door session between Judge Emison and the attorneys.

The judge was dismayed, and not without cause. He knew that the subpoenas Zbranek had requested were bound to be received without enthusiasm by the television stations, and he was not eager to have his custody-cum-murder trial evolve into a First Amendment controversy as well.

Judge Emison decided, for the time being, to impose a gag order with respect to the events of the previous evening. It might not quell the anger, but at least it would keep the sentiments from boiling over in public for a time.

Things were beginning to get truly out of hand.

As badly as things had been going for Zbranek on Thursday, they got worse on Friday. The session opened with the revelation of another compromising blunder on the part of investigators.

Clay Autery, Buck Echols's chief deputy, admitted that he contracted with Jean Murph for more than $1,800 in guard services even though, at the time, he was immersed in the investigation of Price Daniel's death. The premises he had been engaged to guard were none other than Price junior's house on Governor's Road.

As Zbranek sunk lower in his chair at the defense table, Autery explained how he solicited and scheduled off-duty departmental personnel to guard the home for a two-week period shortly after Price was shot. Although his verbal contract with Jean called for guards to be provided at the rate of $7.00 an hour, he acknowledged that he actually paid the officers a dollar less, pocketing the difference as his commission. The fee took the form of two checks, one for $1,600.00 and one for $260.00. Incredibly, Autery went so far as to fill in the name of the Liberty County Sheriff's Department as payee. He offered a simple-minded rationale in defense of this action. "That was where the officers worked," shrugged Autery.

Delighted with the implication that the Liberty County Sheriff's Department was, in effect, on Jean Murph's payroll, Racehorse spent the morning pounding away at Autery in an expansion of what had become his favorite theme in recent days: the pattern of investigative partiality favoring the Daniel family.

Haynes pushed further. His cross-examination revealed that Autery decided not to remove a fifth of whiskey found in Price's truck in a search of the vehicle, although he did remove and inventory other items. Autery also confirmed that there was no thorough search for marijuana in Price's pickup, despite the obvious bearing such a discovery would have had on the case.

Now, Racehorse wanted another matter cleared up. What, exactly, were the circumstances under which Vickie's purse was returned to her by the sheriff's office? Haynes got Autery to admit that before he returned the confiscated purse, he first checked with Zeke Zbranek. It was the logical thing to do, the deputy maintained, since the purse contained keys to the Daniel home as well as a credit card belonging to Price. And after all, Jean was the executor of the estate. Autery would insist after court that there were no sinister inferences to be drawn. Yet once again Haynes had made his point and fashioned the im-

191

age of an uncomfortably direct pipeline from the Daniel
house into the sheriff's office. The implication was that
Jean Murph—no doubt acting as a younger, more energetic surrogate for Price senior—had too high a hand in
the conduct of the investigation.

Chapter Nineteen

r. J. E. Bunce had been Vickie's personal physician for a decade. During that time, Vickie and her children had visited him on dozens of occasions, mostly for such routine medical problems as kids' colds, as well as her own chronic kidney difficulty. As the trial resumed on Monday, Bunce testified about her "acute hysterical reaction" to the death of her husband. Vickie was "crying, screaming, and incoherent" when he saw her about an hour after the shooting in the emergency room at Yettie Kersting Hospital, the doctor said. (It was actually the second time he had seen her that day, since she had brought the children in that very morning for flu symptoms.)

The day before she was discharged, Bunce proceeded, he conducted an examination for the Sheriff's Department to look for bruises, which, the doctor noted, had begun to surface the day after the shooting. His examination revealed a two-inch circular bruise on her left forehead, a two-inch bruise on the left arm, and a half-inch bruise on the left forearm. Bunce had no way of knowing for certain what had caused the forehead bruise, but told Haynes that it could have come from a kick such as Vickie claimed to have received when she attempted to follow Price up the attic stairs.

Vickie was described by her longtime physician as a stoic patient whom he had to question extensively in order to get information about her physical condition. You could read Haynes's pleasure at this revelation from across the room.

The more the doctor talked, the more a sense of Vickie's martyrdom became palpable in the room. Having been her physician during the latter stages of her marriage to Larry Moore as well, Bunce testified that the only time she had ever talked about "one of her husbands" was in June 1979 when he informed her she was pregnant with Bob. She admitted, then, that she had had an abortion in June 1978 because "her husband did not want the pregnancy." Bunce said she was distressed at being pregnant again and requested that he not add to her chart the information about the abortion. He said he respected her wishes and did not record it. With regard to the climate of brutality that had supposedly existed in the Daniel home, the doctor said his records showed no reports of the bruises that might have resulted from the beatings Vickie described in her testimony, but admitted that his knowledge in this area was limited, as he had seen her only once "undraped."

Vickie herself had said nothing to him.

Overall, Bunce's testimony painted Vickie as a woman who suffered in silence despite living under the thumb of a callous, self-centered man. For at least one woman juror, the passage of years would not dull the impact of the doctor's time on the stand. Referring to Price, she would say, "He had her so tormented that she went out and took the life of her unborn baby. And now she has to live with something that, for a God-fearing woman, is just about the most awful thing you can do." Never had the sympathies swung more strongly toward Vickie.

Having laid the proper groundwork, Haynes now focused the physician's thinking on the matter at hand. Yes,

Bunce conceded, she had been through a traumatic ordeal, but no, he did not have any doubts about Vickie's ability to rear her children. It was his belief that Vickie's reaction to the events of that night were not substantially different from those anyone might have experienced under similar conditions.

No further questions, said Racehorse.

Twelve-year-old Kimberly Moore had not held up well at the grand-jury hearing, and both sides were eager to spare the girl, as well as her ten-year-old brother, Jonathan, the ordeal of testifying in open court. Thus, on Friday, depositions had been taken from the children, and they would now be read to the court. The format for the readings was that of a script run-through, with one attorney asking a question and another attorney from the same side reading the response that had been given in the relevant deposition. Neither side was under any legal obligation to read the full deposition, however, so Kim and Jonathan could function as "witnesses" for each side, in turn, simply by virtue of the material from their depositions that was selected to be read. This arrangement also gave the attorneys a chance to add emphasis and coloring that might not have been present had the material been rendered in the child's voice.

Zbranek, as the attorney for the plaintiff in the suit, got first crack. And on Tuesday, he delivered each of Kim's responses with an irony or poignance or naïveté appropriate to the particular passage being read at the time.

Much of what Zeke chose for his presentation countered the general theme of Haynes's defense. Neither the image of a brutal home climate or an undercurrent of sexual confusion appeared in Kim's deposition, and Zbranek was determined that the jury know it.

The girl, for example, said she had never seen either parent bruised, and could remember only two fights during the four years she lived with her mother and Price. Zbranek, in as flat a tone of voice as he could muster, read her description of the now famous TV fight:

Question: "Do you know who hit the first blow?"

Kim: "No, sir."

Question: "Did he hit her with his fist or slap her or what?"

Kim: "With his fist."

Question: "Did she slap him or hit him with her fist?"

Kim: "She hit him with her fist, too."

With these words, Zeke paused briefly, looked up and panned the jury box. He wanted to make sure they understood the significance of this remark: to-wit, that Vickie was no innocent victim. On the contrary, she had been an active participant in the fisticuffs.

Zbranek was disturbed, however, by several curious and important discrepancies between this version of the event and a statement given him by Kim at Larry's home in early March. Whereas the girl's earlier recollection of the fight had both combatants standing up, grappling for position, Kim now placed Price on top of Vickie, on the floor. In the March statement, she was uncertain whether Price had grasped her mother's arms; she now described a scene in which he appeared to have them pinned down, folded against her chest. Previously she had claimed an inability to recall exactly where Price had hit Vickie; she now said she remembered Price's "knee in her stomach," an image that was all the more disagreeable because of Vickie's pregnancy. Kim had formerly described a scene in which she had succeeded in pulling Price off her mother; she now remembered striking Price on the back and being sent to her room.

Zeke wondered who might have been helping the little girl with her memory.

Kim's current version of the TV fight bore remarkable similarities to the last of two fights Kim saw between Price and her mother on the final night of Price's life; as described, the fight of January 19 might almost have been an instant replay.

Once again, Price and her mother had hit each other with their fists. Once again, Price wound up on top of Vickie, whose arms were "twisted across her chest." Once again, Kim came to her mother's rescue. Only this time, Price "pushed me back."

Next, said Kim, Vickie "stood up, and then Price hollered at me and told me to leave the room. To go to my room . . . And I went back to my room, and later on I heard some glass shattering, and I looked out into the hall, and I saw some glass that was spread from this one room, beside the kitchen, out into the hall. And I couldn't see what they were fighting about or anything, 'cause they were in the other room. So I went back into my room." That, Kim had testified, was the last time she poked her head out before the ambulance came. She heard no shots fired.

While Kim's deposition shed little light on the circumstances immediately preceding the shooting, the girl was forthright on other matters. She said that the children had not been deprived of food or clothes, that Price never whipped her or cursed at her, and that her current preference was to live with her father in Dayton because she had grown accustomed to the schools there.

She said she loved her mother.

Also in court on Tuesday were lawyers for the two Houston television stations that had televised the sensational transfer of Franklin and Bob from Vickie to Jean. Out of the jury's presence, the lawyers managed to block Zbranek's attempts to have unedited videotapes introduced into the trial record. Their contention was that the unpublished tapes constituted the reporters' work product—similar to a print reporter's notes—and were therefore protected by the First Amendment. Elma Barrera, one of the reporters, did admit, however, that yes, there had indeed been a prior arrangement for the filming. And no, she did not go to Rita Steadham's house unannounced.

All of which merely intensified Zbranek's conviction that the incident had been a put-up job.

At about this time, a writer by the name of Richard J. Reavis had been dispatched by *Houston City Magazine* to write an article on the events surrounding the death of Price Daniel, Jr. Haynes and Harlan Friend watched with some alarm as the relationship between Richard and Vickie progressed from the courtroom to local restaurants to the Del Ray Motor Inn and elsewhere. Things went from innocent and professional to intimate and confidential in a matter of a few short weeks.

Be wary, Racehorse told Vickie. Writers were notorious for ingratiating themselves, prying out all your deepest darkest secrets, and then crucifying you in the resulting story. Not just that, but it didn't look good. If Vickie wasn't exactly expected to be the grieving widow under the circumstances, neither was she expected to be indulging in some romantic escapade while battling to keep custody of her kids.

Harlan Friend, who had adopted a paternal attitude toward Vickie, took her aside one day. This Reavis feller, he told her, you want to watch out for him. You're vulnerable right now, said Friend, in so many ways. You just don't need to get involved in something like that at a time like this.

"He's not right for you," Friend concluded.

"Oh, Harlan, you've got to stop tryin' to be my daddy," said Vickie. "I need to be around somebody who makes me feel good. Makes me laugh." She gave him an appreciative pat on the arm and left.

Friend remained dubious. If there was one thing he hoped to avoid, it was having his client look like a female Jeff MacDonald.

Chapter Twenty

Did he come up and thump him on his penis?"

The question had been asked by Racehorse Haynes of Jonathan Moore during Friday's deposition taking and was now being read to the court by Haynes. The "he" Racehorse referred to was Price; the "him," little Franklin.

Replied Jonathan, "He was walking out and Frank came in there and he bent down on his knees and started laughing and then thumped him."

"And Franklin didn't have a diaper on?"

"No, sir."

Once again, Zbranek shook his head in disgust. Jonathan had mentioned nothing of the kind during an earlier deposition. Zeke had been emphatic on that very point. And now this. What really got Zbranek was that even if it did happen, so what? Who's to say it wasn't the kind of spontaneous prank that millions of parents indulge in, one of those silly but harmless things adults do at a moment when they have no reason to worry about how their behavior might later look to a courtroom full of strangers. Damn, thought Zeke, if you took every single thing people said and did in the privacy of their homes, and if you held all that up to a magnifying glass, who wouldn't be guilty of at least one or two acts that sounded strange or fishy to others?

Zbranek found it hard to get his mind off the fact that it was April Fool's Day.

Charles Scott Parker, Liberty's mayor, next came forward to testify on Price's behalf. He had not been subpoenaed, he would admit afterward, but rather was acting in accordance with a request from his county Democratic party chairman. The county Democratic party chairman was Zeke Zbranek.

Parker went on to describe Price Daniel, Jr., as a sober and peaceful citizen.

Would you change your feeling about Price if the evidence showed that he beat his wife? he was asked on cross-examination.

The mayor admitted that he would.

"During nonstressful times, Vickie Daniel would make a very good mother," Dr. Kenneth Wetcher of Clear Lake told the packed courtroom after the depositions from Kim and Jonathan had been disposed of. "During stressful times, she would not make a good mother for these children." Jean Murph, on the other hand, was "perfectly normal, fully capable of taking care of children."

Zbranek had decided it was time to play hardball. Prior to the trial he dropped numerous hints about the strength of his psychiatric testimony, and his witness, Dr. Wetcher, was pulling no punches.

Wetcher could not deny that Vickie had impressed him with her charm during their ninety-minute interview, but her personal history gave him pause. He questioned her ability to function under stress. He based his diagnosis, he said, on many impulsive decisions she had made during her lifetime. Paramount among these were her decision to run away from the church-sponsored home just three months before she would have graduated from high school; and her marriage to Price, coming as it did so closely on the heels of an abortive attempt to reconcile with Larry Moore. How, the psychiatrist seemed to ask, could a woman stay married to a man when she considered herself a battered wife? When she feared for the well-being of her children? When she had doubts about her husband's sexual orientation?

As the afternoon progressed, Wetcher slowly and methodically drew the picture of a tense, hyperactive, immature woman, who tended to exaggerate her emotions in order to draw attention to herself; a "shallow" woman whose need for excitement altogether outstripped what life generally afforded. Vickie, the psychiatrist posed, was wont to react to things in an emotional rather than a logical sense. And though there were many people of whom this could be said, in Vickie the pendulum swung so far toward the irrational component that her behavior would be unpredictable and inappropriate. Wetcher further offered his opinion that she was manipulative: either by exploiting her suicidal tendencies (which she might use to frighten people into compliance), or, at the other end of the spectrum, through her immense, innocent charm. Men seemed especially vulnerable.

The textbook name for Vickie's malaise, Wetcher explained, was "histrionic personality disorder." The symptoms of the condition, he felt, were consistent with her lifelong pattern of conflict with the opposite sex, her hysterical reactions, and her compulsive, "flamboyant" behavior.

Wetcher theorized "a serious danger of a number of problems developing" for small boys growing up with a mother who has such a personality disorder. Not only were these dangers significant, but they were exacerbated by present circumstances. If a father is killed, the psychiatrist said, the son may perceive that death as a weakness in men, or may fear his mother dislikes men in general. In such circumstances, a boy might easily develop homosexual tendencies. Or he could overcompensate by brandishing an excessively macho demeanor. As Wetcher phrased it, the sobering choice was between being "weak and passive in order to survive, or overbearing in order to survive." Either way, the risks of lingering maladjustment were real.

Racehorse listened with a burgeoning sense of irritation. He had, in fact, delayed the proceedings for better than an hour by taking issue with Wetcher's credentials and his right to appear in the case. As Haynes saw it, a man who had known Vickie for perhaps an hour and a half should not be allowed to stand in judgment, at such a critical time, especially when the notes of the psychiatrist who had examined Vickie at some length in 1980 were still available.

Now, as Wetcher ventured his opinion on the validity of Jean's fears, Racehorse objected strenuously. He noted that board-certified psychiatrists—an esteemed group of which, ahem, Dr. Wetcher did not happen to be a member—agreed that there was no way for psychiatrists to speak with such certitude of future dangers. Anyone who presumed to do so was acting more as a psychic than a psychiatrist. Moreover, asked Haynes, did the good doctor's diagnosis refer to traits that had been *specifically noted* in Vickie? Or was Wetcher just ticking off an encyclopedic list of *general* characteristics that applied to a personality type he had arbitrarily decided she fell into? Haynes clearly had a point, as the psychiatrist had brought a book with him to the stand, and was spending a fair amount of his time reading from it.

Judge Emison let the psychiatrist's testimony stand. But if Haynes would not prevail here, his attitude—and his eyes—portended a vigorous cross-examination on the morrow.

Racehorse Haynes's assault on the testimony of Zbranek's star witness to date began on Thursday morning, and wore on until the end of the day on Friday.

Haynes portrayed Wetcher as "really reaching" in most of his insights, and was particularly critical of his affinity for drawing inferences that were unsupported by anything in the psychiatrist's account of his interview with Vickie. Time and again, Racehorse showed, Wetcher had disregarded Vickie's own explanation for this or that and substituted his own. One notable instance: Although Vickie told him that financial considerations were behind her family's decision to send her to the church school, Wetcher nonetheless wrote in his conclusions, "It is likely that her decision for going to the school was either impulsive or as the result of some meaningful conflict within a family situation."

How, Haynes wondered, might Wetcher have managed to come to such a conclusion? By the psychiatrist's own admission, nothing in his notes of the interview itself (which Wetcher did not bother to tape) suggested it.

"Experience from similar situations" was the reply.

The lawyer cocked his head slightly, then nodded, his brows furrowed in puzzlement, as he turned toward the jury. Racehorse deemed it unlikely that Wetcher had had much of a chance to assess situations all that similar to this one.

Haynes implied that Wetcher, who had been hand-picked by the Murph camp, bore a preconceived bias against Vickie and wrote his report accordingly. Was Wetcher not aware, Racehorse asked, that Jean Murph was the daughter of Governor Price Daniel, Sr.?

No, he was not, said the psychiatrist, although he did know that her brother was a former Texas House speaker.

During his interview with Jean, had the psychiatrist explored Jean's motives in filing the custody suit?

No, said Wetcher, the question was not in his notes. Jean had simply told him that she felt an eerie kind of guilt about the death—on January 16, she and Price had discussed the awkwardness of his living in the same house with Vickie under the circumstances. Jean now felt there was something she might have done to prevent her brother's death and was determined not to let the children be victimized by a similar lack of action.

Haynes continued to chip away, forcing the psychiatrist to differentiate between conjecture and hard facts, and, before long, Wetcher began to falter. His wording became more tentative. He backed off from his earlier contention that Vickie was impulsive in divorcing Larry Moore. In fact, he allowed that many acts he considered impulsive, if examined individually, would have to be branded normal behavior.

Having come this far, Haynes pushed for total victory. "If you didn't know the reason why she did something, why didn't you ask questions to find out?" he inquired.

"I was satisfied with her verbalization," said Wetcher.

"You were looking to get an end result, weren't you, Doctor?"

"No, sir."

"You cannot state, as we stand here, that Vickie Daniel's children are in danger, can you, Doctor?"

"That's correct," the psychiatrist replied.

By late afternoon on Friday, the relentless sparring between the two men had grown stale and uninspired. Wetcher, despite his several retreats, refused to budge on his fundamental point: that Vickie Daniel suffered from a "histrionic personality disorder." But his pronouncements lacked the ring of authority they had enjoyed under Zbranek's benign guidance.

Haynes, for his part, dismissed Wetcher's appearance as useless to the jury and no threat to Vickie's posture in the case. A day earlier, he had summed up the psychiatrist's testimony to date by saying, "He knew from the beginning who hired him. His message was selected by Murph's lawyers, and maybe subconsciously (he) was programmed to reach an opinion to support their contentions. . . . I wouldn't want to fly an airplane on the precision of his testimony." To those sentiments, he now added the observation that as a total witness, Wetcher had been "off the wall." Haynes promised to produce his own psychiatrists, who would set the record straight.

But even the faithful had had about enough hypothetical-psychological-mumbo-jumbo. As the trial recessed for the weekend, Haynes spoke for the majority when he said the afternoon's session had been about as stimulating as "watching grass grow."

It is axomatic that psychiatrists put on by the defense are expected to bolster the defense's case, and psychiatrists put on by the prosecution are expected to bolster the case for the state. Usually, these expectations serve to rob the testimony of much of its weight.

Only when a psychiatrist witness *fails* to conform to the stereotypical patterns—when he authors viewpoints that cloud or clash with the argument of the side that has put him on the stand—does his testimony suddenly become compelling to the jury. It is as such times, in fact, that psychiatric testimony may gain an impact far greater than usual.

Therefore, *by failing to be conclusive*, Zbranek's psychiatrist had done a not inconsiderable amount of injury to Jean's case. The burden of proof, after all, was on Jean. And yet Wetcher had done little to obliterate the "reasonable doubt" that forms the basis of the American court system.

By failing to prove that Vickie was an unfit mother, he had, in at least a few jurors' minds, gone a long way toward proving the exact opposite.

Chapter Twenty-one

T he strain was beginning to show on Jean Murph. As Jean saw things, it was disgraceful that her facts and Racehorse Haynes's lies were being given equal weight on the scales of justice. Every time Zeke made a point, Haynes drowned it in a sea of misleading rhetoric. No sooner had a witness testified to Price's character than Racehorse would pop up and question the relationship between the witness and Price, or find a skeleton in the witness's own closet.

On Monday, April 6, Jean became Zbranek's twenty-second witness, and at once set about the task of corroborating the portrait of Vickie Daniel as a shrewish, unpredictable woman.

Zbranek knew that, redundant as the testimony was, it would have its cumulative effect. But Zbranek also knew that if Jean was to prevail in this action, they would sooner or later have to shift their emphasis from Vickie's behavior as a wife to her behavior as a mother.

Zeke and his client launched their inaugural salvo on this front on this, the first day of the trial's fourth week.

Asked by her attorney to detail the harsh manner with which Vickie disciplined her children, Jean recalled a 1977 incident involving Kim and Jonathan. The family was staying at a motel in Woodville, Texas, where Price senior was to act as grand marshal in a local parade. In punishment for some offense that Jean could not now remember, Vickie had made the children go stand in the corner of the room. "And," Jean asserted, "she wouldn't let them watch the parade." (Vickie's version of the episode would differ slightly: Jonathan had been screaming and yelling at the top of his lungs in what proved to be a successful attempt to provoke her.)

This alleged act of maternal cruelty left members of the jury looking puzzled. That was it? their expressions said, *that's* an example of disciplinary harshness?

The story was actually counterproductive. There was a ring of self-importance to it. Jean seemed to be saying, how *dare* Vickie deprive these children of an opportunity to applaud the wonder and majesty of the Daniels! Those were not the types of sentiments that would go over well with the eleven workaday townspeople on the jury.

Jean's husband also testified. The Reverend David Murph had married Price and Vickie in New Orleans on November 1, 1976. A member of the Community Christian Church, he was an educated man who had earned a doctorate in history from Texas Christian University. His testimony was imbued with an objectivity and perspective largely unseen thus far. It wasn't so much what he said, but how he said it. It sounded as though he had spent some time examining things from both sides.

On direct examination, Murph had told Zbranek Vickie was basically a good mother, but he did have doubts about her overall stability. Haynes now wanted to know when the concern began.

On January 19, said Murph. But before that, he had noticed she was moody. And there had always been talk in the family, mostly between Jean and Charlotte, regarding Vickie's flightiness. The mercurial Vickie seemed to have trouble deciding how she felt about anything: Price, the marriage, life in general. In that context, then, the killing of Price might be more than just an isolated instance of extreme behavior. Although Murph was willing to concede the possibility that the shooting was accidental after all.

Racehorse asked Murph if he had ever talked to Vickie personally. A minister's testimony carried a lot of weight, and Haynes didn't want such strong credence given to hearsay testimony.

"No, sir," Murph replied. "I don't wish to meddle in that way in her life."

Racehorse had planned to unveil a little bit of theatrics at some point, and he must have felt that the affable, low-key minister presented the ideal foil for getting it into the trial record.

Haynes: "You have heard of human beings calling out in the last years of life—in the final gasp of life—calling out for their mama?"

Murph· "I've never heard it."

Haynes. "Have you heard of a dying man on the battle-field, the last word out of his mouth is 'mother'?"

Murph: "No, sir."

Haynes: "Have you heard little children cry in the night for their mama?"

Murph: "Yes, sir."

The routine was effective, if obvious. But it would provide Zeke with one of his few opportunities for one-upmanship.

On redirect, Zbranek asked Murph, "Have you ever heard children cry for their daddy?"

"Yes, sir."

"Wonder what happened to their father?"

"Yes, sir."

During Racehorse Haynes's seven-hour grilling of Jean Murph, Zbranek took his cue from his more famous rival.

He objected vehemently, if not always sincerely, so as to disrupt Haynes's concentration and momentum. Still, Haynes made headway. Dr. Wetcher had come off inconclusively, at best, and there was an edge to Jean's voice that made her appear less the worried aunt than the unforgiving in-law. Zbranek needed someone whose image and veracity were unassailable. It was time to trot out the big guns.

So it was that, in the midst of Haynes's interrogation of Jean, Zeke produced two surprise witnesses from Austin: Attorney General Mark White, who had known Price since their freshman year at Baylor, and Representative Craig Washington, who was elected to the house in 1972 when Price was speaker. Both men said they appeared as long-time friends who knew Price's reputation to be sober and peaceful.

Racehorse was cynical. The implications of an appearance by the attorney general—in whose office reposed the ultimate responsibility for upholding law and order in Texas—could not be overlooked. Washington, meanwhile, happened to be black, like three of the members of the jury. It was almost like a political ticket.

The testimony of the two politicians was nearly identical. Both men commented on Price's sobriety and peacefulness, as had Liberty Mayor Scott Parker. Both men alluded to Price's inability to defend himself against the defamatory charges then being made; said Washington, "I thought it was necessary for people who know better to say so." With evangelical fervor, the representative announced that he had flown to Liberty because of "this assault on a noble friend whose lips are sealed in death."

Faced with such glossy oratory, Haynes once again finessed. He asked White, as he had asked Mayor Parker, whether his opinion of Price Daniel, Jr., might change if it was true that Price once pushed his knee into his pregnant wife's stomach during an argument over a TV show. White answered as expected—"I find that very difficult to believe about him." But the words were almost irrelevant. By never letting the negative get far out of the jury's sight, Haynes had managed to take some of the luster off the positive.

Thirty cards and letters between Vickie and Jean were entered into evidence. The exhibits were clearly favorable to Vickie's corner. They suggested a sisterly relationship, one of mutual respect and admiration that betrayed none of the reservations Jean claimed to have harbored about Vickie's maternal abilities.

In a letter written in 1978, Jean told Vickie her children were lucky to have a "very good mother." It was praise she evidently thought enough of to underline, and which she doubtless now wished she hadn't written at all, let alone with such zest.

Wednesday afternoon saw Zeke Zbranek take an earnest stab at setting some kind of record by asking a witness a one-hour-and-twenty-minute question.

The recipient of the mammoth query (which was, in fact, merely a summary of the entire case thus far) was Dr. Richard Coons of Austin, another of the last-minute witnesses Zbranek had been producing of late. Dr. Coons, a psychiatrist of some experience in these matters, had been contacted by Price senior in late January. Coons had been an expert witness in at least two hundred criminal trials and about twenty civil trials, half of them child-custody cases. One reason he was so valued as a witness was because he possessed both legal *and* medical degrees. Moreover—and in marked contrast to Wetcher—Coons was board-certified, and a member of a large practice.

The Austin psychiatrist was something less than flabbergasted when the elder Daniel originally came a-calling;

like Haynes, he had already seen the potential for this to develop into "his kind of case."

Now, hoping to apply a splint to Wetcher's hobbled testimony, Zeke asked Coons for a medical opinion of Vickie Daniel's mental health. Haynes was clearly annoyed. This man, he argued before Judge Emison, has *never seen* my client or her children!

Judge Emison allowed that this was an unorthodox situation, but then, it was an unorthodox trial. The psychiatrist was granted an overnight recess so that he might study the material.

As fate would have it, Dr. Richard Coons did not turn out to be the kind of unimpeachable authority Jean's side envisioned. He generally added little that was new and confused some of what was old. Worse, he went over poorly with the jury.

The tone was set with one of Zbranek's first questions. Zeke asked if there was any potential danger of physical harm to children raised by a mother who is histrionic.

"In general, I couldn't answer that," said the doctor. He then expanded on his remark: If the intention was to raise children in a normal, reasonable environment, then it would be in the children's best interests to get them out of any abnormal, unreasonable environment. One juror audibly guffawed. Coons's explanation was the kind of circular, socio-speak verbiage for which simple folks from small towns like Liberty had a low threshhold.

More of the same followed. Basically Coons agreed, from what he knew of Vickie, that Wetcher's "histrionic" diagnosis was on target. She had an abundance of the textbook symptoms. She was emotional; she found ways to draw attention to herself; she craved excitement and activity; she threw tantrums, overreacting to minor events; she was perceived by others as shallow and lacking in substance, despite a superficial charm; she was dependent, constantly seeking reassurance; she was self-indulgent and inconsiderate of others. Moreover, these were character-istics that tended to be passed from mother to child.

Still, the members of the jury looked unimpressed. Worse yet, from Zbranek's perspective, Coons stopped short of testifying that Vickie would be an unfit mother when placed in stressful situations.

On cross-examination, Haynes's first order of business was to make it clear that Coons's opinions were hypothet-ical, and that they had been formed solely on the basis of material supplied by the plaintiff.

Racehorse had a point-blank question for Coons. "Are you testifying as a medical professional that Vickie Daniel is, *in fact*, histrionic?"

"No, I am not," replied Coons. He reaffirmed that his "diagnosis" was predicated on Zbranek's eighty-minute dissertation.

From there, Haynes went on to assail the ultimate sig-nificance of what he would later brand "this histrionic business." He suggested that under the vague criteria that had been advanced in court in recent days, you'd be hard-pressed to find a single event in anyone's life that did *not* qualify as evidence of a so-called "histrionic personality disorder."

Coons disagreed: How about fishing?

Haynes was quick. Why, he could see two right away, he said. A craving for activity and excitement. And ego-centric, self-indulgent behavior.

Coons smiled and nodded.

Racehorse pursed his lips in self-satisfaction.

Jean Murph drummed her fingers on the table.

It was natural and proper that Zbranek should rest his case with Price Daniel, Sr. Cases like this often turned less on evidence than on sentiment. The image Zeke wanted

213

to leave with the jurors was that of the paterfamilias who, as he entered his eighth decade, had had to suffer the pain of having his firstborn child shot dead. No matter what had been said about Price junior in recent weeks— no matter what grievances might have been lodged rightly or wrongly against the Daniel family over the decades— this was not some magisterial land baron up on the stand.

It was a man who had buried a son.

Faltering, sobbing, gasping for breath, the Governor was the embodiment of human grief. His words came with effort as he detailed Vickie's crimes. Not only had his boy's death been "intentional," but he was now the defenseless victim of a calculated plot by the killer and her attorney to disgrace his memory.

But Vickie's offense went even deeper that that. She had breached an unwritten law of human decency as well. "She's not to this day said she's sorry to me," the old man sighed, the hurt thick in his voice.

Zbranek attempted to lead his witness back over the most painful memories.

"During Price's life, did you spend time with him?" he asked.

The elder Daniel broke down. Judge Emison started to call a recess as a misty-eyed Jean looked up at her father with great tenderness. But he managed a muffled "Yes," then added, "Judge, it'll be over soon. You all sit down." As he said this, he motioned with his hand toward the jury, exemplifying the kind of self-assured leadership that came naturally to someone of his accomplishments.

Zeke asked if Price junior was a homosexual.

The Governor's voice showed newfound resolve. "No, Zeke. That's the furthest from the truth in this trial."

Daniel recounted how he had been led by the Sheriff's Department to conclude that the murder was a deliberate act, and how he had guaranteed Vickie's bond nonetheless because he wanted her treated in a hospital, not in jail.

He claimed he still held no animosity, despite the crime. If Vickie were to retain custody, he intended to help her all that she'd let him. "Anything for the benefit of the children."

But she would not again be welcomed into his home until she was treated and "back to her old self."

The Governor's tone changed markedly during Racehorse's cross-examination. No doubt anticipating Haynes's pugnacity, he grew pugnacious himself.

Haynes wanted to know if Daniel had strong feelings about the custody suit. The Governor barked his reply. "Naturally. With your son being killed, certainly."

"Did you tell a psychiatrist that Vickie beat your son?" Haynes asked.

"Yes, I expect I did," said Daniel.

"Did you ever see her beat her husband?" Haynes wanted to draw a distinction between what the Daniels "perceived" and what they could document.

"No, I never *saw* her beat her husband." The Governor placed his emphasis on the word "saw."

Moments later, Haynes and the Governor were discussing the curious alliance that seemed to have evolved between Jean's side and Larry Moore. Daniel had talked with Larry before seeking psychiatric opinions. On the basis of what Vickie's ex-husband had told him, he reported to Dr. Coons that his son was a battered husband.

Haynes asked when he talked to Moore.

Without missing a beat, Daniel said, "I saw him when Vickie tried to get Larry to change his testimony."

Haynes blew up. Not only did the remark violate the hearsay rule, but it was the most egregious form of accusation. Certainly, as a lawyer and public official, the former Governor knew better!

"I'm not as precise as you are," said Daniel, his quiet voice edged with scorn. "Judge, if I made a mistake, I apologize."

Nonetheless, Daniel persisted with his editorial comments. By day's end, Haynes was outraged. During his customary summing-up session for the benefit of the media, he told reporters, "I don't think even grief—bereavement at the loss of a son—should allow a lawyer and former justice of the Texas Supreme Court to continually ignore time-honored rules of testimony!"

Racehorse said he was surprised not so much by Daniel's attempts to get his viewpoints across as by the leeway given him by Judge Emison. He had expected one of the state's premier statesmen to be treated with respect, and perhaps even catered to. But this went beyond that, in his opinion.

"The words were his weapons and his tools," griped Haynes. "He's got to account for that!"

With the debate over the Governor's deportment still raging, Zbranek rested his case. Racehorse would begin his defense on Monday morning.

Jean's side of the civil suit had consumed a full month. Most criminal cases would have already gone to the jury.

About the same time Ann Rogers got a subpoena to testify as part of Haynes's case, she noticed something funny. If, in the past, things hadn't been all that warm between herself and Price's side of the family, at least when she'd pass Charlotte or Houston on the road, they'd wave at each other, neighborly-like.

No more.

Ann would see them coming and start to wave, and it would seem to her they'd bend over all of a sudden and pretend they were trying to pick up something off the floor of the car. After a while, she decided to goad them by beating them to the punch. Soon as she saw them coming, she'd dive for the floorboards. She joked about it with Pat, her husband, who thought it was pretty amazing that they managed to avoid a head-on collision.

Ann figured the whole thing was pretty silly. But she also realized something for the first time: There were those who worshiped Price Daniel, Jr., and those who didn't.

It was that simple, and, like the old sixties hippie ethic, if you weren't part of the solution, you were part of the problem. A person stood on one side of the road or the other.

Try to stand in the middle, you could get run over.

Chapter Twenty-two

Mary Cain, Mark Morefield, and some of the others who worked at Price's Main Street office were at their desks around lunchtime on Monday, April 13, when a scene right out of *Kojak* unfolded before them. Two or three cars swerved off the road and up onto the dirt in front of the double-wide trailer. In a symphony of slamming car doors, a pack of men got out and jogged over to the rear of the trailer. Leading was a man Mary could not identify, but a half step behind was Racehorse Haynes. Remaining seated in one of the cars was a woman whom Mary took to be Vickie Daniel.

With Mary and the others straining to watch from inside the trailer, the men proceeded to slide open the door covering the hot-water-heater enclosure. From her vantage point, Mary could not actually see inside the enclosure. A moment later Haynes emerged and trotted back to his car. He smiled and held aloft what appeared to be a fairly large crumpled paper bag.

The bag looked to be stuffed full of something.

As the convoy drove off with the same dispatch that had marked its arrival, the office workers looked at one another and shrugged. "Now what in the world was *that* all about?" Mary thought aloud.

Later, when word filtered back of what the bag supposedly contained, she would be furious. She was convinced that Racehorse had had it hidden under his bulky raincoat all along.

Haynes would describe it as a most fortunate coincidence that on this first day of his side of the case, a hidden satchel of marijuana and other damaging material supposedly belonging to Price Daniel, Jr., made itself available to the defense team.

He explained that the idea for the spur-of-the-moment search was a "hunch" he acted on after Joe Liles, a construction-company owner who had been subpoenaed to testify on a different aspect of the case, told Andrew Lannie he knew where Price junior had hidden marijuana in 1979.

Ironically, it was Vickie, as Price's survivor, to whom the attorneys had to turn for permission to inspect the area Liles had indicated She assented, agreeing to accompany them on their mission just in case Haynes's authority should be questioned And when the cover was opened as Racehorse told it, there was the bag, in plain view.

The defense lawyers strutted into court after the noon recess with Haynes displaying his find like a trophy. "I didn't expect to find anything!" chirped a jubilant Lannie. "I thought it would be removed by now." The search had yielded an unexpected bonus as well. Besides the substance Haynes identified as marijuana, the brown paper bag contained cigarette-rolling papers and a girlie magazine. Judge Emison did not allow the bag to be opened in court because Liles had not personally seen the contents after Haynes made the discovery, and there was the possibility of tampering. But Haynes insisted, "It looks like the noxious weed," reminding everyone that he had "defended over one hundred cases [involving it] myself."

Zbranek didn't know whether to express his disbelief

through tears or laughter. How convenient that the bag held something pertaining to each element of Haynes's basic line of defense! "Anyone who doesn't think that it was planted would be a good candidate for the next set of New York City bonds," he fumed. True, Zeke had not yet checked with any of Price's associates to see if the hot-water heater had been opened since January 19. But the whole thing was just so incredible. And to think that Liles was at the center of all this! The man, after all, was on probation after pleading no-contest in an attempted murder case.

Jean's anger equaled Zbranek's, but she was resigned to such dispiriting surprises.

"I knew something like this would happen," she hissed. "And there will be more."

Liles continued to inflict damage on the stand.

He said he had lived in Liberty from 1970 until 1979, working as a mobile-home salesman, and knew Price junior fairly well. He claimed he first saw Price smoking pot in 1975 at the abandoned service station adjacent to the company where he worked. The station was used as a storage area by the mobile-home company—and also, according to Liles, by Daniel, who kept his stash concealed in a rest room. Then, in 1979, Liles remembered, he saw Price take a large bag of marijuana from the hot-water-heater closet located outside the rear of the mobile home. He had made this observation twice, from about twenty feet away. On each occasion, said Liles, Price put the bag of pot into his suit coat before leaving in a silver pickup truck.

Jean nudged Zbranek. Price hadn't owned the "silver" pickup—which was, in fact, *blue* and silver—until February 1980. Zbranek nodded. More evidence, he felt, of the witness's basic unreliability. Or of the fact that he had been

221

coached in his testimony by someone who managed to get the dates screwed up.

Racehorse asked how Liles knew this was marijuana Price was smoking.

"It smelled like marijuana," he replied, "and I have burned personally a lot of marijuana." As muffled laughter rose around him, Liles clarified his remark. He had burned the weed, *not* smoked it, while he was a trusty of the county Sheriff's Department, serving a contempt of court conviction associated with the shooting of his estranged wife. He went on to describe the clear plastic bags that Price carried as containing "long leafy plants that had a slender leaf with tiny seeds in it." Sometimes the substance was green, sometimes gold.

Zbranek grew edgy. Unsavory or not, the detailed nature of Liles's answers gave him a certain credibility.

Liles then twisted the knife.

He testified that Price junior "put his hands on my private parts" in May 1977, while Liles was managing a mobile-home sales office in Beaumont.

"He said that for sexual favors he would represent me in my divorce proceedings," Liles explained. Or, if Liles preferred, Price might try to help him effect a reconciliation with his wife.

Liles recalled being disgusted by the solicitations. "I told him to take his hands off me or I'd knock the, ah, you know, out of him." After the fondling incident the two did not talk again until 1979, when Liles hired one of Daniel's associates to represent him in the divorce action.

For the most part, Zeke opted in his cross-examination to steer clear of the pot allegations, since he couldn't know what ace Liles might have up his sleeve. Often, to react defensively to such charges was to give them undue credence, and there was no sense reinforcing harmful testimony.

Basically Zbranek saw the situation as a game of my-word-against-yours. The only way to win, he knew from experience, was to demonstrate that the guy was simply a habitual liar. Properly handled, this strategy would alleviate the need for a risky attack on the individual elements of Liles's testimony.

Zeke thus concentrated on the fact that Liles had plea-bargained a sentence of ten years' probation for shooting his wife three times in the buttock. He wasn't so much interested in proving that Liles had done the deed as that he had offered an inplausible explanation in his defense. Liles claimed his wife pulled her boyfriend's .38-caliber pistol on him, and the shots were fired during a scuffle over the gun. Zbranek was dubious. How, he mused, do you shoot someone in the ass in a scuffle over a gun? Three times, no less.

And if Liles had lied under oath then, why not now?

During the afternoon, Zeke expended a good deal of effort trying to communicate his doubts to the jury, prompting a series of objections from Racehorse. Finally, Judge Emison had heard enough.

"Do you want to litigate that crime as a part of this matter?" the judge asked tartly.

"No, sir," said a chastened Zbranek.

He let the matter drop. But he was satisfied that he had given the jurors something to think about.

Haynes's dramatic discovery became a prime topic of conversation throughout Liberty and East Texas, displacing even the ecstatic hubbub over the flawless inaugural launching of the space shuttle *Columbia,* from nearby Johnson Space Center.

Zeke Zbranek was not the only one who had his doubts about the legitimacy of the find. Soon after hearing of the incident, Sheriff Buck Echols ran out to the trailer office to take a firsthand look at the water-heater closet. What he found made him angry.

There was, he would later insist, dust all over the place. The whole interior of the enclosure was coated: top, bottom, and sides. Certainly, if the bag had lain undisturbed since late January—it was now April 15—there should have been a noticeable absence of dust in the spot the bag had occupied. At the very least, the dust should have been thicker outside the perimeter of the area where the bag had reposed for nearly four months.

Although Haynes believed that Zbranek's psychiatrists had drawn no blood, he nevertheless felt compelled to put on some psychiatric testimony in Vickie's defense. Custom demanded it.

Dr. Grady J. Browning, director of Browning Psychological Associates, had some twenty-eight years' experience in the field of child psychology. He had examined Vickie for about eleven hours in mid-March, and now, on the basis of that examination, proclaimed her to be a normal, healthy woman who did not suffer from any alleged histrionic personality disorder. Dr. Browning explained that a battery of tests, including the Minnesota Multiple Personality Inventory, the venerable Rorschach, and sixteen Personality Profile tests were given to Vickie, Jean, and Jean's husband. All results were completely normal.

Browning's assessment of the marriage and Vickie's attitude toward Price could hardly have differed more from those of the psychiatrists recruited by Zeke and the Daniels.

"She tried to do everything to please him because she loved him very, very much," said the doctor. But she was chronically rebuffed. What's more, her most acute needs—for tenderness, gentleness, and "a feeling of being Number One"—were not being met by Price. No less disheartening, as recounted to Browning by Vickie, was her late husband's attitude toward the children. He showed little genuine affection, hoping instead to buy their loyalty through presents.

In the end, said Browning, there was just no reason to take the children away from Vickie. Generally, there were but two conditions—abuse and abandonment—that would lead Browning to support the removal of custody from the natural mother. Neither condition fit the case at hand. "In my opinion," said Browning, "Mrs. Daniel would be a good mother to any child."

A shouting match developed between Haynes and Zbranek. The tensions had been building for weeks and now erupted into open hostility over the mysterious crumpled paper bag.

"Just because you're a lawyer doesn't give you the right to snatch whatever you want from private property!" complained Zeke. He felt that the seizure of the bag had been conducted illegally. Vickie's consent had nothing to do with it. Haynes should have alerted police and let them make the search. And he should have notified Jean, who, as executrix of her brother's estate, certainly was entitled to some advance knowledge of what was going on. Clearly, no hanky-panky could have occurred with Jean and a handful of sheriff's deputies looking over Haynes's shoulder.

Racehorse was indignant. "You know full well that no laws have been broken! The search was perfectly legal." Barely had Haynes begun to expand on his belief (contending that the laws to which Zbranek alluded did not apply in civil cases), when an angry Zeke interrupted him.

"You're not the only one entitled to talk here!" he bellowed. Zbranek's forehead was beet red.

Undaunted, Haynes shouted back at him. "It ain't no illegal search, and that's that!"

The situation deteriorated from there, and Judge Emi-

225

son deemed it advisable to recess the trail for the day.

As he left the courtroom, Zeke was questioned by reporters about the specific contents of the bag. He was in no mood.

He snapped, "I don't know what's in the bag. Whatever's in the bag is what they planted there!"

When Mary Cain was on the stand, Racehorse had asked about a trip she and Price made to Houston shortly before his death. Mary's answers were routine enough, and Haynes had left the issue hanging for the time being. Spectators had wondered exactly what Haynes had up his sleeve. On Thursday, a car salesman named Randy Blackwell provided the answer.

Blackwell said he saw Price and Mary acting very much like lovers when she picked up her new car at the Houston dealership where he worked.

The two of them, Blackwell testified, were holding hands and "touching each other." Then, when it came time for them to go their separate ways, Price unloaded some clothing from her car to his, and they kissed each other good-bye, "on the mouth."

"I thought they were going together," Blackwell added. "I thought they were boyfriend and girlfriend." He described Mary as "a very nice-looking lady." A couple of the male jurors nodded in accord.

Blackwell's testimony was the prologue to a day of Haynes's unleashing what amounted to a parade of rebuttal witnesses.

Larry Moore's own sister, Yvonne Croft, testified she never saw her brother with scratches on his body. Larry's boss during 1974 and 1975 came up and swore that he had never seen Larry scratched, either. Vickie's sister Patsy Denman told of two separate occasions during Vickie's marriage to Price on which she had seen Vickie with bruises on *her* body. In 1978, there were the bruises on Vickie's arms after Price allegedly grabbed her. In the summer of 1980, there were the baseball-sized bruise above Vickie's tailbone and another bruise on her right shoulder. Vickie was reluctant to tell Denman about the bruises but later admitted "that Price had kicked her in the back."

Haynes then moved to the Daniels' influence. Larry's sister said her brother told her Price senior offered Larry "the use of his evidence" in a suit against Vickie to get permanent custody of their daughter. Denman then reprised her story about Price senior's threats to "intervene" if a suitable custody arrangement could not be worked out between Vickie and Jean. She further noted Eckols's threats to arrest Vickie if she attended Price's funeral. Denman said Eckols told her he was acting "under orders" that "if she goes to the funeral, I will have to arrest her." Denman claimed that Jean wielded her executrix role like a club. She had even refused to allow Vickie to have Bob's bed or the children's toys!

With the Great Toy Controversy now out in the open, Vickie's lawyers pressed Judge Emison for a decision on whether or not Jean could withhold the children's playthings as part of Price's estate. Though legally Jean was in the right—minors in Texas could not really be said to have ownership of personal property—her stance struck observers as petty.

Zeke contended Haynes had been told more than a month ago that Vickie could take anything she could prove was hers—the key word being "prove." Vickie insisted she'd bought a certain toy but could produce no proof, and Jean was skeptical.

Well, I don't care who bought what, Judge Emison said, in effect. The kids are entitled to have their toys. Vickie was granted permission to return to the house and retrieve the items. Judge Emison made particular note of a seventy-dollar spaceship identified by Vickie as Franklin's favorite toy.

Zbranek was miffed. "The problem is, Judge, they get their way when they want it and we never get our way!" he whined.

Suddenly, from the plaintiff's table, Jean let out a deep and soulful sob. It was the first time she had publicly surrendered to tears since the trial began. The dam having finally, irretrievably collapsed, she now sat crying at the counsel table, her body heaving as her shaking right hand cradled her head.

Vickie turned to Haynes's associate C. B. Hanby in puzzlement. "I don't understand," she whispered. After all that had been said and done, why now?

Hanby thought he understood. The toys, he explained, were a "hold" the Daniel family had over the boys, an enticement for them to visit the ranch. With that incentive removed, the Daniels would have to find less material ways of keeping their loyalty.

Buck Eckols noted that Vickie continued to maintain admirable composure. Everybody seemed susceptible to her . . . charm, or mystique, or whatever you wanted to call it. A witness would say something against Vickie, and she would sit there at the defense table and shake her head. Not melodramatically, but subtly, almost imperceptibly, as if she were talking to herself. As if to say, Now, you *know* that just isn't true. And looking over at the jury you would see that they'd bought it. Now and then the jurors would seem to check her reaction before making up their minds about the testimony.

To Buck Eckols, the trial was getting to be a waste of everybody's time. He saw the verdict as a foregone conclusion.

Chapter Twenty-three

An article appearing in the *Houston Post* over the weekend proved that the sheriff did, indeed, have his finger on Liberty's pulse.

According to the newspaper, "the overwhelming opinion of local residents, including elected officials and civic leaders who asked for anonymity," was that the trial should not have been held until after Vickie had first had her day in court on the murder charge.

"Regardless of how one feels about who should have those kids," the *Post* quoted an unnamed local businessman, "the overriding consideration at this point is Vickie has been accused of murder, not convicted of murder.

"There is no one—well, maybe I should say very few—who think Vickie is an unfit mother or that she ever did one thing to harm her children."

Never one to miss an opportunity, Racehorse Haynes took the familiar climb up onto his soapbox. "I took this case because I saw this lady being run over by the system," he told the *Post*. "If I play a small part in helping her keep her children—as a father of four kids I can tell you she loves all of her children and is an excellent mother—then I've accomplished something."

Ann Rogers had not been the only recipient of a phone call warning that those who failed to protect Price's image might not retain their good standing in the family. Late in January, Ann's brother-in-law, David Parker, was put on notice as well, except in his case, the call came directly from Jean. She had heard that he was going around town spreading rumors about a romantic involvement between Price and Mary Cain. Word was he had even told the story to one of Mary's friends in a neighborhood bank.

Parker was not intimidated. "I can think of nothing I said that was not true," he told her, just like that. In the ensuing months, he continued to be forthright with Jean and the other Daniels who would take up the cause on Price's behalf. The only information he held back was that he and his wife were chiefly responsible for bringing Haynes into the case. Had the Daniels known *that*, it might have started an all-out war.

As the trial moved into its sixth week, Racehorse called Parker to the stand. With Jean giving him the evil eye, Parker described how his relationship with Price had gone from one extreme to the other over the years. In recent years things had gotten so bad that he once threatened "to beat the hell out of Price."

Much earlier, though, Parker had seen things—little things, indications. He enumerated for the court the number of times he could recall seeing Price drunk—twice at his home, twice at Baylor, and once in Austin. He told the bank story, about how Price's indifferent handling of the application procedures for their new banking venture had cost him his job at a Liberty savings and loan.

In late 1975, Parker claimed, he caught Price smoking a joint in his office.

What Parker found most memorable was Price's reaction.

"He offered *me* one," testified Parker, who said he declined. "He was very relaxed, kind of cocky, I guess . . . on top of the world."

"And how did you react to all this?" asked Racehorse.

"I was a little angry and disgusted, to be perfectly honest with you."

With the jury out of the courtroom on a motion by Zbranek, Parker was asked by Haynes if Price had any explanation for his use of the illegal substance.

"He said he made the law, but he didn't live by it."

Parker then testified he saw bruises on Vickie twice. The first time was just prior to Vickie's temporary stay at the Del Ray, in May 1979. Parker noticed neck bruises that "looked like choke marks." The second time was after the shooting in January. Parker went to Yettie Kersting Hospital and saw a "reddish, flush, swollen area" on her forehead, and on both sides of her face.

The subject turned to Jean's campaign to protect Price's memory, and a letter from Jean to Susan Parker was introduced into evidence. Jean had written: "You see, Sue, Price was the greatest, I'm crazy about him and loyal and I'll stand behind him against *anyone*"—"*anyone*" being underlined—"who tries to tarnish his name, even if it's by repeating gossip to someone else (in this case, to me!)."

Parker concluded his day's work by impugning Vickie's first husband, Larry Moore. As someone who had known Larry since childhood, Parker was here to say that Larry was locally known as a kind of shiftless character.

And when it came to telling the truth, said Parker, Larry's reputation was just plain bad.

Haynes produced Dorothy Williams, the sixty-six-year-old matron who had cared for newborn Franklin in 1977. Credibility-wise, Williams had two things going for her. First, she was a grandmotherly southern black, and she carried all the endearing physical and psychological baggage that went with the role: One could just picture her a-scttin' by a cozy fire, readin' scripture. Oh, sure, she could be crusty, but she was nothing if not truthful. She looked to be the kind of woman who might preface every sentence with "As God is my witness . . ." Second, and perhaps more important, she was one of the very few witnesses perceived to have absolutely no vested interest in the case.

Her portrait of Price was compelling. And damning.

The nanny said the very first time she met Price, his walk was not "straight."

Was he drunk? she was asked.

Well, his breath sure smelled like he'd been drinking. "Either that or he's a diabetic," she ventured.

She also said Price had an uppity air about him, that he seemed to enjoy talking down to people. She remembered one night when Price came in under the weather, and Mrs. Daniel told her husband she didn't like him driving after drinking.

" 'You high-school dropout, don't be telling me what to do!' " she quoted Price, "and he struck her." Williams pantomimed an open-handed blow to the left cheek.

"I was there seven days and he wasn't polite any night," she said.

Why, Williams was asked, didn't she do something about a situation that so obviously distressed her?

"I wasn't there to keep *him*," she snorted, "I was there to keep the baby."

Haynes's parade of character witnesses continued. On Monday, he had produced Emy Addison and Virginia Leonard. Both women knew Vickie through their involvement in Cub Scout programs and felt she was a good mother. In reply to another of Racehorse's favorite questions, each of them said she would allow Vickie to care for her children "to this day." On Tuesday, he trotted out two partners in a child-care venture, Diane Ashton and Lucille Powell. The familiar litany about the excellence of Vickie's "parenting skills" was repeated.

Then came another twist.

Racehorse effectively called himself to the stand. Still battling to get the brown paper bag into evidence, he was determined to offset testimony by Houston Daniel. Houston had brought the ownership records pertaining to the Main Street office property and insisted they showed Vickie had no community-property rights in the trailer and therefore was not empowered to grant a search of the premises. Such information appeared to preclude the admission of any evidence yielded by the unauthorized search. Racehorse figured his own persuasive powers were the only hope. For almost ninety minutes, he offered an impassioned recap of the circumstances of the discovery and its relevance to the matter at hand.

Zeke clearly relished having his nemesis in a subordinate position, under oath, and at first, cross-examined him hard. Why, asked Zbranek, did he not call the police to make the search?

"We didn't know it was there until we opened the door," said Racehorse.

"You mean you expected you wouldn't find anything?"

"Yes," said Haynes. He had been surprised to find the bag still sitting there.

Racehorse may have been even more surprised by what happened next, for Zeke asked him a most peculiar question: Did his suspicions about the sympathies of local law enforcement have anything to do with his decision not to call the deputies first?

"That is one of the things that occurred to me," Haynes replied, sounding almost grateful for the chance to express the sentiment. "That it might be ripped off."

It was not the first time Zbranek had raised an issue that seemingly could hurt Jean's cause.

Finally, Judge Emison ruled that the bag could be admitted and opened. An exultant Haynes carefully placed the contents into three Ziploc storage bags. One bag for the "marijuana," one for the rolling papers, and one for the porno magazine.

Racehorse, at his theatrical best, held the marijuanalike substance up and slowly inspected it, milking the moment for all it was worth while allowing those in the gallery to get a good view. The jury snickered as the exhibits were passed among them, although one of the two women declined to inspect the bag with the magazine.

Buck Eckols had been subpoenaed by Haynes, who disdained the sheriff's handling of the case. Though he didn't expect much cooperation from the sheriff, Racehorse figured at the very least he might have the pleasure of making the old boy squirm a bit.

Racehorse began by implying yet again that the Daniel family had manipulated the entire investigation to its own advantage. Eckols, his contempt for Haynes clear, denied he took orders from Price senior. What about the funeral business? asked Racehorse. Could Eckols deny he was acting on the family's orders that Vickie not attend the funeral? Did he not tell her sister he'd arrest Vickie if she showed up? Haynes was making too much of it, said Eckols. The family was simply afraid she would be hysterical and start a disturbance. Eckols decided (incorrectly, as it developed) the arrest threat was the surest way of guaranteeing her nonappearance.

The sheriff was then asked to comment on the bag of stems, leaves, and weeds.

"Do you know what this is?" asked Haynes coyly.

"Couldn't say," Buck retorted. He was determined not to give an inch.

"Do you think it could be marijuana?" Racehorse pressed.

"Could be anything," said Eckols, holding firm. But if it *was* pot, it was indeed "a very sorry grade." Not the finer weed from Colombia. Buck Eckols wanted it known that Price Daniel, Jr., would not have been caught dead with such a pedestrian stash. Literally.

During recess, Zbranek picked up on Eckols's remarks. Said Zeke, "If it was Price junior's stuff, it would be good stuff, not cheap stuff."

"That's right," Jean added, triumphantly. "Price bought only the best."

Vickie's lawyers were amused by the reasoning. "It's kind of sad," said one of them. "They're really grasping at straws now."

The defense rested.

Zeke Zbranek was not quite finished, however. Jean remained concerned that their earlier attempts at a psychiatric offensive had misfired. And so, notwithstanding an earlier admission that they might be "wearing out" the jury with this protracted inquiry into Vickie's mental health—and perhaps believing that, as the old saying goes, the third time's a charm—Zbranek put on yet another psychiatrist.

Like Dr. Coons, Dr. George Willeford, Jr., of Austin had not interviewed Vickie. He spoke in a crisp, authoritative voice, and said that one part of the multiple-personality-inventory test administered by Haynes's witness, Dr. Grady Browning, had been misinterpreted. Vickie was not, as Browning claimed, perfectly normal. Rather, contended Willeford, the MMPI's "Scale 6," or paranoia scale, showed Vickie was resentful and expressed hostility and brooding. Willeford also took issue with Browning's contention that Vickie was bright, alive, and sensitive to the needs of others. On the contrary, he insisted, she was self-centered and morose.

Willeford also disputed Haynes's heartrending portrayal of the psychological damage that would inevitably result from "tearing the children away" from their home.

"A psychological home does not have to be with the natural mother," said the psychiatrist.

Nonetheless, as forthright as Willeford was on direct examination, he was for the most part no luckier than his predecessors once Racehorse went to work. He had to acknowledge that he had no formal training in interpretation of MMPI scores and relied for such insights on an associate in Austin. This was duly noted by Haynes: Not only had the man *not* examined the woman whose mental health he was now impugning, but he was in effect giving hearsay testimony. With each successive psychiatrist, Zbranek's case seemed to be getting farther and farther removed from scientific accuracy.

Willeford also admitted that he, like Coons before him, had met more than once with Price senior in his Austin office. The image established—of Price senior scouring the city where he wielded such tremendous influence in search of psychiatric allies—was not helpful to Zeke's quest for credibility.

No one could be immediately sure, but all opinions pointed to the case's being the longest custody suit in the annals of Texas jurisprudence. No one knew this better than the eleven men and women who would soon have to render a verdict.* During the selection process, prospective jurors had been told that the case would run no longer than two weeks.

By the end, it had consumed a full six weeks. And the final arguments still remained.

The amount of testimony had been vast. The evidentiary phase of the trial had consumed some ten thousand pages of court reporter's notes—as many transcript pages as the far more celebrated murder trial of serial killer Ted

---

*One juror had been dismissed for possible conflict of interest.

Bundy two years earlier. All told, the case included more than six hundred exhibits.

Besides its length, the case had been amazing for the starkness of its contradictions. Few of the forty-one witnesses called by Jean Murph and Zbranek would give an iota of credence to the testimony of the eighteen witnesses called by Racehorse Haynes. And vice versa. It was as if the witnesses on the respective sides of the case had known, and were describing, entirely different people.

The irony was that because the majority of the testimony was so determinedly black or white, the whole case had become one enormous gray area. No one could say with any certainty that they felt they had found the truth. People who had known Price and/or Vickie for years suddenly felt that they knew them hardly at all. Seldom had either of the principal attorneys tried a case that had so few gray areas, and in which so little common ground could be found.

Chapter Twenty-four

B y giving Zbranek the freedom to go off on what reporters were calling "rabbit trails" (principally those leading back to the evening of January 19) Judge Sam Emison had more or less allowed Zeke to try a murder case, as Haynes had foretold from the outset. Conversely, by permitting the defense to conduct its lengthy inquiry into the personality, life-style, and suspected vices of Price junior—none of which, in the final analysis, bore much relevance to the matter at hand—Judge Emison had allowed Racehorse to deflect much of Zbranek's evidence. (There were those who felt that Zbranek had largely overlooked a golden opportunity to demonstrate that Price's behavior *did* have something to do with the case—but not in the manner Haynes supposed. For if Price was truly the drug-crazed child molestor Haynes had portrayed him to be, why had Vickie tolerated him around her children for so long? What kind of mother would let her kind spend their daily lives in that kind of environment? This line of reasoning was raised briefly during Zbranek's questioning of his first psychiatrist, Dr. Wetcher, but then quickly dropped—possibly on the instructions of Jean Murph.)

For his charge, begun shortly after noon on Friday, Judge Emison took great pains to ensure the jurors understood their mission.

It began simply enough. Judge Emison told the eleven jurors they had to find on the basis of the evidence who should have permanent custody of the children. They could vote for one of three possibilities: for Vickie, for Jean, or for neither woman.

This, however, was where the complications set in. In the arcane world of family law, a vote for either woman would have in effect given the loser "possessory conservator rights," similar to those of a parent who does not have primary custody in divorce action. If the vote went for Vickie, Jean would have visitation rights, and vice versa. Only a vote for *neither* woman—thereby denying the fundamental merit of the entire suit—would have preserved the status quo, leaving Vickie with full control. Thus Vickie's position, as she listened to Judge Emison clarify the point, was a most paradoxical one. In order to claim she had been totally vindicated, she would have to hope that the jury voted not for her but for "neither woman."

Judge Emison stressed that an outright victory for either side could be achieved only through a minimum margin to 10 to 1. Should the jurors be unable to muster ten votes for any of the three options, the judge would have to declare a hung jury, and, at Jean's option, the case could be retried. Under those circumstances, Judge Emison could place the children temporarily in the home of his choice.

Should it come to that, Racehorse Haynes was not particularly worried. The trend of the trial, plus his twenty-six years of experience in court, let him to believe that Judge Emison was leaning Vickie's way.

It was the jury—that uncertain equation of eleven randomly selected hearts and minds—that always worried Haynes.

Zbranek, for his part, had already decided that in the event of a hung jury, he would not recommend a retrial at this time. Maybe, if Vickie were to go on to be convicted of murder, his thinking might change. But right now, it seemed to Zeke that everybody'd had about enough of this.

Of course, the final word on the subject would belong to Jean.

Before a standing-room-only crowd, including a hard-core group of thirty who had been there faithfully for every session, Judge Emison called for the attorneys' final arguments. The format gave Zeke the last word; he did not waste the opportunity.

"She hurt them in a way she can never repay!" he began with great emotion, his tone and cadence evoking the outrage of one of the tent evangelists indigenous to Texas. On the one hand, he said, there were the facts. On the other hand, there was Haynes's *manipulation* of those facts. He reminded the jury that in a civil case, he did not have to prove his case beyond a reasonable doubt; he merely had to show "by a preponderance of the evidence" that Jean should prevail. Which, he insisted, he had done. In the most outspoken terms, he alleged that Vickie and her lawyers had "fallen flat on their faces and haven't produced one credible witness to support their innuendo!"

Rousing to a finish, Zeke allowed his diplomatic veneer to crack. *"Vickie Daniel has had one abortion, two marriages, one divorce, and one shooting!"* he railed. "Out of seven interpersonal relationships she has had in the past fourteen years, all but two have turned out wrong. . . . She has got to be told she can't go through life scratching and clawing and shooting people and then tell big stories without somebody saying, 'Girl, you gotta clean up your act!' "

Reporters came away impressed. For weeks there had been a feeling among the veteran observers, who would fill nearby Yvonne's Restaurant to overflowing at the close of each session to take stock of the day's proceedings, that Zbranek was no match for the wily Haynes. Now, though, a few reporters thought they had seen a juror or two nodding during Zeke's oratory.

Maybe, just maybe, Zbranek had salvaged something after all.

As the jury began deliberations, the various players in the drama tried to find ways of holding off anxiety.

Vickie fussed absently with her dress, and leaned over for a word or two with Karen Bussey, a free-lance writer who had been covering the trial for a local publication. It would be noted that she betrayed little evidence of any great turbulence within.

Racehorse, clutching a copy of *Modern Synopsis of Comprehensive Textbook of Psychiatry* and his trademark curved pipe, divided his time between signing autographs and fielding reporters' questions. When someone asked him jokingly how he made out on the trial, fee-wise, he pegged his compensation for defending Vickie at "about a dollar an hour, one two hundred fiftieth of my regular fee."

Meanwhile, other reporters were pressing Zbranek for a postmortem. They suggested that some of his tactics had been inconclusive, while others had plainly backfired. Zeke defended himself.

"There was no other way I could show what we consider is wrong with Vickie, by that I mean her mental makeup," he said. "We had to show she has a mental disorder. I believe we did. I feel great about our case. I feel terrific that the thing is over. It's been like riding a roller coaster."

The press turned back to Racehorse, who was shaking his head at Zbranek's continuing disparagement of his client. "Vickie is not frothing at the mouth. She is a decent human being. I've seen the two little kids with their mother and I can tell you there is love—a deep love—between them.

"They are Vickie's little children. You have to jerk yourself into the proper context. . . . What if they were *your* children?"

Later, however, as word came that deliberations had begun, Haynes got opening-night jitters. "I've shown in this case I should have stayed in Houston," he fretted. "I have a trepidation that I have been less than adequate in my presentation."

Jean was asked if she was satisfied with the trial.

"Yes, I'm satisfied," she said evenly, "I really am. If I win, then we'll at least have salvaged something out of tragedy. If I lose, I'll say an extra prayer each day for the children and I'll live on."

Reporters remarked at her seeming nonchalance. Gone was the fire in her eyes that for the past six weeks had urged sympathetic witnesses on or issued bitter challenges to opponents.

The jurors began deliberating at 9:15. Just one hour and twenty-eight minutes later, at 10:43, and with the courtroom, if anything, more packed than it was before, they sent word that a verdict had been reached.

Chapter Twenty-five

T he tears that streamed down Vickie Daniel's face were her first real outpouring of emotion since she testified in early March.

She had been vindicated. Quickly, and by a unanimous vote, the jury had settled on the "neither woman" option, thus leaving Vickie with full and unabridged control of little Franklin and Bob.

The jury foreman had a simple, direct explanation. "There was no evidence in our opinion that she was an unfit mother," said Jackey Leo Stansel.

Judge Emison looked relieved. His main concern throughout was that the jurors not allow themselves to go off on emotional tangents, that they find the right answer for the right reasons. "And I think they did," he would say afterward.

Jean simply sat there, head cocked to one side, showing no discernible emotion. She appeared less despondent than dumbstruck. Possibly it had something to do with the implications of the dispatch with which the jurors had decided. Clearly, she must have realized, little if any thought had been given to what occurred on January 19.

In fact, this would be affirmed soon enough by a second juror. Leslie Bartlett was the music director of the First United Methodist Church, the house of worship from which Price's body had been taken to its final resting place along Governor's Road. Bartlett announced that the jury did not for a moment consider whether or not the shooting was intentional; they accepted Haynes's oft-repeated argument that the criminal matter was irrelevant. But speaking strictly for himself, Bartlett ventured an opinion on the murder charge anyway. "There was," he asserted, "simply not enough evidence to remove all reasonable doubt."

Later, Jean would register surprise at the verdict, and at the logic that allowed jurors to view the possibility of a woman's having committed murder as separate and distinct from her fitness to be a mother to the children of the man who had been killed. "I'd do anything for those children," she said. "I think the boys have a mom with lots of problems." When reporters pressed for her views on an appeal, Jean was noncommittal. "We haven't made that decision yet," she told them.

That was what she said. What they heard was, This thing isn't over by a long shot.

As soon as the verdict was read, Vickie was swamped by well-wishers. A letter containing more than fifty signatures and $154 in cash collected that day was presented by a Liberty woman named Marguerite Pinckney. Many of the signatories had been present since day one, lending their support. In one of the more remarkable and overt displays of jury sympathy on record, the eleven men and women formed a haphazard receiving line to congratulate Vickie. She literally had to hug and kiss her way out of the courtroom.

"I'm so happy, I can't wait to get home!" she gushed before the knot of reporters. What did she intend to do now? they asked. To just try to wind down and lead a life that was as normal as possible, Vickie replied. How did she feel about the unanimity of the jurors' findings? In a word, she was overwhelmed. "The best thing they could have given" was how she described the verdict.

For Racehorse Haynes, this was one of the sweeter victories of his career. "I have an unbroken and unbridled faith in the jury system, and we saw it work here tonight," said Haynes, who so often sounded as though he were speaking with the expectation of having his words jotted down for posterity. ·

Was he surprised by the unanimous verdict?

No, he said, he had expected it.

The press found Harlan Friend already thinking of the next hurdle. The day's developments appeared to improve the chances that Larry Moore's suit could be settled out of court (inasmuch as the jury's verdict seemed, at least on some level, to be a slap in the face to Larry and a thorough repudiation of his testimony). Perhaps, Friend felt—he wouldn't hope for this too strongly, but it never hurt to be optimistic—even the murder case could now be laid to rest. After all, Zeke had essentially presented the state's murder case, and the jurors had rejected it, hadn't they? When someone reminded Friend that the jurors claimed not to have even really discussed the evidence pertaining to Price's killing, Friend was still dubious.

Zeke Zbranek stood off to the side, looking somewhat disoriented. Eager to know what was on his friendly adversary's mind, Friend edged over.

"Hell, yes, I'm surprised," Zbranek confessed. "I truthfully don't understand it. We had our problems back there, sure. But I really thought we'd win it in the end."

Indulgently, Friend smiled. "Zeke," he said, sighing and shaking his head, "you were never even in the ball park on this one."

Arriving at her sister's house late Thursday, Vickie found little Bob still awake, waiting for her. She rocked him to sleep in the dark, talking to him gently, and looking forward to the weekend, when all four of her children were to be reunited for the first time since January.

In the ensuing days, many saw the filing of the suit itself as a gross miscalculation. Jean had obviously failed to predict how her attempt to deprive Vickie of custody would galvanize sentiment in Vickie's favor.

If any one element leaped up from the newspaper analysis of the trial, it was the broad admiration Vickie had earned for herself through her trial testimony. A Houston radio station found a man named Lewis who felt Vickie should "sue somebody for a zillion dollars for defamation of character." The *Post* interviewed a woman named Janie Lanaford, who claimed to have observed all but one day the of six-week trial and "agreed with the verdict one hundred percent." Lanaford had a succinct analysis of the dynamics of the trial: "When people start slinging mud, you more or less go with the underdog."

Perhaps most remarkable of all was Vickie's success at impressing people with her fairness. She had said some truly terrible things about her late husband, and implied some less than wonderful things about his family. And yet no one seemed to sense any rancor, no one seemed to feel she was the type to hold a grudge. This was in marked contrast to the conclusions many had drawn about Jean. Vickie struck virtually everyone as honest, eminently sensible. The very voice of reason. The kind of person who would do something simply because it was the right thing— the *commonsense* thing—to do.

As Lanaford put it, "If she gets convicted of murder, I feel like she would ask Jean Murph to take care of her children."

As if to prove everyone right, Vickie announced on Friday that she would not deny visitation rights to the Governor and Mrs. Daniel. Even though the verdict had left her without any legal obligation to arrange for such visitation.

"Oh, I'm sure, yes, I definitely want the kids to see their grandparents. It is as important to me as it is to them," she explained. "I want the boys to have a wonderful relationship with their grandparents. They love each other very much."

"The verdict, at this time, does not influence my opinion on the murder indictment."

District Attorney Carroll Wilborn was by no means ready to concede defeat. On the matter of the impending murder trial, he merely said he wanted to study the testimony and see the exhibits from the custody trial, noting they could "have an effect on my plans in the prosecution of the case." Wilborn had not personally heard any of the testimony in the trial; instead he had received most of his information from newspaper accounts and conversations with some of the key players.

"Anybody," he said, "would realize that with the intense cross-examination by Mr. Haynes there has been evidence created that I was not aware of from the grand-jury testimony and law-enforcement efforts."

The remark was interpreted by many as an implicit slap in the face of Liberty Sheriff's Department, perhaps suggesting that Buck Eckols and company had not presented the district attorney with as good a case as a prosecutor might hope for.

Chapter Twenty-six

F or Vickie Daniel, the trial had aroused ambivalent feelings. As someone who, growing up, did not even have grandparents, she had always envied people like the Daniels, with their strong familial bonds that stretched back generations. While her failure to get sympathy from her in-laws had been (to say the least) frustrating, Vickie also found their tunnel-visioned devotion admirable. Touching. How nice it would be to have everybody—your mother, your father, your siblings, most of your aunts—put you up on a pedestal like that. For this reason, Vickie had no trouble imagining the devastation all of them must have felt at Price's death. She grieved especially for Price's mother, who had always impressed Vickie as the true center of the family, the one constant source of calm, understanding, and pure, unqualified love in the midst of a caldron of smoldering ambitions.

On the other hand, Vickie found it hard to fathom why the Daniels went about some things the way they did— why they just had to have their way. In some respects, she realized they couldn't help themselves, especially Price. They were raised to think they were special, and when they grew up, they expected you to think they were special too.

251

The one bright spot for Vickie in the trial—besides the verdict—was her relationship with writer Dick Reavis. During the trial, their friendship had flowered. Vickie had always had a certain empathy for writers. As a child, she herself read a lot and wrote stories and poems. Which didn't mean she always trusted writers or their methods. With Reavis, however, she felt entirely at ease (at least at the outset), even though she knew he was writing a magazine article about her. There was, of course, the physical attraction, for Dick Reavis was a throwback to the kind of ruggedly male types who had always caught Vickie's eye in the days before Price. In addition, he helped her get her feet back on the ground.

With everything else going wrong, she badly craved a refuge from all the chaos. It wasn't just the trial. Her mother was gravely ill, and all along, Vickie was squeezing in hospital visits between her court sessions. Then her mother passed away, with nobody at her bedside. Vickie had been up there with her for three days in a row, but she had finally died alone.

Vickie was understandably bitter. All those children, she thought, and nobody there at the end. One sister even had gone up to Colorado to ski! Nothing like that would have ever happened in the Daniel family.

What good does it do to wallow in self-pity? Dick Reavis would ask her. Just take life as it comes. He helped her regain her confidence, told her she was a capable person, bright and strong and self-sufficient.

Vickie was enthralled by Reavis's circle of friends. He knew a rich assortment of people: bikers, Bohemian types, photographers, toughs. Never before had Vickie been exposed to such characters, and she was fascinated by their diversity and vitality. She saw them as a welcome departure from the pragmatic, businesslike types who had been Price's friends. These were the kind of people who talked about the tree in the forest and whether it made a sound when it fell. Price, she knew, would be interested in the tree only if it happened to fall on one of his rental properties. Or if he could chop it up and use it for firewood.

The relationship was not without its psychic costs, however. Running with Dick Reavis and his entourage demanded that certain notions about relationships be jettisoned. One time, as she sat in a restaurant with Reavis and a group of other women, she was gripped by the strangest awareness. "You know," she thought, conducting a visual survey of those around her, "he might have been to bed with *every* girl at this table!" But for some reason, with Reavis, it didn't matter. She found her sudden insight amusing, rather than vulgar. Almost charming, actually.

In those quiet hazy moments just before the onset of sleep, she would ask herself, Why couldn't it have been this easy with Price?

Despite the bitter feelings spawned by the trial, Vickie had no intention of barring the Daniels from their grandchildren. Indeed, one of her first acts after the jury's verdict was to announce that Price senior and Miss Jean would be permitted liberal visitation rights.

Nonetheless, in the middle of the week following the verdict, the Governor drew up an intervention document seeking to formalize some sort of visitation arrangement.

Daniel filed the document personally. He asked for "reasonable access" to Franklin and Bob, and also demanded that the boys' mother not allow her young children to be taught to "dislike or hate anyone concerned with the possession, access or visitation." (This was presumably a reference to some heated discussions between Vickie and Jean, during the course of the trial, over who was acceptable for picking up and delivering the kids.

253

Among Vickie's least favorite candidates for this role was Mark Morefield, who had offered moral support to Jean during the messy televised exchange of Wednesday, March 25.)

The Governor's definition of "reasonable access" was generous indeed. He requested visitation for one week each during the Easter, Thanksgiving, and Christmas holidays: three-day visits during February, May, June, and October; and a full month in the summer during the annual Daniel-family reunion-roundup in Liberty. It was further requested that, as executrix of Price's estate, Jean Murph should also be entitled to reasonable access. Should her visitations conflict with the Governor's own, then he would waive his rights to see the children on those dates. It struck Harlan Friend that Daniel was attempting to salvage for his daughter, through quiet legal maneuvering, some small part of what the circuslike court proceedings had failed to achieve.

Friend and Lannie considered the document as nothing more than a bargaining position. Perhaps if this matter could be resolved to everyone's satisfaction here and now, Jean, who had left open the option of appealing the custody verdict, could be persuaded to give up her crusade once and for all. Perhaps the Governor and his daughter might even prevail upon the district attorney's office to rethink its posture on the first-degree murder indictment. In any case, both men agreed that the demand, taken literally, was outrageous. The boys would be away from Vickie for more than sixty days each year. Said Friend to the press, "He knows Jean Daniel Murph is entitled to nothing. The jury was very specific in its unanimous decision that Mrs. Murph was to have no visitation rights. Period."

During the custody trial, Vickie had been staying with relatives, mostly her sister Rita Steadham in Baytown. After the verdict, she took up residence in an apartment there. She described it as "a horrible, ghastly place, a terrible place with no furniture, nothing." For a time, she slept on a borrowed mattress. It was the best she could do under the circumstances. Things got so bad at one point that she applied for child-welfare payments, and was enrolled in the federal Food Stamp program at the rate of $183 per month.

Rita Steadham complained bitterly to the media. "If Jeanie is so concerned about the welfare of these boys, why has she given Vickie only fifty dollars since January? I wouldn't call her concerned." But nothing changed. A good buddy, a man who had given Vickie her first job when she was sixteen, had to loan her the money for the rent.

It was such occasional acts of philanthropy that broke the bleakness of the period. Shortly after she moved in, two girls came by and performed a kindness Vickie would come to label "the nicest thing anybody's ever done for me."

She had been standing outside the dreary apartment, staring into space, when one of the girls approached, startling her.

"You're Vickie Daniel, aren't you?"

As she nodded reflexively, Vickie was apprehensive, believing she detected something ominous in the tone. She felt alone and distraught and more than a little paranoid, and so her first thought was that these girls had it in for her; perhaps they had even been dispatched by someone to do her harm. But Vickie by this point lacked any will for further hostility. The trial had taken the fight out of her.

Go ahead, she thought, kill me right here.

Thus she was shocked by the girl's next remark: "Listen, we just wanted to say that if there's anything we can ever do to help you, let us know." What made the whole thing especially poignant was that the young girls didn't exactly look like Rockefellers themselves.

Vickie invited them in. "I'd offer you somewhere to sit," she told them, "but I don't have anyplace." After a brief chat, her guests mentioned that they thought it would be nice if they could all have a little bit of lunch together.

"Well, that's another thing," said Vickie. "I don't really have anything to eat."

Whereupon the girls went out to remedy the deficiency. They returned shortly with a chicken and some string beans. Unfortunately, she hadn't expected them to come back with something that needed to be prepared. She had nothing to cook the stuff in. Out again went the girls. When they returned once more, it was with what would strike Vickie as "the rattiest old pots I'd ever seen." But after all this, she wasn't about to get fussy over their cookware. So she fixed lunch for the three of them.

There was another incident, too, right after Vickie went back to work at Dairy Queen (which had become a kind of safety net, a home away from home for her). She was now a curiosity there. Folks'd eye her sidelong as they ate, and more than once the whispered conversation at the counter would come to an abrupt halt as soon as she strutted forward and said, "Can I help you?" Other customers were entirely too pleasant, smiling too hard to put her at ease.

Once, right after her financial woes had made the papers, a lady in a Jaguar, a beautiful, statuesque blonde in an ermine coat—the kind of woman you just didn't see around town—drove up, came in and bought an ice cream with a fifty-dollar bill.

Vickie excused herself to get change, but when she came back her mysterious benefactress had disappeared as suddenly as she had arrived.

256

* * *

The official inventory of Price junior's assets and obligations was filed in Liberty County Probate Court in late May. It showed that Vickie stood to receive something less than $16,000 as her share of the estate. Harlan Friend and the rest of Vickie's legal team openly disbelieved the sum, as did the media. The *Houston Post*'s account noted that "Vickie would receive $15,375 from community property acquired *during her four-year marriage to the scion of one of Texas' most powerful political families*" [italics added].

Price's total assets were listed by Jean as $732,397 and his liabilities as $152,562, leaving a net worth of better than half a million dollars. Included among the items were $282,000 in real property and just under $400,000 in stocks and bonds (mostly in banks, trailer parks, and realty-development firms). Two checking accounts contained $2,342.73. (A third account, bearing $777.09, was later unearthed.) Of that, however, Vickie's claim was limited to her share of checking accounts, the estate's $3,000 equity in a modest rental property in Liberty, a couple of dozen acres of land, and the 1980 Mercury Zephyr wagon, which, Friend grumbled, Price had purchased for her use but which Jean still refused to relinquish.

Adding insult to injury, the $15,375 did not take into account $5,000 advanced by Jean back in January for Vickie's cash bail. That would have to come wholly out of Vickie's portion of the inventory. Therefore, after the estate was reimbursed, Vickie would be left with roughly $10,000.

"That's ludicrous!" steamed Friend. "We're going to have to contest it. We're going to be able to show she had a community-property interest in a good portion of the property listed as separate. Vickie contends they did not report all of the property in the inventory.

"It's going to be a lot of work," the lawyer added, referring to the task of uncovering and analyzing all of Price's holdings, obligations, and sources of income, "but it *will be done* until we get a final accounting."

Having grown accustomed to a life-style from which she now stood to be dispossessed, Vickie saw herself as caught between two worlds, and not really comfortable in either. True, Price had never let her live in the lap of luxury. But the house, the grounds, the shindigs at the Governor's ranch, being married to a big-time lawyer and politician—it was bound to creep inside you after a while.

Because of Dick Reavis's relaxed approach to life, Vickie had felt she could tell him anything. She even confided that, at times during the trial, she suspected she was being used by her lawyers for their own purposes—that she might be regarded as a stepping-stone, with which to further their own careers. That summer, an incident made her aware of the irony of her saying such things to Dick.

On this occasion, Vickie had planned to stay overnight with one of Reavis's female friends, but then changed her mind. While rummaging through a desk looking for something on which to leave a note explaining her departure, she found the manuscript he was preparing. Feeling a wee bit unethical, she read it nevertheless. In general, his article was gracious in its handling of Daniel idiosyncrasies. In particular, Vickie felt it glossed over what she considered to be Price's uglier faults.

Vickie phoned Dick the day after reading it—told him she hadn't really meant to, but—and said some changes were in order. In essence, his response, as she would remember it, was Let's not rock the boat. Any changes at this late date might kill the whole deal.

Vickie laughed it off. But she felt the episode had confirmed something about writers.

On June 19, five months to the day after Price's killing, all parties with custody interests assembled at the courthouse, where Judge Sam Emison tied up the several loose ends. He began by overseeing a settlement of Larry Moore's lawsuit seeking custody of Kim. Although officially custody of Kim would now revert to Vickie, the teenager would remain for the time being with Larry so that she could continue attending Dayton schools.

Next came an hour and a half of generally cordial negotiations guaranteeing the Governor and Mrs. Daniel twenty-seven days' worth of annual visitation with Franklin and Bob. The Daniels, who were already seeing the boys every other weekend, would have three days each at Christmas, Easter, and Thanksgiving; two nonconsecutive weeks during the summer; and two weekends at other times during the year. The Governor thus obtained a bit less than half of what he had asked for in his April intervention document.

Reporters were eager to know how Vickie was doing financially. She told them her attorneys had recently managed to obtain for her the contested Mercury station wagon but that the $640 per month she had begun receiving for the upkeep of the two children was simply insufficient. "If they don't give me a fair amount of money to support the children, I'll go back on welfare and Food Stamps," she said.

Did she expect to go to trial on the murder charge? someone asked.

"Oh, definitely," Vickie replied. "The Daniels will never let it pass by. They feel people need to pay their dues."

Well, then, did she expect a criminal jury to follow the civil jury's lead and find her innocent of murder charges?

"I hope so. I hope so for my children's sake. I could never intentionally kill anyone, especially Price. I have to

259

live with that and it's not easy. I have nightmares and I can't sleep."

But the interview ended on an upbeat note, with Vickie saying that if nothing else, she was at least happy to have the custody trial behind her.

"I'm satisfied," she said wearily. "I think it's finally over."

Two weeks later, Jean Murph filed a motion for a new custody trial.

Chapter Twenty-seven

I n early August, Vickie's entire defense team changed.

Racehorse Haynes bowed out, passing the torch, with Vickie's blessing, to his associate Jack Zimmermann. Haynes met with reporters to explain. He faced a busy court calendar; decisions had to be made, and Zimmermann got the call. Since Zimmermann was not used to working with co-counsel, Lannie and Friend would also withdraw. Besides, they were civil lawyers. This was no longer a civil case.

The press speculated, though, that the two local attorneys had been the last to find out about their withdrawal from the case. "I don't know all the facts, but it appears Zimmermann wants to work alone," said a somewhat perplexed-sounding Harlan Friend. Friend added that he would continue to represent Vickie in matters pertaining to the will.

It turned out, in fact, that Zimmermann would not work alone. He would be assisted by C. J. "Buddy" Hanby, the civil-law expert who had been at Haynes's side during the custody case.

Desperate for insights into Zimmermann, the press hounded Racehorse for details. They received an uncharacteristically terse response: "He's a crackerjack lawyer and,"

Racehorse emphasized, "a partner in this firm. That should tell you something. The record will reflect he has done an outstanding job."

Most of the press was understandably sorry to see Haynes go. He had provided no small amount of drama, and on more than one occasion—particularly during the week or so that the psychiatrists were at center stage—he had kept things going with his barbed wit and sideline antics. There was not the slightest trace of an impish smirk on Zimmermann's face. He spoke with a certain economy and was not given to offbeat metaphors and florid verbal outpourings.

Yet when he stepped before reporters, fixed them with a steady stare, and said, "I do *not* like to lose," nobody doubted they were in the presence of someone to be reckoned with.

Jack B. Zimmermann was a product of the spit-and-polish professionalism demanded of graduates of Annapolis and Marine Corps officers. Born in San Antonio (a favorite Daniel vacation haunt), Zimmermann had honed his scrappy, odds-bucking nature as a five-foot-nine-inch, 145-pound All-District halfback at Alamo Heights High School, and later at Navy.

Between his junior and senior years at the Naval Academy, he was assigned to the U.S.S. *Enterprise*. Zimmermann fell under the spell of the marine detachment aboard the vessel because he saw that particular branch as "more professional" than the navy. Eagerly, he accepted a regular commission in the Marine Corps. Trained as an artillery officer, he was one of five marines assigned to three-year Hawaii tours. Though it was considered at the time a plum assignment, Zimmermann would soon learn differently. "We took a ship from Oakland and had no television, no radios or newspapers," he would recall. "When we arrived we were shocked to find out our unit had shipped out for Okinawa and would be the forward unit to clear Chu Lai," the first major marine landing in Vietnam. Zimmermann received two Bronze Stars during the second of two tours in Vietnam, one of them for action near the DMZ where casualties were the rule.

He returned from Vietnam in 1969, got his master's from Purdue and his law degree from the University of Texas in rapid succession. He then returned to the Marine Corps at Camp Lejeune, North Carolina, where he made a name for himself as a prosecutor.

Zimmermann joined the law firm of Haynes and Fullenweider in July 1978. And now, three years later, he faced what was clearly the biggest, most visible case of his career. He wasted little time in taking a posture at least as aggressive as that of his more celebrated predecessor.

"Vickie is innocent right now and she's going to be innocent when she walks out of the courtroom when the trial ends," he informed the press following a pretrial hearing before Judge Leonard Giblin, a Beaumont native imported to hear the murder trial.

Judge Giblin, known as an old-fashioned judge in the tradition of the Old West, forewarned Zimmermann and Wilborn that he intended to conduct the trial "strictly" by the rules of evidence and criminal procedure. He was determined to avoid the circuslike publicity that had attended the custody trial. "Emotions are going to run high . . . mostly, I guess, because of the parties involved. I intend to make sure Mrs. Daniel receives a fair trial. I believe in it." Judge Giblin had been weighing a gag order, but he told the two attorneys he'd decided it would be best if they had a chance to visit with the press "on a case of this nature."

"However," he warned, "I don't want [the case] tried outside the courtroom!"

The judge then expanded on his vision of the climate

263

in which the trial was about to unfold: "I see myself throwing the flag quite often. . . ."

A few reporters who knew the judge from past trials in his own 253rd Circuit Court shook their heads. The line on Judge Giblin was that he was the kind of a guy who might like to take advantage of the grandstanding opportunities that enforcing fairness—"throwing the flag"—would afford him.

Although by failing to impose a gag order, Judge Giblin had left the matter of public statements largely to the discretion of the individual attorneys, one of Zimmermann's first acts was to muzzle Vickie, who was coming off a decisive victory in the custody trial. She was, for the moment at least, in the catbird seat. There was nothing to be gained by having her speak, but everything to lose.

Not that Zimmermann or his client was all that worried. In fact, the mood around Vickie's camp might have been summed up by a photo of Zimmermann and Vickie that appeared in the *Post* on October 4, the day after both sides had heard Judge Giblin lay down the law.

In the photo, lawyer and client looked as relaxed, self-assured, and convivial as Hollywood types arriving at the Dorothy Chandler Pavilion on Oscar night.

When Jean, through Zbranek, filed for the second custody trial in early August, she had cited "undisputed evidence" that Vickie "unlawfully shot and killed Price Daniel Jr."

The motion alleged a series of errors, chief among them that the unanimous verdict for Vickie was not supported by the weight of the evidence and that the "act alone" was prima facie evidence that Vickie lacked the "stability, judgment and rectitude" to properly rear her children. Further, Zbranek chastised Judge Emison for offering a permanent custody verdict in preference to the temporary hearing Jean had originally sought (although Zbranek would later admit that, in fact, it had been *he* who erred by letting himself get roped into the arrangement).

Now, however, with the murder trial imminent, Jean decided not to seek a new trial or even to appeal the verdict in the original suit. She recognized what a bad move a refiling would be strategically. Public sentiment had galvanized against the Daniels; you could feel it in the streets. No sense piquing the underdog mentality any further, this close to the trial. Besides which, if Vickie was convicted, there was an excellent chance Jean and the Daniels would end up with the kids anyway, and without a fight.

"The case is dead," Zeke Zbranek announced. "It's over." Though his feeling for the Daniel family was clear, he sounded almost grateful. There was, in his voice and in his eyes, the unspoken sentiment, "Now maybe I can put this all behind me and get back to my wills and dented fenders."

"I really feel this lady has been put upon by the system," said Zimmermann in early October. "The conduct of the investigation will probably be an appropriate area of inquiry for the upcoming trial." (A source quoted by the *Post,* and identified as being "close" to the investigation, was even less circumspect: "It was easy to go after her. She was a non-person. The sheriff did not know her. She was not known by politicians or law enforcement. She was a nobody married to a somebody.")

Zimmermann had been prepped by Haynes on the circumstances of the custody trial, and as he waded into the testimony himself, he was shocked. As far as Zimmermann could determine, never before in state history had a court allowed virtually all the evidence from a criminal trial to be scrutinized, in advance, in a civil suit. Although many thought this actually put the defense at an advantage, Zimmermann didn't necessarily agree. Haynes had had to reveal some of Vickie's trump cards as well. Prosecutors were thus given a chance to come up with a strategy for surmounting those arguments in the criminal trial. Further, Zimmermann worried about the possibility of getting a fair trial in a town that had been so inundated with material.

But what upset Zimmermann most was that, even looking at things from a prosecutor's point of view, the evidence simply did not appear to warrant the present charge. Manslaughter perhaps, but not first-degree homicide. Why hadn't a plea-bargain been offered? Especially since about 95 percent of the criminal cases in this jurisdiction *were* plea-bargained . . . ? Why was this case the one where the state had opted for an all-or-nothing stand? Especially after the embarrassment of the custody suit, the lack of a plea-bargain in a case this iffy suggested again some higher forces at work behind the scenes.

The one factor for which Zimmermann had to be grateful was Wilborn. The Liberty district attorney was the most respected figure in local law enforcement. He was thought of by his colleagues—even his adversaries— as smart, industrious, and above all fair. "I do this because I can contribute to society," he was once quoted. "I'm not dependent on the job. I have other resources to support my family." He often said he did not prosecute if he did not believe in the case.

The statistics seemingly bore him out. During his very first year as an assistant D.A. in 1972, he had won seventy-two of eighty cases in which he participated. The public had faith in Carroll Wilborn. He had been elected to his current post by a wide margin in November 1980, around the time that Vickie was preparing to file her second divorce action against Price.

Zimmermann knew that Wilborn would be a tough opponent, but he expected the man's innate sense of fair play to work against any machinations attempted by those in power.

Jury selection for the murder trial of Vickie Daniel got under way on Monday, October 5. To no one's surprise, the fireworks began almost immediately.

It started innocently enough, when the Daniel contingent—the Governor, his wife, Jean Murph, Houston and Charlotte Daniel, as well as Laverne Capps, the Governor's personal secretary of long standing—sat up in the front row of the courthouse to await the start of proceedings. Nearby was newsman Bill Buchanan, who thought he noted some confusion among the Daniels—as if they were searching for something they had misplaced. Buchanan would recall leaning over and asking Jean what the trouble was.

"I don't seem to have my call list," she replied, referring to the list of community residents who had been summoned as prospective jurors.

"No problem," said Buchanan, who promptly handed over his copy.

Jean and her father scanned it. After a moment, the Governor sighed and shook his head slowly from side to side.

"Where have I been?" he asked rhetorically, gesturing toward the list with an almost helpless look. "I don't know any of these names." Buchanan heard the remark as the wistful lament of an aging politician whose finger had slipped from the pulse of what had once been his staunchest constituency.

Jean and her father pored over the list, and every once in a while the light of recognition came into their eyes. "Oh, I think I know this one," said the Governor. "Yes," added Jean, "and isn't this so-and-so's son?"

On the opposite side of the courtroom, to Vickie's attorney it looked as if the group was huddled over the list in a conspiratorial manner. Jack Zimmermann was convinced by the way their eyes darted from the list to the jury box and back that some devilish plot was afoot.

Zimmermann strode to the bench and demanded that the charges against his client be dismissed. Price senior, he argued, had made it clear by his conduct that he was attending the first day of selection for the express purpose of "denying Vickie a fair trial." Zimmermann claimed the Governor's goal was to "intimidatingly influence" prospective jurors not just by his presence but by his daunting looks.

Price senior was called to the stand to explain his behavior. In a voice tinged with indignation, he denied any intention of influencing prospective jurors in any way. As he sat back down, he shook his head in disbelief.

Judge Giblin denied the motion to drop the charges, appearing mildly annoyed that the onset of hostilities could not even wait until the trial began. But he did acknowledge that he was prepared to excuse the remaining one hundred seventeen jurors and either move for a change of venue or grant a postponement.

Zimmermann demurred. In his heart of hearts, he did not really want the trial moved or postponed. Nor had he honestly expected Judge Giblin to dismiss. He was primarily interested in getting his concerns on record. His mentor, the inventive Haynes, used such tactics often; he even had a colorful name, "hickeys," for controversial rulings that could eventually be reversed on appeal, thus affording him the chance of snatching victory from the jaws of defeat.

Zimmermann also hoped to put the Daniels on the defensive right at the outset, an objective he achieved through Judge Giblin's next directive: All the Daniel family members would be sworn as prospective witnesses. As such,

under the terms of an agreement already in place between Zimmermann and Wilborn, they were barred from
attending the jury-selection process.

This turn of events left Price senior shaken. He started
back toward the bench to argue, but Jean took her father
by the arm and deftly guided him out of the courtroom.
A scene would not help matters, for if the custody trial
had proved anything, it was that *the Daniels,* and not Vickie,
had the most to fear from a jury.

The jury call included a fifty-two-year-old housewife who
had come to Liberty in 1979 after living abroad for a dozen
years. On Tuesday, she was selected as the first of thirty-
two potential jurors, possibly in the belief that if there was
no one around who'd never heard of Price or Vickie Daniel, the next best choice was someone who'd been away
for a while.

After Vickie was introduced to the remaining panel,
Zimmermann reaffirmed the customary presumption of
innocence, reminding the jury that the burden of proving
Vickie's guilt was totally Wilborn's. "A crime cannot be
committed by accident," stressed Zimmermann; beyond
that, the perception that one's life is in danger "is a highly
subjective judgment." One juror, later excused, thought
Zimmermann's oratory contradictory. Either Vickie had
shot Price by accident, or she had shot him out of fear for
her safety—which, the juror wanted to know, was it? "He
seemed to be saying, well, it was an accident—and if it
wasn't, she shot him in self-defense." The man was reminded of the apocryphal defense put forward by an attorney whose client's pooch was accused of biting a
neighbor: "Ladies and gentlemen of the jury, my client's
dog doesn't bite; my client's dog wasn't out that day; my
client's dog was on a leash; and my client doesn't have a
dog."

One day later, an eight-man, four-woman jury was

seated. The makeup of the panel underscored the difficulty involved in finding "ideal" jurors in a small town like Liberty. Among the group was the wife of a county sheriff's detective and a cousin of one of the lawyers who represented Jean Murph in the custody case.

The jury would not be sequestered, Judge Giblin announced. He then offered the familiar admonitions about reading, watching, or listening to media reports on the case, and told the jurors to eschew discussion among themselves until the time had come to reach an official verdict. "And if anyone approaches you about the case," the judge instructed, "I want to know about it." At this, Wilborn frowned.

Outside, the district attorney was asked whether he was surprised that it had been so easy to locate twelve jurors who had not already formed an opinion on the case.

"At least," he said archly, "that's what they told the court and the lawyers."

Chapter Twenty-eight

J ack Zimmermann was not quite ready to begin. He had a series of further motions to make with respect to the evidence against his client. His principal concern was Vickie's decision to give up her Fifth Amendment rights during the custody trial. It was Zimmermann's belief, after having had several weeks to conduct a full review of that case, that all of Vickie's testimony, including depositions, should be blocked from introduction in the current case. Vickie had felt trapped, Zimmermann explained. Her understanding was that if she remained silent, Judge Emison had the prerogative of simply taking it upon himself to award temporary custody to Jean Murph. Zimmermann argued that considering the options facing her—take the stand or risk losing her children—Vickie's testimony was hardly voluntary in the accepted legal sense. Rather, it ran much closer to a statement extracted under duress, and such statements were universally inadmissible. Racehorse Haynes, who had careened his Porsche into Liberty just for the occasion, took the stand to echo his colleague's posture. In his patented grand manner, Haynes volunteered that Jean's suit had backed Vickie into a terrible corner.

"She said she would do *anything* to keep the children," said a plaintive Racehorse.

The ruling that Zimmermann demanded from Judge Giblin was unique. In the annals of criminal justice there had never before been a case in which virtually all the evidence from a criminal trial had been previously unveiled in a civil case. "I only ask that you give grave and proper consideration to the precedent we are about to set," implored Zimmermann.

After a night's tormented sleep, Giblin ruled in Zimmermann's favor: Vickie's testimony from the custody case, depositions included, would be admissible only to impeach her present testimony. That is, should she decide to take the stand again, which was very much in doubt.

This was a crushing blow for Wilborn. Without her testimony, the role of plausibly reconstructing the events of January 19 fell squarely and solely on the state's shoulders. (Theoretically, Wilborn might even have to prove that Vickie was *there* that night.)

Only with Vickie's testimony would Wilborn get a chance to expose what he saw as the fundamental paradox of her story. She had contended at the custody trial that she ran and fetched the gun in order to make Price leave the house. But all available evidence—from the keys Price had dropped to the clothes in the pickup to the fact that the pickup door was open—suggested Price was already *in the process of leaving when the shooting occurred*. If he was already on his way out, why had Vickie needed the gun?

Such were the questions, it now appeared, that Wilborn might not have the chance to ask.

Nor did the district attorney's worries end there. Judge Giblin had also been listening closely to Zimmermann's complaints about the conduct of the murder investigation. Securing of the property had been haphazard, at best. No search warrant was issued to cover the activities of sheriff's investigators who arrived in the days after the shooting. One of the department's own men had been put on retainer by the Daniels to watch over the property!

Accordingly, Judge Giblin limited prosecution exhibits to items seized during the first twenty-one hours of the investigation. During that time, he ruled, there had been unbroken supervision—such as it was—of the crime scene by the Sheriff's Department.

By barring evidence after this early juncture, Giblin decreed that only a few items from the custody case would be admissible: the .22-caliber rifle, bullet fragments taken from Price's body, two bullet casings, the .410 shotgun, a key case, a jacket, and a small number of items on Price's person. Only photographs taken during the first three visits, when the house was presumably in the same condition as when the incident occurred, would be allowed.

Particularly hard hit were the investigative efforts of Marvin Powell. (With ten separate searches over the first ten days after the shooting—every one without benefit of warrant—C. I. Powell had established himself not only as a most thorough sleuth but also as the most flagrant and conspicuous transgressor as well. When asked, later, why he had gone to the house so often without a warrant, Powell simply responded, "I was not told *not* to go to the house.") Among the items Powell recovered that would be barred under Judge Giblin's ruling were the legal papers that supposedly formed the centerpiece of Vickie's heated arguments with Price that night, personal notes penned by both Vickie and Price, the mysterious brown wooden box, roof decking where the disputed warning shot exited the house, and a Dixie cup containing a mixed drink Price had reputedly made that night (and which Bill Buchanan said he saw Buck Eckols sample).

Wilborn claimed to be unshaken. "We've got the guns, the bullet, the hulls, and the scientific reports," he proclaimed. And there was even a silver lining in the bench's judgment. Exclusion of the wooden box probably meant

Wilborn would have to endure less of the marijuana angle that Haynes had dredged up during the custody trial. What's more, Judge Giblin would let stand Vickie's statements to Oscar Cantu wherein she confessed firing the fatal shot. That alone, Wilborn felt, had to block any attempt by Zimmermann to argue that his client was in a total fog when it happened.

But privately the district attorney was disappointed. Things did not seem to be going his way. Jurors might be disposed to think, If the evidence found after the twenty-first hour was unreliable, how solid was the rest?

Wilborn's opening statement on Wednesday, October 14, gave new meaning to the word *succinct*. He took a mere ninety seconds to outline the state's contention that the act under consideration by the jury was "not only an unnecessary killing, but also a criminal homicide." That said, Wilborn wasted not a moment in once again filling in the courtroom with the events of January 19.

Up to the stand trudged Anderson and Cantu to reprise their twin accounts of finding the body and grappling with Vickie. The material itself should have been compelling enough, certainly to a jury that had not heard it before—at least first-hand—but there was something missing in their presentations. Cantu in particular was tired of the hoopla, and it showed in his voice.

Oscar was not alone in the sense of mounting ennui. Like a summer rerun of Dallas, the case now lacked the melodrama and suspense of the first go-round. And Haynes's absence didn't help.

Of the eighty spectators who turned out—perhaps a third of what the custody case typically drew—only a few dozen stayed long enough to hear Zimmermann tell reporters, after the day's session, that the testimony thus far "doesn't appear to show any degree of guilt."

. . . .

* * *

KPXE's Bill Buchanan had not been called as a witness during the custody case, and by at least one account, had felt a bit slighted. He now got his chance to remedy the oversight.

Wilborn led him through the chronology of his involvement at the shooting scene. The characterization of Vickie, holding her own against three grown men on the floor, was vivid and helpful to the state's cause. But Buchanan had a disconcerting tendency to keep coming back to Vickie's concern for her fallen husband. "She kept screaming for us to leave her alone and go help Price," said the newsman more than once. He added that her state of mind, based on almost two decades of observing hysterical people at personal tragedies, "was as extreme as I have ever seen." Nor did he have the slightest doubt whatsoever that her hysteria was genuine. Buchanan could not testify as an expert witness on this point, for he was a radio personality, not a medical doctor or a psychiatrist; from a legal standpoint, decisions about the exact nature of Vickie's mental state were clearly out of his domain. And yet he would remain firm, as the years went by, that "nobody can fake the kind of behavior I saw from that woman in that house on that night. Anybody who tells you different just doesn't know what he's talking about."*

As Zimmermann stood to begin his cross-examination, he had to feel euphoric. Normally cross-examination provided a defense attorney with the opportunity to recoup, to mitigate harmful testimony that came to light on direct examination. But thus far Buchanan had said so little that was detrimental to Vickie's case. Zimmermann could instead feel free to explore new territory without so much

*Nurse Nancy Bell, who arrived at the scene as Buchanan and the EMTs were grappling with Vickie, would later testify that Vickie was "uncontrollable," and that her hysterics were, in Bell's professional opinion, "very much genuine."

as a backward glance. And there were indeed several items he wanted to cover.

Most of all, Zimmermann sought to raise the possibility that it was not Price but Houston, arriving earlier than everyone else, who had opened the pickup door and left it ajar. This was an important point to make. Did Vickie shoot Price to *prevent* him from leaving, as the prosecution contended? Or did she shoot him in the chaotic aftermath of an unsuccessful attempt to *force* him to leave? Zimmermann urgently wanted the jurors to believe the latter. To get them to accept that, he would need to demonstrate that someone else—and who better than the loyal brother, Houston?—had tampered with the pickup before sheriff's investigators arrived.

Did Buchanan happen to notice if the truck's dome light was on when he first pulled up? Zimmermann inquired.

No, he did not notice it until after Houston attempted to gain entry through the carport door.

Did Houston look at the body on the kitchen floor?

No, Houston did not look down, said Buchanan—either Houston did not want to see his dead brother, or he already knew where the body was. The implication of the latter possibility was clear: If Houston had already seen the body, then most likely he had also reconnoitered the murder scene and the house in general. Which, in turn, would mean he had more than ample opportunity to "do a little shiftin' and shufflin'," as Ann Rogers had once put it.

Wilborn objected and was sustained. Buchanan, after all, had no way of knowing exactly what Houston's behavior signified. But the point had been made. And heard.

Friday belonged to Marvin Powell. It was a long, tedious descent through the murky abyss of investigative blunder, such that by day's end Carroll Wilborn might well have wished he had stuck with cattle ranching.

The veteran sheriff's deputy, who after the Daniel incident had left the county's employ and gone to work for an oil-tool company, described a comedy of errors, although the way Powell told it, none of it was his fault. His very best efforts at doing his customary, solid job of detective work were undermined by a combination of bad luck, bad timing, and especially, interference from on high. Powell's buck-passing played right into Jack Zimmermann's hands, determined as the attorney was to seize upon the smallest suggestion of Daniel clout.

"With respect to your investigation of the Daniel shooting," Zimmermann asked, "did people tell you what to do and what not to do?"

"Yes, sir."

"Did interference by other people interfere with your judgments?"

"No," Powell replied, "it didn't interfere with my judgment, but it interfered with me carrying out my judgment."

The witness then outlined for Jack Zimmermann the magnitude of investigative carelessness. Powell allowed that when he showed up at the Daniel house about an hour after the shooting was reported, it was not secured. Nor, despite Sheriff Eckols's threats to Bill Buchanan and others, were there any security locks or other measures implemented to seal the crime scene as the inquiry proceeded. By Powell's count, at least a dozen people, including nurse Nancy Bell, Houston and Charlotte Daniel, and assorted media types, had free access to the house and grounds prior to the investigator's arrival.

Unfortunately, one individual not present was Vickie. Thus Powell was deprived of the all-important opportunity to correlate her statement with observable evidence while the crime scene was still fresh (not that a statement would have been possible, given her condition). Then there were the telltale oversights, among them, that no fingerprints were taken either in the home or from Price's pickup.

Asked for his own explanation of why only the rifle was dusted for prints, Powell gave forth with another reply that had onlookers shaking their heads in disbelief: "I didn't feel like it was necessary."

In any case, the prints taken from the gun did not match Vickie's.

Not all of the blame was laid by Powell on the Sheriff's Department. He said a request by lawyer Andrew Lannie to preserve the scene as it was found also hindered his evidence gathering. Lannie could not get a coherent story from his client and he didn't want the house disturbed until he'd had a chance to get back there and piece things together for himself.

Zimmermann spent no small part of the day in a painstaking reconstruction of the chain of custody, hoping to paint a vivid picture of evidence tampering. He was skeptical of the department's handling of the celebrated wooden box found in Price's attic. How did it happen that the box arrived at the crime lab in Beaumont minus the green specks Powell himself had noticed, and reported, when the discovery was made? What was Powell's theory? "I don't have any," replied the former C.I., insisting that he had not destroyed any evidence. Powell did say that access to the office where the evidence was kept was limited to Sheriff Eckols and Deputy Clay Autery. Eckols's sympathies were well known, and Autery was cashing a paycheck from Jean Murph at around the time the box was being logged into evidence.

Along with New York's Milton Halpern and L.A.'s Thomas Noguchi, Dr. Joseph Jachimczyk of Harris County was one of a handful of forensic pathologists who, in 1981, enjoyed national reputation. In Jachimczyk's case, the reputation was not one he might have chosen for himself. In the celebrated Joan Robinson Hill case, he had been called upon to determine whether or not Dr. John Hill might have killed his socially prominent wife by, among other things, slipping her a bacteria-laden chocolate eclair. But his handling of that autopsy was a matter of controversy. More recently, Dr. Joe, as he was locally known, had come under fire for his stewardship over the Harris County medical examiner's office. So it was with mixed emotions that Jachimczyk stepped back into the spotlight to deliver expert opinion at yet another prominent trial.

Jachimczyk's trepidations may have accounted for the equivocal tone of his testimony. He stated that:

The trace-metal test taken on Price's hands revealed a pattern on the right hand that might have been consistent with his grabbing the barrel of the gun. Then again, it might not. Medical science was not that precise in its reconstructive capabilities, explained Jachimczyk. The pattern could also be consistent with the holding of clothes hangers or a pipe of some sort. The tests did not appear to indicate that Price had been going in and out of the house, opening the door of his pickup truck or handling the four locks on the kitchen door. Then again, you couldn't say for sure, inasmuch as the washing of one's hands would remove trace-metal deposits.

The brusises on Price's body, especially those on his knuckles and near one of his nipples, might have been an indication of his having been in a fierce struggle; Jachimczyk had noted similar abrasions on the bodies of thousands of people known to have been fighting just before their deaths. Then again, the bruises might not be all that significant. Some of them could have occurred when he fell after being shot.

One of the jurors would recall thinking, as Dr. Joe was excused from the witness stand, "Well, I'm glad we cleared that up."

Chapter Twenty-nine

P rice Daniel, Jr., went to his grave without being fingerprinted, and the trial next became a contest to see who could shift the blame fastest.

The fingerprints were a crucial piece of physical evidence. As Marvin Powell explained during his turn on the stand, the Sheriff's Department had taken nine readable "lifts" from the rifle. The lack of Price's fingerprints, in conjunction with a fruitless after-the-fact search of the files in Austin, Houston, and Washington, D.C., precluded defense efforts to prove that Price had indeed grabbed for the gun.

Powell said he had expected Dr. Jachimczyk to lift prints from Price's corpse during the autopsy. But the fingerprints were not taken, even though Jachimczyk admitted that the oversight was "an exception to common practice" in the office of the Harris County M.E. Sergeant J. D. Satcher, an identification expert with the Harris County Sheriff's Department, explained that on January 20 he phoned Deputy Clay Autery and requested the prints after learning that Jachimczyk had unaccountably failed to obtain them. Taking the prints from Price's body would have been a "relatively simple procedure" that would have in no way disturbed the body, Satcher explained. Nonetheless, the prints never arrived. Wilborn—by this time clearly losing patience with the competence of those whose case he was now attempting to hold together—termed it "another investigative mess-up . . . something that should have been done and wasn't." He said he hadn't even learned of Satcher's request until the week after Price was buried.

Later, however, Wilborn recovered his composure before reporters. He declined to fault his subordinates for the state's foundering presentation of the physical evidence. Rather, he once again focused on the circumstances of the shooting. "I can't help it," he sighed, "if there were only two witnesses to this killing and one of them is in the ground."

Houston Daniel testified and remembered having arrived at the house about 7:30 P.M.—a time that had been fixed as the moment of his brother's death. He was informed by emergency medical technician David Bautsch that his brother was "gone," which he at first took to mean that Price was not at home. (Several people in the gallery snickered at the remark.) The EMTs directed him to the bedroom wing of the house to take care of the three children. Kim at that point told him "something that made me concerned," but for reasons having to do with the hearsay rule, Houston was not allowed to share her comment with the jury. (She had told him about the fights she witnessed between Price and her mother.) The kids seemed all right, so Houston left them after a while and circled around the back of the house to the carport. He wanted to see if he could "find Price and help him." That was when he located the pickup truck with its passenger door open. He said he touched nothing. His voice was firm, resolute.

Zimmermann was dubious. He asked Houston if he might have opened the door of the truck.

"I am absolutely certain I didn't," Houston replied.

Dr. Jerry Bunce told the jury Vickie was under his treatment from about 8:30 the night of the shooting until she was released from Yettie Kersting Hospital on January 23. He repeated his story about the bruises that developed over the first thirty-six hours of her hospital confinement, and described his unease at documenting her injuries for the Sheriff's Department. "I felt it compromised the doctor-patient relationship," he explained. C. J. Hanby, the only member of the defense team who had played a hand in both trials, asked Bunce if he had a theory about battered women who fail to report their injuries to their doctors. Earlier, Wilborn had suggested that it was curious how, in all the time of her supposedly turbulent marriage to Price, Vickie never once complained to Bunce about any physical abuse.

The doctor shook his head, and a knowing look briefly crossed his face—a look that said prosecutors should not presume to venture into territory so far removed from their fields of expertise.

"The battered woman," said Bunce, "does not report, does not seek help—except as a last ditch."

The testimony of a child in open court is always an event of great dramatic tension. When the trial is a murder case involving one or both of the child's parents, the drama is that much greater. Thus Wednesday, October 21, became one of the rare dates on which attendance at the Liberty County Courthouse swelled to a number reminiscent of the custody trial. One would have thought the whole world wanted to hear what thirteen-year-old Kimberly Moore had to say.

For district attorney Carroll Wilborn, the testimony of Kim Moore promised something besides drama. Wilborn

had long suspected the child knew more than she was telling. It wasn't just that her recollections of that evening, as
expressed in five prior statements to investigators and
lawyers, seemed to be in a constant state of evolution. Nor
was it that her story grew ever more favorable to her
mother as time went by. It was something about the way
the girl told her story. Wilborn's years in law enforcement
had taught him that as a rule, children were highly transparent storytellers. The average child was not, by nature,
a convincing liar; more to the point, the average child
had not yet learned the subtle distinction between telling
a bold-faced lie and simply withholding some of the truth.
A child hiding something would usually exhibit the same
guilt or discomfort as a child who was fibbing. You could
just *feel it* somehow. Wilborn had always had that feeling
with Kim.

During a polygraph session with the girl the previous
week, his suspicions had borne fruit. And now, before God
and the jury, Wilborn would lead Kim through her story—
what was, he believed, the once-and-for-all true story—of
what really happened in that huge house on that glum
night in January.

Wilborn did not plunge right into the essential details,
which might have alarmed the girl. He wanted to give
Kim time to build up her confidence, as well as her credibility. The more details she could provide about what had
gone on earlier that day, the more likely the jury would
be to accept her recollection of what transpired later.

Wilborn had Kim describe the kind of day January 19
had been for her. In a soft voice, she began by painting
what might have been the portrait of a routine day in the
life of any American teenager. In the afternoon, her
mother had picked her up at school, as was customary,
and they had arrived home at about four o'clock. She said
she studied for perhaps half an hour and then went to
her room to watch television.

Sometime later, hearing her mother and Price "fussing in the next bedroom, she came out to see what was up and found the two of them in the midst of an earnest wrestling match. Price shoved her mother down onto the bed, grabbed Vickie's foot, and twisted it. Acting on instinct, Kim shoved him off. Satisfied that she had defused the situation, Kim returned to her room where her two siblings, Franklin and Bob, were still watching TV.

When she later went to the kitchen to get some water, "Mom and Price were fussing and pushing each other," she testified, explaining that both combatants were angry and loud.

After going back to her bedroom and spending a "pretty good while" there, Kim said she heard her mother call and went to the front hall.

Vickie was on her back with her arms across her chest and Price on his knees holding her by the wrists.

For the second time that evening she shoved Price off Vickie. Except this time, he shoved her back. When she lost her balance, her mother managed to catch her and break her fall.

"Price hollered at me and told me to return to my room," she said. Frightened, she retreated down the hallway and closed the hall and bedroom doors behind her.

Soon she heard glass shattering. Again leaving her room to investigate, she saw broken glass strewn in a widening pattern down the hallway from the dining room. Too scared to check further, she sought refuge in her room once more.

Sometime later, she was on her way to the kitchen yet again and noticed the attic ladder down in the hallway. Price was up in the attic "digging through some boxes"; at one point, she said, he looked down at her. Zimmermann shifted uneasily. There was an eerie undercurrent to her testimony—as if she were not just telling the story, but actually watching it happen—reliving it. She was also giving a more detailed rendering than in the past. Still more worrisome—he didn't know if it was his imagination—she appeared to be avoiding eye contact with her mother. A sixth sense present in all good trial lawyers told Zimmermann that the teenager was leading up to something. Perhaps something she had not divulged before.

He could not have been more right.

"I saw Mama coming out with a gun . . ."

In all his days in court, and on the gridiron before that, Jack Zimmermann had never been hit this hard. Through five previous statements Kim had mentioned nothing about the rifle. The lawyer steeled himself for the worst, while beside him, his client sat with her jaw clenched tight.

". . . She didn't say anything. She looked very angry." Kim had not seen her mother that angry before. The girl described how her mother went to the attic ladder and looked at Price, who was holding a small white bag.* "She said, 'Put the sack down or I'll shoot.' She told me to go to my room. I said, 'Please don't,' and she told me to go to my room."

Kim paused for just a heartbeat. She then quoted her mother as warning Price, " *'If you don't believe I'll shoot, I will!'* " Even in her cracking adolescent's voice, the words were ripe with menace.

Kim said she could hear them arguing until she returned to her room and closed the door behind her. Then she heard nothing further from without. Moments later Vickie came to her room holding a rag over her mouth, "like she was sick." Don't let the boys out of the room,

---

*The bag apparently contained keys, photographs, and sundry other items, and was eventually found by sheriff's investigators in the attic under some insulation. How it got back there remained a mystery, since Price's clothes tested negative for fiberglass remnants.

Vickie admonished. Just before going back outside, she added, "And keep the door closed."

Kim was too worried and confused to stay put, however. After a few agitated moments, she opened the door and looked down the hall. That was when she saw Vickie kneeling at the foot of the stairs, praying.

Minutes later, when the ambulance arrived, Kim sized up the situation. "I knew my mama shot Price."

There was by now a steady murmur building in the gallery and a thunderstruck Jack Zimmermann could almost feel the heat of the jurors' eyes on his client.

Zimmermann's first priority was to find out what had made Kim change her story. On cross-examination, he asked her how the district attorney happened to come by this new information.

"Somebody's pressured you, haven't they, Kimberly?" pressed Zimmermann.

"No, sir," she said.

Brushing away tears, Kim said she first told about seeing her mother with the gun when she went to take "the polygraph" last week.

Zimmermann had scored. The accuracy of a polygraph, or lie detector, was not recognized for courtroom purposes. And yet juries tended to side with law-enforcement personnel in giving lie-detector tests quite a lot of credence. Hence, the fact that one's revelations had surfaced originally during such a test might be considered sufficient grounds for excluding the testimony, as it would be given undue weight by the jury. It was another "hickey" situation: Either Judge Giblin would now rule the child's testimony inadmissible, or an appeals court—if it came to that—would hold that Vickie's right to a fair trial had been breached by allowing such testimony into the record.

But Zimmermann was not content to let it go at that. Kim's recollections were the first truly new and startling information revealed since the custody trial. No doubt the jury had been strongly affected by it—Zimmermann could read as much on their faces—and no command from the bench to "ignore those remarks" would erase their impact. Zimmermann, therefore, resolved to ask Judge Giblin either to declare a mistrial or to render an instructed verdict of not guilty.

After making his motions and being assured by Judge Giblin that due and proper consideration would be given, Zimmermann spoke to the press. He was still visibly shaken. He had been well aware, of course, that children were invariably the most unpredictable, and therefore most precarious, element in any trial. But he had considered Kim's testimony bedrock solid.

"I'm really offended by someone getting to that kid!" he fumed. "I'm offended as a father that someone has convinced a thirteen-year-old girl to change her story in the middle of a trial!"

By "someone," did he mean Wilborn? a reporter asked. Zimmermann said no, he was certain that Carroll Wilborn would not have anything to do with such shenanigans.

Did he suspect the Daniels, then?

But it was too late; Jack Zimmermann was already on his way out of the courtroom, striding angry, purposeful strides.

With Kim's testimony complete, Wilborn rested his case. He had saved the best for last, hoping to leave the jury with the image of a vindictive, demanding woman who knew exactly what she was doing when she killed her husband. It was a portrait that could not be all that easily dismissed, considering its source: Vickie's own, presumably sympathetic, teenage daughter.

Wilborn believed that Kim's testimony had gone a long

way toward setting the record straight. Yes, there had been a fight that night, and perhaps it was true that Price had overstepped himself. But Kim's portrayal made the final confrontation between husband and wife—*the only one that mattered, from a legal standpoint*—sound far more deliberate than Vickie had implied in her testimony at the custody trial. The jury, Wilborn knew, would also be interested in the fact that the threats Kim heard Vickie issue were conveniently absent from her otherwise detailed account of the shooting.

If Kim could be believed—and Wilborn saw no reason why not, especially in view of her performance on the polygraph—it was clear that Vickie was not hysterical, nor even irrational, in the moments immediately preceding the shots. Angry, yes; irrational, no. Maybe even blind with rage. So what? Rage alone was never sufficient grounds for taking a life.

To Carroll Wilborn's mind, there was a simple chronology to the whole affair. Vickie made a demand, Price refused, she shot him. Didn't even matter if Price *had* grabbed for the gun, in this context. It was like a drugstore holdup.

Wilborn summed up for reporters. He had rested his case after calling just seventeen witnesses and introducing a mere ninety pieces of evidence, many of them photographs. Compared to the custody trial, this one had been a veritable quickie.

"I put on the case I had," he explained, his voice strong and steady, even if the words themselves had a slightly defensive ring to them. "I'm satisfied it proves the elements of the prosecution to the jury.

"I have not alleged premeditation. The state only has to prove she intentionally or knowingly caused the death. By that I mean she intended to cause the result. Or she intended to cause the act that caused the result." A bit tartly, he added, "She has experience with guns and knows they will kill animals and people."

As a result of all this, there was no question in his mind about her guilt. That was what he said. And yet for Carroll Wilborn, a man incapable of seeing just one side of an issue, there must have been doubts. He felt compelled to add, "But I'm not the jury."

Chapter Thirty

J udge Giblin denied Jack Zimmermann's motions. He would not declare a mistrial, nor would he direct the jury to find a verdict of not guilty.

Zimmermann was contentious. The impact of Kim's remark about the polygraph, he argued, was "grossly negligent" because "it bolsters that witness's testimony to the jury." The jury was bound to focus on the statement and place undue weight on Kim's testimony in general. Furthermore, a verdict of not guilty did not strike him as an excessively harsh penalty to bestow on the prosecution. A thirteen-year-old girl who had never before testified in court should have been cautioned by Wilborn about mentioning the lie-detector test. Since it was the district attorney's oversight that gave rise to this mess, it was only fair that the district attorney suffer the consequences.

Judge Giblin maintained that he had reviewed several cases that seemed to constitute precedent; his research led him to believe that there was no basis for such rash actions at this time. Zimmermann was granted a recess until Monday to allow the defense to review or revamp its strategy in the light of developments.

In assessing his strategy, Zimmermann now had three choices: rest without calling any witnesses; have Vickie testify and call other witnesses; or call other witnesses but not Vickie herself. "We've been on the defensive so far, not on the offensive," Zimmermann told the papers. To clarify his position, he offered a slightly cryptic analogy to baseball: "We must now decide, are we tied, are we behind, or are we going to bat?"

He promptly declared that had this been the first time around for Vickie, he would have had no reservations about resting his case and delivering his final argument on Monday. He took this position based on the economy of Wilborn's prosecution: the scant number of witnesses and the subdued tenor of the bulk of the testimony. The state, in Zimmermann's view, had simply failed to meet its obligation of proving guilt beyond either a reasonable doubt or a moral certainty. "Vickie was caring for two sick little boys that night," he observed. "She had taken them to the doctor hours earlier. She was cooking dinner for three children. Does that atmosphere suggest an intentional shooting? A murder?"

Even so, the publicity produced by the custody trial had been sensational enough to give Zimmermann pause. Sure, the jurors had been admonished not to discuss or read the papers, and he was satisfied they were complying with the bench's directive. What Zimmermann wondered was, How many could honestly say they had been oblivious to all the details of the custody trial (many of which had been rightly excluded by Judge Giblin from the current proceeding)? How many could say that none of Zeke Zbranek's impassioned oratory had made its way back to them at some time in the past? Long before they ever got their jury-call notices for this trial?

And, of course, there was Kim. To the jury, Kim's testimony was a matter of conscience: here was a loving, devoted daughter who nonetheless saw "the truth" as her highest allegiance. It wasn't so much the specifics of what

Kim said, but the emotional vividness of the narrative she had spun. Through a child's innocent eyes, the jury had seen Vickie get the drop on Price—seen her standing there menacing her husband with a rifle. Regardless of the lack of corroborating physical evidence, that had to be reckoned with.

As he headed into the weekend, Jack Zimmermann knew he couldn't let Kim Moore's testimony be the last that was heard before deliberations began.

"The jury," he proclaimed, "wants to hear both sides."

Jack Zimmermann called his star witness, and Vickie Daniel did not disappoint. Distraught and at times hysterical, she stuck to the story that had been her strong suit all along, weaving a most extraordinary series of recriminations into a graphic picture of a marriage made in hell.

She had married Price in spite of her better judgment, she said, and he had lost interest in her almost from the moment the marriage began. (She recounted the fact that they did not have sex until their union was a day old because Price was "ill" on their wedding night.) Price ate alone. Instead of talking, they "wrote notes." When Franklin was born, Price took her to the hospital but did not visit during her recovery and the Governor and Mrs. Daniel had to take her home. When she and Bob were hospitalized for eight days at his birth, Price showed up only once to see them. She got the feeling Price might have ignored her completely had it not been for physical abuse, which progressed from slapping matches to all-out fistfights, and the unorthodox sex—"anal sex and oral sex all the time . . . he wouldn't do anything else." Vickie kept coming back to the sex. In explaining why her first divorce filing came at such an odd juncture—just three months after the birth of their first child and in the midst of Price's political comeback attempt—she said, simply, "I didn't want to have anal sex." Yet almost as bad as the sexual or physical abuse was the belittling, the psychological torment—being left out of conversations, being called "stupid," being blamed for his political failure, being coerced into getting an abortion. Though a divorce would have seemed unavoidable, almost necessary, it was always put off because that was Price's wish; he always wanted to wait.

With only minor deviations, her testimony about the shooting was a verbatim replay of her version at the custody trial: Price had gotten angry and grabbed her by the throat after she said she would not sign the divorce settlement until Lannie had first read it. She got away briefly, but Price knocked her to the floor, then turned against Kimberly when the girl came to her assistance. "Get her out of here before I do something to her!" she again had Price saying.

Her voice began to falter badly as she told the jury how she insisted that he leave; whereupon Price began hunting through the attic for his "stuff." She reminded him that she had flushed it months earlier, but he took off to the attic to investigate further. When she followed him to the stairway, "he kicked me in the head, in the forehead." She fell down and he jumped on her and began pummeling her. "It felt like he was hitting me everywhere."

He then looked at her and growled, "I ought to kill you."

Although she had feared him for most of the marriage, she was more afraid now than ever. She ran to the carport, tried unsuccessfully to get the locks undone, reached into the hallway closet for a gun. She was "scared he was coming to get me."

Slowly, she crept through the house to the stairway and pleaded for him to leave.

If anything, her having armed herself only strengthened his resolve to stay. "He said he was going to stick it up my ass. . . . He acted like he didn't care." She told him she was going to shoot; he smiled at her defiantly.

She aimed at the roof of the attic and fired.

Price started coming down "real fast" and said he was going to kill her.

She backed away to her left, knowing another beating was imminent, wanting desperately to avoid it. She shut her eyes.

"I don't remember anything else," she told Jack Zimmermann. There was just that "funny sound, like when you shoot bullets through the water."

"Do you remember pulling the trigger?" asked Zimmermann.

"No, no," she said, now breaking into deep sobs. "I don't remember." Nor did she recall ejecting the spent cartridge. Her last memory of the encounter at the attic steps was of "flinching away from him."

Her narrative resumed at the point where she reopened her eyes to see Price walking away. She put the gun down in the "frog room," heard what she thought was the sound of Price unlocking the carport door, and crept to the kitchen to see if he'd gone.

"I saw him at the back door on the floor. . . . I told him to get up"—she sobbed convulsively, and her voice began to fail her—"but he was hurt, he was bleeding on the floor. I wanted him to get up, and *he wouldn't get up*."

For his cross-examination Wilborn wanted to seem polite and to avoid at all costs any behavior that might be interpreted as badgering the witness. The result was what many observers fancied as one of the more solicitous crosses on record, particularly in a case of this nature. Many of the hard questions Wilborn had been mulling went unasked. Several times the district attorney paused to ask Vickie if she was all right. More than once he smiled at her. It was not a smirk, nor a look of condescension or sardonic contempt, but an open, sweet smile. He asked Vickie very little that might have been considered challenging or laden with hidden purpose.

He concluded his interrogation by asking Vickie two questions that, he must have felt, went to the heart of the matter. "Are you sorry you shot Price Daniel junior?"

Vickie's face reddened; her body shook as she struggled to control her sobbing. It was, some thought, a remarkable question for a prosecutor to ask. What had he expected Vickie to say? And if the answer brought forth a torrent of emotion from her—as it did—well, that would only serve to heighten jurors' perceptions of her remorse.

Zimmermann rose to object anyway, feeling the query was in poor taste, but Wilborn was already en route to a second thought.

"Really, Vickie, what it gets down to is this: But for you getting that loaded gun and cocking it at least once and firing twice, Price Daniel junior would be alive today, wouldn't he?"

Zimmermann shot up again. A conference at the bench ensued. Vickie, still shaken and no doubt also perplexed by Wilborn's strategy, nodded silently in the background.

The three witnesses who followed Vickie Daniel to the stand all had stories to tell Zimmermann about various marks they had observed on his client from time to time. In each instance Vickie had left them with the impression that the marks were the result of physical abuse by Price.

Ann Rogers recalled a time midway in the marriage when Vickie came to her home wearing dark glasses; even inside the house, Vickie initially refused to take her shades off. Then, under Ann's probing, she raised the glasses to reveal a dark bruise below her right eye. Ann recalled Vickie's words as "Price got carried away."

. . . .

Patsy Denman said she observed bruises on her sister twice, once on her left arm in 1978 and one on her back, above the buttocks, after Bob was born in February 1980. "Price had kicked her," Denman said of the back bruise. "She wouldn't talk about it."

David Parker said he saw Vickie twice with bruises, once at his home in October 1977 and once at church in June 1979.

Parker went on to repeat the anecdote about catching Price smoking pot in his office. He added that "during the period of time I was associated with him on a daily basis, he drank daily."

An assistant district attorney felt it only fair to put such denunciations in perspective. The accuser, after all, was Susan Daniel's husband, and Susan was Bill Daniel's daughter. As, by the way, was Ann Rogers. It was common knowledge that Bill and his brother, Price senior, had been on the outs for some time. Parker, however, insisted that he personally had no ax to grind. In fact, he had helped Price in his campaign for state attorney general—long after most of the incidents that had caused tensions between the two of them.

If Carroll Wilborn was growing edgy over the testimony, he got edgier upon receipt of several new defense exhibits. An FBI report noted that the round that had felled Price could not be matched to the rifle from which it had supposedly been shot. Although Vickie did not dispute having fired the fatal bullet—thank Heaven the state hadn't been forced to try and prove *that*—the finding could only solidify the jury's impression of a haphazard, inconclusive investigation.

Of even more concern was a second test. Zimmermann's colleague, C. J. Hanby, had taken detailed measurements of the shooting scene that appeared to show that the butt of the rifle could have been slammed backward against a door molding at a critical point in the struggle. Theoretically, the sudden jolt might have caused an inadvertent discharge.

The new test demonstrated that the rifle with which Price had been killed could discharge accidentally if its bolt was jarred.

Three physicians testified.

Dr. James Gullett said he referred Price to a urologist in mid-1977 after he diagnosed venereal warts; Vickie, at the same time, had been referred to a rectal surgeon. Dr. Gullett explained that the usual cause of such viral warts in the rectal canal was anal intercourse. Generally, he found the virus in homosexuals. Dr. John David Wright, a urologist, said he treated Price for "small" warts on July 7, 1977. Dr. Harold Randolph Bailey, a rectal specialist, testified that he too had diagnosed the venereal-wart virus in Vickie's anal canal. However, he did not treat her because she was expecting a baby at the time—Franklin would be born in a matter of weeks—and the medication would have been harmful to the child. Dr. Bailey agreed with his colleague, Dr. Gullett, that the virus was transmitted by homosexual contact among males.

Lips pursed and heads nodded at the apparent corroboration of Vickie's testimony about Price's sexual tastes.

A baroque trial called for a baroque finish. On a breezy Wednesday afternoon, October 28, Judge Leonard Giblin laid the groundwork.

For some time, both sides had been privately concerned about the jury. Lately, an impression had been building within Zimmermann and Wilborn, based on some of the jurors' observed reactions to trial testimony, that the panel might include a couple of people likely to disregard principles of law and render their decision on emotional considerations.

For Zimmermann, the particular object of concern was one Margaret Penry. The fifty-nine-year-old teacher's aide from nearby Cleveland, Texas, had suffered a loss of her own. Sometime ago, her husband had been a homicide victim. The accused killer was then acquitted of murder, despite Penry's own highly charged testimony. The information about Penry's personal tragedy had come to light shortly after the trial got under way. Both sides had vowed to press on anyway. Now there were second thoughts. Could someone who felt she had been cheated by the system assess a case of this nature with detachment and objectivity? Might she listen a bit too closely to the state's case, and be a bit too skeptical—perhaps even contemptuous—of Zimmermann's efforts to mount a defense?

"It's not her fault," Wilborn told Judge Giblin as the principals assembled in chambers. "She answered all of our questions, both prosecution and defense. We just did not ask the right question."

Was this, then, another motion for a mistrial? asked Giblin.

No, upon reflection, Zimmermann had decided that he could not countenance returning to square one, and subjecting his client to yet another trial. "I don't think she could handle it emotionally," he asserted. "It is a tragedy to her. She's had to live with it every night. I'm not going to make her do it again."

Carroll Wilborn agreed, if for different reasons. The state's position had become tenuous. If Penry was convinced of Vickie's guilt—and word had filtered back that she was already taking a hard line—then even if she managed to swing the sympathies of her fellow jurors to her side, an overturn on appeal was a distinct possibility. If, on the other hand, Penry dug in for battle and became the lone panel member holding out for a guilty vote, then a hung jury loomed. Either way, the state couldn't win. Besides, it was expensive to try a murder case, and each time they dragged Vickie back before a jury the natural sympathy for her plight would only grow that much stronger.

"I stand a better chance of seeing justice done in this case by submitting it to the judge," posed Carroll Wilborn.

Judge Giblin mulled that. Waiving the jury in mid-trial was highly exceptional. It happened, but not often.

The judge turned to Jack Zimmermann. "You've got to roll the dice," he told him. "It's a decision of taking a chance with twelve people or one person. All I'm going to do is look at the evidence and make the decision."

Before the end of the hour-long meeting, an agreement had been reached. Vickie would waive her right to a trial by jury and leave the verdict up to Judge Giblin.

During a recess, Carroll Wilborn explained the action to the press. "This case has principles of law concerning an accident and an illegal act that sometimes is hard for a jury to understand. We believe it is in the best interest to place the case before one person learned in the law. In my opinion, it was the best decision to go with the court."

Judge Giblin was more succinct. "They trust my decision. It's as simple as that."

Over the next few days the press sought out jurors for their reactions. An informal survey of the eight-man, four-woman panel showed that seven jurors were emphatic about Vickie's innocence. (Indeed, when it was announced that the panel was being disbanded, several of the ex-jurors sought out Vickie and Jack Zimmermann to shake hands and offer encouragement.) Three were undecided "but leaning toward not guilty," and the remaining two female jurors, one of whom was Margaret Penry, were steadfast in their perception of Vickie's guilt.

Dayton's James Horne spoke for the majority. "The state didn't prove to me that she intentionally shot him. She was provoked into the shooting."

"I believed her with a shadow of doubt," added John L. Ward of Cleveland, the "shadow" not surprisingly having to do with Kim's testimony. But, noted Ward, "having children myself, the daughter could have confused the events that night. I think we all generally felt the little girl was confused."

The strongest dissenting view came not from Margaret Penry but from a juror named Lynn Allen, in a *Post* sidebar article under the headline WOMEN ON DISMISSED JURY SAY THEY ARE CONVINCED OF GUILT.

"I believe she was abused, but not all women who are abused shoot their husband," lectured Mrs. Allen, twenty-eight years old and the wife of a Liberty County sheriff's deputy. "She knew what she was doing and she was not that scared of him that she needed to get a gun and kill him." Allen felt her marriage to a law-enforcement officer better enabled her to sort out the information provided by the state. Nonetheless, her position softened when it came to punishment. If convicted of murder, Vickie stood to receive life imprisonment, plus—rather anticlimactically—a fine of up to $10,000. Judge Giblin, however, did have the option of assessing a probative sentence instead. And that was how Allen felt he should rule. "I do not want her to go to prison," she said. "I believe probation is a just punishment."

As for Margaret Penry, she would say simply, "I believe she's guilty." Reporters pressed for elaboration. No doubt disgruntled over the publicity she had received as the proximate cause of the jury's dismissal, Penry snapped, "Just my opinion."

Finally, the press sought out Vickie. Zimmermann had been keeping her on a tight leash, but the time seemed right for a statement. And for once, Vickie herself felt like speaking out, getting something off her chest. She felt so isolated from the rest of the world. Even her relationship with writer Dick Reavis had soured—he had written her a marriage proposal, she had dispatched a Dear John via return mail.

As she summed up her feelings about putting her fate in the judge's hands, her tone grew increasingly fatalistic. "I've lived through nine months of this, one tragedy after another. First Price. Then they tried to take my children away. Then my mother—she was my best friend and I loved her very much—she died. The days and days of court sessions, and then this trial. Physically and mentally, I am exhausted.

"I do not feel well. I do not have enough time to spend with my children, now the most important people in my life. I'm ready for it to be over. One way or the other, it must end."

Chapter Thirty-one

J udge Leonard Giblin was an old-fashioned man with two abiding loves, his family and the law. When it came to his slant on the latter, Giblin was about as close to a hanging judge as modern Texas had to offer. He himself joked that he was so law-and-order oriented he "couldn't hardly say the words 'Not guilty.'"

Since childhood Leonard Giblin had pictured himself as a Texas Department of Public Safety trooper. After high school he applied to the DPS academy, where he passed all the academic tests and reported to rookie school, only to be sent home the first day because he was an eighth of an inch shorter than minimum DPS regulations. He next set his sights on the FBI. He believed he could clerk there for a time, attend college, and ultimately become an agent. But less than a year later he left the bureau after being told his eyesight was unacceptable. On the trip home, his new bride suggested to the crestfallen Giblin that he think about law school as an alternative to law enforcement.

"Thanks to good parents who paid all my expenses, I accomplished that dream," Giblin would recall. In 1974, his dedication and popularity at the grass-roots level won him election as county judge, and he had been a fixture in the East Texas judiciary ever since.

Like many of the sociologists who he felt were too soft on crime, Giblin believed the decline of the family structure was responsible for most of the problems of modern society.

"Respect for the system no longer exists," he would bellow. "It starts in the home and continues in the schools. In the past, if you got in trouble at school you got in trouble at home. Today there is no discipline in the home or in the school."

To Jean and the Governor and the rest of the Daniel sympathizers, Judge Giblin seemed the perfect man for the job.

Seconds after the judge took the bench on Friday morning, October 30, Daniel family members and co-workers from the Daniel law firm entered the courtroom en masse. A carefully timed power play couldn't hurt at this point. Only the final arguments remained to be made. A show of solidarity at the last minute could convince a wavering man of the right way to go.

The final arguments went on for three hours. Zimmermann argued pretty much as expected. There was no concrete proof that his client had committed murder. The shooting itself was accidental, and in any case, had been provoked by Price's own brutality. His client had feared for her life, and the safety of her three children, two of whom were ill to begin with. The doubt in the case was not only "reasonable," but overwhelming.

During the prosecution's turn, Wilborn suddenly backed off from the hard line he had taken on the homicide charge. He told Giblin that at the very least, the case exhibited "all the signs of voluntary manslaughter"; he maintained that the validity of finding Vickie guilty of the lesser charge had been certified by the tenor of defense logic in recent days. Hearing this, the Governor wept quietly in the front row, saddened by Wilborn's last-minute diffidence.

The final arguments ended. After a short recess, Judge Giblin returned and instructed Vickie to stand to hear his verdict. Unsteadily, she pulled herself up between Zimmermann and Hanby.

Judge Giblin fixed her with a hard stare. Even from the rear of the courtroom, where the media huddled shoulder to shoulder, the tremor in the judge's hands was discernible. He took a deep breath and opened his mouth to deliver what he would later describe as the most difficult decision of his career.

"Mrs. Daniel, I find you not guilty."

Vickie burst into tears. The courtroom filled with exultant screams, soon to be drowned out by thunderous applause. Many of the three hundred onlookers leaped to their feet and cheered.

"Court is adjourned!" Judge Giblin yelled, clearly startled and straining to be heard over the ruckus.

To Jean Murph, it felt like a kick in the stomach. Worse than the verdict itself was the jubilance. A man was dead. Was there no respect for the grieving?

Vickie must have felt it, too. After quickly hugging Jack Zimmermann, she attempted to push her way through the crowd toward the Governor and his wife, who were in the process of making a quick exit from the courtroom. Unable to intercept them in time, she decided to make an overture through the press.

"Somehow I will tell the Daniel family I love them," she cried. "I understand what they did. If I were in their shoes I would have done the same thing. I'm happy about the outcome but sad because of someone else's disappointment. I hope and pray they will say something to me first.

"I can only tell you what was in my heart. I am not guilty."

A charitable Vickie even had praise for the prosecution's lawyers, saying, "They did their job." Only when it came to Buck Eckols did the animus seem to rise in her voice. "I think I was treated unfairly by Sheriff Eckols," she said, lowering her eyes.

She knew, of course, that her troubles were not yet over. Not by a long shot. Among other things, the considerable matter of Price's estate remained to be resolved. But right now, she wasn't thinking about that. Her only plans were to go home to her Baytown apartment and spend a quiet night with the children.

"None of the family is commenting," steamed Houston Daniel, cornered by reporters at the base of the courthouse steps. But Jean, who had all along comported herself as the voice of justice, could not keep her feelings locked up inside.

"She killed someone and got away with it," Jean seethed. "I think it was definitely an unfair decision based on the facts. I think it gives people a license to do whatever they want to do."

A few steps away, Carroll Wilborn concurred. "I think we place a higher price tag on a human life," he went on. "I just hope it doesn't give us a rash of shotgun divorces. I would hope we don't see that result. I don't think we will. But I don't know."

To Buck Eckols, the verdict was a slap in the face. Eckols had little to say publicly, for he had come to resent the press on several grounds. They had, in his view, misquoted him on more than one occasion during the two trials. Even worse, as Eckols saw things, was the way the press had blown out of all reasonable proportion Vickie's salacious accusations against her dead husband.

But even though he declined to speak for publication—damned if he'd give the bastards the satisfaction—the sheriff was mad. He looked at the acquittal through the eyes of one who life had cheated. In high school, Buck had lost a full scholarship to Rice when the coach found out he was working rodeos on weekends. The lousy $70 he earned had cost him his amateur status. That had been his big sin. And now he watched as a woman who had killed someone got off scot-free.

There's no justice in this world, thought Eckols.

For ex-Governor Price Daniel, Sr., all that remained was to compose himself in anticipation of a visit from little Franklin and Bob. The children would be spending several days at the ranch beginning Saturday morning, as directed in the accord reached with Lannie and Friend in mid-May.

All along, Price senior had been portrayed as the purposeful avenger. The media always homed in on that unmistakable clout, on the notion that, in the end, the system be damned, he would have his way.

The Governor resolved, now, that he would not look back in anger. The time for that was past. And the fact was, the boys needed a mother. He and his wife would have to learn to live with that. They would have to put away the frustration and the bitterness, and somehow find smiles with which to greet their grandchildren. Forget the wounds, begin the healing.

Chapter Thirty-two:
Epilogue

I had arrived in East Texas on January 20, 1986, and promptly gotten off on the wrong foot by telephoning the home of ex-Governor Price Daniel, Sr., to try to arrange an interview. Somehow, despite my yearlong immersion in the case, I had managed to forget the anniversary of Price's death.

Still, Mrs. Jean Daniel fielded the call with aplomb, and even surprising cordiality. She told me that the Governor was not at home, and she doubted at any rate that he would have much to say to me. It was a part of his past he did not like to confront anymore. As our brief conversation went along, she admitted that she feared for her husband's health. The Governor was well into his seventh decade and not a particularly robust man—there had been recent surgery on his carotid artery to alleviate a circulatory problem in his head—and she didn't want him getting riled up all over again at this late date. Be that as it may, she promised to relay my request. Feeling exceedingly squeamish about my inadvertent show of poor taste and timing, I apologized and wished her well. She responded in kind, sounding as though she genuinely meant it. I asked her how she could be so gracious. Even in her one brief reference to Vickie, there had been not the slightest trace of malice. She drew a quick breath, thought for a moment, and said, "We live for the living."

Later that day, I phoned back and spoke with the Governor himself. Mrs. Daniel had indeed told him of my call, as promised. Although he was gruff, and clearly less than thrilled with my having appeared out of the blue to scrutinize that most tragic chapter in the Daniel saga, he spoke with passion and clarity about Vickie and his son and—especially—his grandchildren. He expressed the fervent hope that I would not say or write anything that might in any way affect "those poor innocent young children." Finally, he was scornful of the view that Price junior had not been cut out for politics.

"My son was *not* unsuccessful at politics," he said emphatically, "he was unsuccessful at marriage."

I began to try to contact Vickie Daniel. I had heard that, at least outwardly, after the trial Vickie's relationship with the Daniels had simply picked up where it left off. The kids were dropped off at the ranch for their regular visits with the Governor, or for the annual August roundup. Vickie would exchange polite words with the parents and siblings of the man she had killed. Still more amazing, Jean Murph, of all people, seemed, on some level at least, to accept her sister-in-law. From time to time, the two of them would even sit down over a pot of coffee to discuss various matters relating to the children's support.

The situation was simply too extraordinary to ignore. I had to talk to Vickie. Nonetheless, I was told by a polite Jack Zimmermann, still her attorney of record, that she had no desire to talk to anyone from the media. In the five years since the shooting, she had, through Zimmermann, routinely declined all offers for interviews.

I gave Jack Zimmermann the standard writer's line: that the book would be written with or without his client's cooperation, that I had already initiated discussions with people from "the other side," notably Jean Murph, and that Vickie's interests would best be served if she at least responded to some of the things that were being said about her by Price's allies.

After several phone calls, Zimmermann remained convinced that no accommodation could be arranged, but said there was one slim chance of getting Vickie to open up. It seems there was a mutual code of silence; the Daniels and Vickie, recognizing that their futures were bound together by the children, had agreed in the wake of the murder trial that neither would speak out against the other.

I sent Jack Zimmermann salient portions of a rambling, nine-page letter I had received from Jean Murph not long before.* In the letter, Jean called Vickie a "murderer," and alluded to a catalog of damning acts on the part of her former sister-in-law. She appeared to have lost none of the vitriol for which she became noted during the two litigations of 1981.

Within days, there was a message on my answering machine. Over the long-distance crackle could be heard the fragile drawl of a youthful-sounding woman. The voice said, "Mr. Salerno, could you please call me back. This is Vickie Daniel." She left a number whose prefix marked its origin as the town of Highlands, Texas, another of Houston's many colorless eastern suburbs.

Since Vickie had taken the initiative of cutting her lawyer out of the picture, I had no reservations about phoning her directly. She sounded surprised to get my call, told me she was still a little leery about talking to me.

*In all fairness to Jean, I should mention that she was furious at my sending the letter, which she believed she had written in strict confidence. I had no such understanding. The letter was a remarkable testament to Jean's idolatry of her brother, which had not diminished in the slightest. In fact, over time, Price had apparently become for her a mythic figure. Responding to my assertion that some people felt he had "a classic Napoleonic complex," she insisted that he was nearly six feet tall! Jachimczyk's autopsy put him at five eight, and none of the friends or acquaintances with whom I spoke personally estimated his height at much beyond five nine.

After all, there was the code of silence to think about.

I told Vickie that a code of silence works only when it is bilaterally observed. In this instance, it seemed a little silly for Vickie to be keeping mum, inasmuch as Jean had already made it quite clear that she continued to regard Vickie as a killer and fully intended to have the record set straight. As a matter of fact, Jean had once said, "I'm going to see that the right book is written someday if I have to write it myself!"

Before long, Vickie decided that she wanted to "clear the air." It had been five years since she had really opened up to an outsider; maybe the time was right. Plus, she thought it might be therapeutic for her to get some of her feelings off her chest. (Perhaps this had something to do with the psychology class she was taking at the time.) And too, there were the kids to think about. Frank and Bob were getting older, starting to ask questions. "How can I let them grow up only listening to what their grandparents say?" she implored.

Over the next few weeks, I spent some seven hours talking on the phone to Vickie Daniel. Perhaps the most striking aspect of our conversations was Vickie's remarkable chameleonlike nature. One time, she was tentative, guarded. Next phone call, she would be voluble and forthcoming, and I would think some great barrier had been crossed. But then by the next call—or sometimes even within that same call—she might close up again. There would be mood swings as well. On some occasions she would be open, sweet, quite charming. But at other times she brandished a sarcasm that bordered on hostility. Jean had forewarned me of Vickie's "near-schizophrenic" changeability, but experiencing it firsthand was something else again. I was immediately reminded of a couple of stories I'd heard from Bill Buchanan and Sheriff Buck Eckols.

Shortly after the trial, Buchanan had run into Vickie in front of one of the shops on Main Street. He walked up to her with an outstretched hand and a neighborly smile, and asked her how she was doing.

"You've got a lot of nerve talking to me!" she shot back.

Buchanan was nonplussed. They'd always been so cordial, he remarked. What could she possibly be referring to?

"You know you've been following me every time I come to town!" she said.

"Why, Vickie, I haven't even seen you since the trial."

"That's a lie and you know it! You know darned well you've been following me every time I come to town."

Buchanan tried to make headway for a while. But he soon realized there was no point and gave up. They never spoke again.

A year or so after the verdict, Buck Eckols and his wife had encountered Vickie and her kids at a roadside rest stop. *Oh shoot,* thought Eckols, *here it comes.* The sheriff fully expected an awkward confrontation. Instead, Vickie greeted them warmly. "It was like we were long lost friends," Eckols would recall. "She actually came over and put her arms around me, as if I was maybe her best buddy in the whole world." She told them she was on her way to a nearby camping area. Then she packed the kids in the car, waved out the window, and drove off with a big smile on her face, leaving Eckols and his wife standing there openmouthed.

Later, something in Eckols's sheriff's nature made him check on Vickie's story about the campground; he wasn't aware of any such facility in that neck of the woods.

"Ain't that something?" he said, putting down the phone and turning to his wife. "There's no campground out there anywhere!"

* * *

Despite Vickie's emotional changeabilities, a picture began to emerge of a woman who had finally put some things
in perspective. And a most intriguing perspective it was.

She spoke about the "relationship" she had implied under oath between her husband and a young black handy-
man Robert Broussard:

"At the time, what I said was what I thought was true.
. . . I used to think, Why was [Price] so much better to
him than those little children? But since then, seeing how
people interact with other people, and trying to figure
out Price in my own mind . . . You see, Robert put him
up on a pedestal, he idolized Price. Which is the way I
used to see him once, but I didn't anymore. Price so badly
needed for people to see him that way. He needed to sur-
round himself with people who saw him that way. And
once I stopped, I think Robert took my place for that purpose. . . ."

She spoke about Jean's undying rancor: "Jean told me
out of her own mouth, 'It's not the crime of Price's death;
it was what you said about him. You crucified him with
your mouth, Vickie.' That's the exact words she used with
me. She could forgive me for his death, but she couldn't
forgive me for what I said."

About Price's dependence on alcohol, and his resultant
distaste for the campaign trail: "He *hated* being cooped up
in a room making speeches and talking to people all the
time. He would lean over and say to me, 'I gotta get outta
here. I gotta get a drink.' He always kept a bottle in the
suitcase."

About the "unorthodox" sexual practices of which she
accused Price during both trials: "If you're naïve, you don't
appreciate it and you find it offensive. . . . Maybe Price
just wasn't the man to teach me, or maybe, like somebody
told me, he was just a clumsy lover. I felt like a prosti-

tute—not wanting to do something, but I was his wife and I had to do it. . . . I now realize that when you meet the right man, you want to do things you never thought you'd do. . . . What helped me was sitting around and talking to other women about it."

About the clear disparity between her avowed revulsion for Price's sexual tastes and Price's promise, in the Del Ray peace pact, to provide "more sex" and to "remember her special cravings and wild desires": "That was just his way of making a point. Another person might have said it straight out, but Price would say it sarcastically. . . . In other words, it was just his backhanded way of complaining that as far as he was concerned, I had no interest in sex."*

About the night of the shooting: "I've thought back and thought back to everything, and if there's one thing I've concluded, it's *never let me get hungry*. If I seem to be hungry, feed me! . . . Even before that night, we'd go here, and they'd talk and talk and talk and talk, then we'd go there, and they'd just talk and talk and talk and talk, and meanwhile, I'd be getting so hungry. I couldn't stand it after a while."

A face-to-face meeting was arranged; I was to travel to Vickie's home in Highlands. I could not deny I had some trepidations. The woman's behavior could be puzzling, to say the least.

As it developed, the meeting did not come about. Vickie

---

*Vickie had actually been irritated by, and uncomfortable with, the incessant focus on sex, but the lawyers felt it would have a helpful impact on the jury, and they were correct in that assessment. Hardly a word was whispered, hardly an eye was blinked during the racier moments of Vickie's testimony. Some of the jurors' reactions went considerably beyond the scope of the trial's inquiry. "Richard," said Vickie (who, like most of Haynes's friends, called him by his given first name), "told me afterwards that one of the male jurors mentioned to the bailiff that he'd like to help me with my sexual problem."

called at the last minute to cancel, claiming that pressure had been brought to bear by Jean Murph. (Jean later denied this.) Try to understand, she pleaded. Jean still wielded tremendous control over her finances. If she wished, she could make life truly miserable for Vickie and the children.

In our final phone call, just days after the meeting was to have taken place, Vickie grew contentious and obfuscatory. She accused me of "spinning my wheels" in my efforts to get at the truth. She unaccountably depreciated the worth of most of my observations about the case—the very same observations she had praised during our previous phone calls—and implied a certain deviousness to my methods: "You played a certain tune with me which I didn't hear, and I'm hearing it now for the first time." After having spent the better part of one hour-long conversation talking about writer Dick Reavis's crucial role in her emotional recovery, she suddenly scoffed at his importance: "It's so funny how he lived so far away, and yet he was so blown up by some people in my life, when there was one [man] that lived right here in the same town that no one seemed to know anything about!"

She went so far as to take issue with the fundamental premise of my interviews with her: "I think you're giving me more credit than what I duly deserve about some things. I would just love to be this mysterious woman . . . but it just really wasn't that way at all."

More to the point, perhaps, she gave the impression that my poking around had rekindled her awareness of the story's commercial possibilities. Shortly after the verdict in 1981, the film rights were actually sold to some local interests, but the deal never went much beyond the talking stage. Now, however, she alluded to the fact that she might have someone writing her life story under contract. If that was true, she would obviously be ill-advised to give everything away to me for free.

At the last, we hung up uneasily; the rapport that I thought we had established during our hours of searching conversation was gone.

Despite Vickie's chastisements, and her transparent attempt to recant much of what she had voluntarily shared, I sat down to make sense of our phone conversations. The implications, I came to realize, were stunning.

• At the trial, Vickie had leaned heavily on the suspicious relationship between Robert Broussard and Price. Now, she wasn't sure at all. She had come to see things more philosophically, had come to realize that Broussard's real value to Price was spiritual, not physical.

• At the trial, she had made Price out to be a sexual deviate. Now, she was confessing that she had simply been woefully naïve and unprepared for his advances. Indeed, though she had not said it in so many words, she even hinted at a certain liking for the kinds of bedroom activities that were such a turn-off during her life with Price.

• At the trial, she had portrayed Price as a child molester. Now she was saying that the lawyers had prevailed upon her to "stress" events that might have led to such an impression.

• At the trial, she had blamed the shooting itself on Price's brutal aggression. Now, though, she seemed to be insinuating that the whole tragedy might have been sparked by something as mundane as her and Price's inability to quit arguing and sit down to supper. *Never let me get hungry,* she said, the menace clear in her voice. I recalled how, even early in the marriage, she had been displeased with the way Price's business meetings would often put their dining plans on hold: "They'd do all this talkin' and talkin'," she had said, "and meanwhile my stomach'd be growling and I'd be getting irritable." Above all, I recalled the green peas and spaghetti that simmered on the stove above Price's body that dismal night in January.

317

I wondered whether everyone would have felt as sorry for her if she had said such things back in 1981. And I wondered whether the courtroom decisions would have still gone in her favor.

On my last trip to Liberty, I saw the house.

The current owner, a local businessman, was nice enough to invite me out to the property along with Oscar Cantu, whose wife was in the man's employ. It was no skin off his back, he said, since he'd had it on the market anyway. He explained that it had not been "a particularly happy home" for him; his marriage had soured and fallen apart. Evidently, the house had not made a particularly happy home for anybody. The former owner, who had purchased the house from Price's estate, suffered through a bankruptcy there when the oil business went sour. Long before that, Price and Diane had seen their marriage crumble. And of course, there were Price and Vickie. . . .

I was given a tour of the expansive residence. I saw the famous attic stairway, so much smaller and flimsier than I had pictured it. I felt the goose bumps rise as Oscar Cantu showed me where he had stood, peering through the stairway slats at Vickie, on that foggy night five years earlier. I saw the "frog room," now restored to its original function as a guest bedroom. I saw the carport door where Price lay, and the spot in the foyer where the EMTs and Bill Buchanan grappled with Vickie.

"The house has changed a lot," said Cantu, sounding almost apologetic. "There's carpet in spots where there used to be tile, or vice versa. And the decorating is completely different, of course." He ventured his understandable opinion that the house looked a whole lot more cheerful now than it had then.

But clichéd as it sounds, there was still something about the place. Outside, the day was quite pleasant, warm for that time of year, and yet there was a chill inside that wouldn't quit. I could hardly help recalling what Vickie once said about living there.

"No matter how high I put the thermostat," she had told me, "I could never seem to get that house warm."

In a story replete with question marks, the biggest one, in the end, concerns Price Daniel, Jr. Several people described him as utterly unfathomable—"the most truly difficult person I ever tried to know," to quote one. To be sure, a number of the major decisions Price made in his life were beyond comprehension, even by the small circle of people who considered themselves his confidants. He revealed so little of what he was feeling that most people were left to draw inferences from the superficial aspects of his behavior: the way he dressed, looked, spoke, aligned his books, set his watch, kept vigil over his checkbook, corrected the newspapers.

"To describe Price that way is to describe what he *did*, not what he *was*," protested a friend. "The thing is, he could be a truly warmhearted individual if you got to know him, and if you didn't get put off by that exterior of his. . . . Sure, he liked to have his checkbook add up to the penny, but he was also the kind of guy, if he thought you were in a fix, he'd give you the shirt right off his back. . . . This one day, we were talkin' near the courthouse, and there were these black boys comin' by. Price, I guess, knew one or two of them. He always favored the underdogs, you see—I think in some ways he identified with 'em.

"Anyway, it was a pretty cold day, and one of the fellows didn't have a jacket on, and Price asked him why. And the boy says, ' 'Cause I don't have one, Mr. Price.' So Price reaches into his pocket and gives the boy the money— I think it was maybe forty dollars or fifty, but at least forty, a couple of twenties—and tells him, 'Here, son, you go and get yourself a coat.' That was the side of Price Daniel that you don't hear much about. . . .

"The problem was, he just wasn't comfortable with his situation. He was following in footsteps, huge footsteps, and I suppose he must have felt like he didn't measure up. And yet being the perfectionist he was, he also probably felt that he had to keep on trying. . . .

"For most people, being Price Daniel junior would have been a blessing. Not for him, being the way he was. You know that expression, a blessing in disguise? For him, it was a curse in disguise. It was a blessing that turned out to be a curse."